Lawyers – The Quality Agenda
Volume Two

Assessing and Developing Competence and Quality in Legal Aid –
Transaction Criteria

Avrom Sherr
Richard Moorhead
Alan Paterson

LEGAL AID BOARD

London: HMSO

© Crown copyright 1994
Applications for reproduction should be made to HMSO

ISBN 0 11 380083 5

Companion volume:
Lawyers—The Quality Agenda
Volume One

The Report of the Birmingham Franchising Pilot

ISBN 0 11 380084 3

Printed in the United Kingdom for HMSO
Dd296636 7/94 C20 G3396 10170

Foreword

The Birmingham Franchising Pilot formally concluded in 1992 and at that time we published the major outcome of the research carried out during the pilot, transaction criteria in nine green form categories of work. The transaction criteria contained in this volume update those criteria and also reflect the further development work carried out over the last two years, including extensive consultation with practising solicitors.

The research report we publish in Volume 1 contains many updated sections reflecting additional work and data gathered and analysed since we first commissioned research some 4 years ago.

Franchising is a quality assurance scheme combining a variety of measures to provide this assurance. Transaction criteria are an important component because they provide a focus on the client's case file and give essential clues to the work which has actually been done in individual cases. As our confidence increases through the development of the quality assurance measures in franchising, we aim to devolve more of our statutory powers to franchisees. We also hope that our ability to differentiate between services at different levels of quality will enable high quality work to be properly recognised and rewarded.

The publication of the research report provides an opportunity to understand fully the development of the transaction criteria and gain an insight into franchising itself. We are in no doubt that this piece of research will influence the quality of legal work for many years to come, there are already signs of improvements directly attributable to the criteria and franchising.

We look forward to further developments.

John Pitts
Chairman
Legal Aid Board
July 1994

Contents

The transaction criteria apply equally to advice agencies (with or without solicitors) as well as to solicitors in private practice. Any reference therefore to "lawyers" or "firms" should be taken to refer equally to advisers and advice agencies. Throughout the criteria the generic term "lawyer" is used to refer to all people working on a file. It can include work done by legal executives, non-solicitor advisers and caseworkers, counsel, clerks etc.

Legal Quality Assurance Standards

An Introduction to Volume Two from the Researchers

Legal Aid Franchising is a revolutionary approach to the provision of legal services. It sets up a "preferred supplier" relationship with firms of solicitors and other legal service providers in which the quality of work carried out is assured to the clients. Quality and competence are assured through Standards for Practice Management, and monitoring of work through legal aid applications, costs and the basic information contained in solicitors' files.

The quality standards criteria in this volume are composed of detailed criteria (transaction criteria) which competent legal advisers would be expected to meet in particular transactions. They include standards for work up to full certificate stage in Personal Injury, Matrimonial and Crime and for green form advice and assistance work in the remaining six franchise categories. The criteria were initially developed and tested as part of the Legal Aid Board's franchising experiment which is reported in part in Volume 1, and taken further into Full Certificate work subsequently. The criteria are generally based around a review of files and a survey of literature and have been revised as a result of extensive consultation with experienced practitioners, the Law Society, consumer and other interest groups. Procedures are being put in place to ensure that all transaction criteria will be kept up to date. The transaction criteria are published here in order to advise practitioners of the quality standards which will be expected of them by the Legal Aid Board and to encourage public discussion and comment. Comments should be sent to Legal Department, Legal Aid Head Office, 85 Gray's Inn Road, London, WC1X 8AA.

A previous volume (*Transaction Criteria*, HMSO, December 1992) covered earlier drafts relating to the initial advice and assistance provided under green form as well as ABWOR and emergency civil legal aid, where appropriate. Those areas have been amended as a result of consultation and updated to cover changes in the law. They are now joined by transaction criteria for full certificate personal injury, criminal and matrimonial litigation, as funded under full certificates.

The Franchising Experiment

As will be seen from the report of the research in Volume I, the initial project involved the restructuring of payment arrangements and the devolution of certain of the Board's powers to legal aid practitioners alongside the introduction of quality monitoring for organisations (law firms, advice agencies and law centres) seeking to gain legal aid "franchises". Although termed a "franchise" there was no exclusive arrangement and firms within the experimental area were not required to seek franchises to be able to practice legal aid. Monitoring of firms took three forms: a consideration of the organisation's basic systems of work and management structure; monitoring of the quality of work submitted to the Board by potential franchisees (i.e. the quality of their bills and applications); and monitoring of the quality of advice and assistance given to clients, through the use of the transaction criteria and client questionnaires. The details of the scheme as operated during the Birmingham experiment are fully set out in Volume I. The details of Legal Aid Franchising as it is currently operated are published by the Legal Aid Board in the Franchising Specification and differ from the initial experiment in some marked respects. Practice Management Standards are a pre-condition for entering franchising and firms are expected to have systems drawn up and in place before they apply for a franchise. Before signing a contract firms will be audited for their compliance with transaction criteria as contained in this volume, and monitored for their refusal and rejection rates on applications and bills. Research into quality assurance approaches continues with the assessment of measures relating to the outcomes of cases. In this way a range of aspects of the quality of legal work will be assessed. Transaction criteria, as laid out in this volume relate principally to the process of work carried out by looking for basic information to be found on files.

Defining Legal Competence

Chapter 2 of Volume 1 looks more closely at the definitions of legal competence and quality, dividing these into Structure, Inputs, Process and Outcomes. The Practice Management Standards deal with the first two elements and Transaction Criteria considers the process of legal work. Research on outcome measures continues. Chapter 3 of Volume 1 explains in detail the researchers' method of preparing the transaction criteria, together with an appreciation of concerns expressed by the profession. In particular Chapter 3 discusses the problems of sub-dividing the world of competence into the manageable proportions of transaction criteria and accepts that the sum of those parts might still not be considered to match up to the whole of a lawyer's assessment of quality. The approach used in the audit of transaction criteria is intended to be helpful, in the sense that it is sufficiently detailed to provide exact comment and advice on areas of work which are consistently missed or not reported in the files. The assessment received by each firm on its transaction criteria audit pinpoints not only specific criteria which have been missed, but also systematic omissions (occurring frequently on the same criteria across several files) set out against specific files and therefore file workers. The pre-contract audits carried out during 1994 have shown the criteria to be a supportive and instructive management tool, as well as a tool for assessment of quality.

Developing the Transaction Criteria

Defining, articulating and measuring the competence of legal work was a complex and exacting task. Only fully qualified lawyers are capable of assessing the complexities of a legal case and devising a system for such assessment. The lawyer's work product was the most appropriate source of data within the context of franchising and accordingly case files were selected for this purpose. The first stage in the designing of quality criteria involved reviewing a number of files within each chosen subject area. The aim was to base the quality criteria firmly in the context of legal aid work as it is carried out within firms and other organisations. The review of files was followed by an initial drafting process involving knowledge gained from the review itself and from literature dealing with the issues each type of case raised. Initial drafts were then circulated to practitioners and interest groups. Numerous lawyers expert in the various fields were covered; they, and specialist Law Society groups have contributed to the drafting of the checklists. We express our most sincere thanks to them. As this process of consultation developed, we were able to reconsider the initial drafts and pilot the criteria on legal aid files using researchers uninvolved in the drafting process. Upon this basis drafts of transaction criteria were produced for use in the assessment of firms participating in the franchising experiment, and final drafts refined on further consultation with the profession. This process is explained more clearly in Chapter 3 of Volume 1, following the "Delphi technique" within medicine.

Thus the aim has been to produce a series of quality criteria applicable to specific types of legal work (transactions) handled by franchisees. Satisfaction of the criteria will be a requirement of a franchise. [Details of the required levels and dates from which compliance will be necessary will be published by the Board in the Franchising Specification.] It will be noted that the transactions contain numerous and detailed elements which should be satisfied. It is not the expectation of the researchers or the Legal Aid Board that organisations be required to conform at a hundred per cent rate of compliance. The precise level of compliance to be required may differ between different types of work and will be fixed by reference to the scores obtained in the audits carried out on over 10,000 files during the pre-contract audit phase in the spring and summer of 1994. The level set is likely to be in excess of the 65% compliance originally suggested. The aim was to set the initial standard at a comparatively low threshold. Organisations will be expected to improve and the standard of compliance will rise as use of the quality criteria develops an understanding of the approach both within the Board and within organisations. The Board has given a clear assurance that required compliance rates will be raised only where it is necessary to assure the requisite level of quality, and not to limit arbitrarily the number of franchisees.

Feedback

It is intended that an ongoing process of improvement will be achieved through co-operation between legal aid organisations and the Legal Aid Board in seeking a better legal aid service. Clearly a system which simply set standards and policed them would breed hostility within the profession. The system for implementing the criteria is thus of central importance. The approach recommended and to be adopted by the Board uses the transaction criteria initially as a means of problem diagnosis, following which organisations are encouraged to take remedial action once difficulties have been pointed out.

A co-operative liaison relationship between the Board and organisations was a feature of the initial franchising experiment and appears in general to have fostered a level of trust and understanding with potential franchisees, which might have been thought of as unlikely given the political climate within which legal aid reform currently takes place. The process of monitoring and feedback should secure genuine improvements in quality which it is hoped will benefit organisations and clients alike. The liaison relationship is one of the means by which transaction criteria could be amended to take account of developments in the law generally and in legal practice. It is important to stress that, as with much else in the legal world, the criteria laid down here are not static and will need to change and develop. Practitioner feedback on these matters is something which will be central to this process of development. The Board wants to encourage this.

Using Transaction Criteria

The approach is therefore not intended to be rigid. The transaction criteria are a first step in the articulation and monitoring of the quality of the process of legal work. It is possible that some lawyers may be in for an unpleasant surprise if incompetent work is discovered and exposed. The more foresighted will recognise that this is a point of departure. Organisations will have a basis upon which their own performance can be monitored and improved. Organisations may wish to develop the uses of transaction criteria by incorporating them into their existing quality systems. Periodic self-assessment using the criteria may prove a beneficial working tool. Similarly, organisations may use the criteria as one of the sources for their training programmes. The Legal Aid Board will have a means of assuring that the clients, on whose behalf it purchases legal services, are receiving a quality assured service. Ongoing co-operative improvement will make the assessment more sophisticated and deepen the understanding and definition of professional competence through a range of quality measures, heightening the ability of organisations to manage their practices and improving the service provided for clients.

Auditing Case Files

No lawyer likes to see their work set out like a plumbing manual but detailing the standards enabled an agreement to be reached on a more objective approach. By the checklist method we sought to incorporate empirical work and the expert knowledge of consulted practitioners into the fashioning of the measuring tool. It is hoped that this tool comes closer to measuring elements of quality of the process of legal work than most other proxies, and will also engender good practice, organisation of work and training. Clearly checklists have to be used with care during the quality assessment and in continued use they will need to adapt as more results are gathered and practices within firms evolve. Nonetheless, as a basis for auditing files, this approach seems the most feasible and likely to produce meaningful results. The use of trained auditors will clearly be more cost efficient than qualified practitioners. But more qualified staff are necessary for the interpretation of the results of the full assessment across all the franchise requirements. The Board's staff structure provides this differentiation of expertise but the Board has also agreed that a specialist panel may review transaction criteria results if failure to comply at the required level leads to an organisation's franchise being refused, suspended or terminated. This provides an extra assurance for practitioners.

When they are used in audits the criteria will be in a slightly different format appropriate for use as an audit tool. The substance is identical, and the "mark books" used by auditors will be left with the organisation so that all decisions are open and clear.

Review Process

The process of using the criteria, monitoring their use, and feeding back the results to organisations will provide a basis for the development of the criteria. A review process will be instituted to ensure that the criteria are kept up-to-date and new editions of the criteria published regularly. This means ensuring that new quality criteria can be included as well as allowing an opportunity to recognise when certain criteria have become obsolete. It will also provide an opportunity for organisations to help progress and refine the transaction criteria. Thus the definition of competence will evolve within a system of quality assurance that could provide real benefits to clients, legal aid practitioners and the Board.

Enhancing Quality

It is perhaps unreasonable to expect organisations to be happy about a system for assessing the quality of their work, but all firms and interest groups approached for consultation proved amenable and helpful, and seriously interested in enhancing their work by understanding the criteria for assessment. In the initial experiment and continuing research, the transaction criteria proved to be a reliable and effective means of monitoring competence, comparing well with peer assessment of files. Although many journals and text books have become much more practical in recent years, there is very little opportunity for the profession as a whole to discuss how best its work should be carried out. Opening up an assessment tool to full professional scrutiny for the first time provides such a forum. Now fully available to the profession, it is hoped that transaction criteria will have a strong effect in enhancing the quality of work carried out under legal aid.

Professor Avrom Sherr
Richard Moorhead

Centre for Business and Professional Law
University of Liverpool

Professor Alan Paterson
University of Strathcylde

Chapter One:
Personal Injury

This chapter sets out transaction criteria applicable to all stages of a personal injury case. The criteria are based around a review of files and a survey of literature on personal injury litigation in general legal practice[1]. They have also been revised in the light of extensive consultation with experienced practitioners, the Law Society, consumer and other interest groups.

The criteria cover work done for plaintiff clients both under green form and under full legal aid certificates. Individual lawyers must consider when further work should be carried out under a full certificate and apply at the appropriate stage.

Five sets of quality issues are addressed. These are:

- Getting Information from the Client

- Strategic Decision Making

- Client Counselling and Advice

- Procedural and Practical Steps

- Transfer of Files and Complaints

The issues are considered at a number of specific stages throughout the file:

I   Initial Instructions and Investigations

II   Discovery and Pre-action Stages in Medical Negligence Cases

III The Start of Proceedings (Issuing Proceedings/Receiving the Defence)

IV   Payment into Court

V   Settlement of the Case

VI   Going to Trial

Transfer of files and complaints (questions 111–112) are applicable to all cases and are considered throughout the file.

Although much of the work for personal injury cases is similar enough to merit the use of a single transaction, there are specific categories of cases which will require particular types of approach. For example, information gathering is split first into three categories: general, the accident itself and the clients' injuries. The section relating to the accident itself is further split into sub-categories covering: road traffic accidents, accidents at work or school, client falls, and faulty goods. Auditors will use the most appropriate of these "fact" categories in each case. If the accident involves a fatality to the client's spouse, cohabitee, or other relative, then the section on fatal accidents must also be completed.

Beyond the first stage (initial instructions and investigation) the operation of each stage will depend upon the characteristics of each individual case. Section IV (payment into court) for example will only operate where there has been a payment into court. Equally, section III (the start of proceedings) will only apply where proceedings are actually issued.

Unless indicated otherwise the criteria here apply equally to High Court and County Court actions. References to 'Statement of Claim' should be taken to mean not only Statement of Claim but also Particulars of Claim and Counterclaim unless the text clearly indicates otherwise.

Outcome Measures

The Board is interested in exploring the relationship between the outcome of cases, their cost, compliance levels with the transaction criteria, and other franchise requirements. Although there will inevitably be differences on individual cases, it may be possible to define a statistical relationship between outcomes, cost and levels of compliance which will allow effective comparison between firms to be made. Draft outcome measures for Personal Injury, Matrimonial/Family and Crime are contained in chapter 10.

I   Initial Instructions and Investigation

This section covers the initial fact gathering, advice and action in a personal injury case. The work may be completed under a green form and/or under a full civil certificate.

A.   GETTING INFORMATION FROM THE CLIENT

General Information

			Yes	No	N/a
1.	Does the lawyer know:				
	1.1	the client's name?	[ ]	[ ]	[ ]
	1.2	date of birth?	[ ]	[ ]	[ ]
	1.3	address?	[ ]	[ ]	[ ]
	1.4	telephone number(s)?	[ ]	[ ]	[ ]
	1.5	unless the client is a minor or pensioner, the client's national insurance number[2]?	[ ]	[ ]	[ ]
	1.6	does the lawyer know if the client has any accident, general insurance, or other cover for legal expenses?	[ ]	[ ]	[ ]

The Accident Itself

All Accidents

2.	Did the file demonstrate that the lawyer had some understanding of how the injury was caused, including, where possible:				
	2.1	the place(s) of the incident?[3]	[ ]	[ ]	[ ]
	2.2	the date(s) of the incident?[4]	[ ]	[ ]	[ ]
	2.3	the time of the incident?	[ ]	[ ]	[ ]
	2.4	the identity of parties involved in the incident?	[ ]	[ ]	[ ]

		Yes	No	N/a
2.5	the addresses (where possible) of the parties?	[ ]	[ ]	[ ]
2.6	how the incident was caused, including the events leading up to the incident and the incident itself?	[ ]	[ ]	[ ]
2.7	what the client was doing at the time?	[ ]	[ ]	[ ]
2.8	whether there were any witnesses to the incident (and, if so, names, addresses or possible contacts)?	[ ]	[ ]	[ ]
2.9	any official involvement (in particular any information on the police, factory or other relevant inspectors that were called: e.g. names, numbers, police station)?	[ ]	[ ]	[ ]

3. Road Traffic Accidents[5]

N/A [ ]

3.1 Did the file demonstrate that the lawyer had some understanding of all of the following:

		Yes	No	N/a
3.1.1	if possible, details of all vehicles involved (make, type, registration number, etc.)?	[ ]	[ ]	[ ]
3.1.2	if possible, how many passengers there were in the client's vehicle and the vehicles of any other parties?	[ ]	[ ]	[ ]
3.1.3	if possible, the insurance details of all vehicle drivers in the accident?	[ ]	[ ]	[ ]
3.1.4	the traffic conditions?	[ ]	[ ]	[ ]
3.1.5	the light and weather conditions?	[ ]	[ ]	[ ]
3.1.6	how the client and any other parties reacted after the accident (especially what was said to (or by) the other side or to the police by way of 'admission')?	[ ]	[ ]	[ ]

3.1.7 if the client was travelling in a vehicle:

N/A [ ]

		Yes	No	N/a
3.1.7.1	in which seat the client was travelling;	[ ]	[ ]	[ ]
3.1.7.2	whether they were wearing a seat belt;	[ ]	[ ]	[ ]
3.1.7.3	if they were not wearing a seat belt, an explanation for this.	[ ]	[ ]	[ ]

		Yes	No	N/a
3.1.8	if the client was driving, whether or not there are any prosecutions pending against the client in relation to the accident?	[ ]	[ ]	[ ]
3.1.9	if it is known whether proceedings are pending against the other driver?	[ ]	[ ]	[ ]

3.1.10 if the client was driving during the accident, does the lawyer know:

N/A [ ]

		Yes	No	N/a
3.1.10.1	if the client had current motoring insurance;	[ ]	[ ]	[ ]
3.1.10.2	what type of insurance this was (fully comprehensive, third party, etc.); and	[ ]	[ ]	[ ]

	Yes	No	N/a
3.1.10.3 the certificate number and name of company;	[ ]	[ ]	[ ]

4. Accident at Work or School   N/A [ ]

4.1 Did the file demonstrate that the lawyer had some understanding of all of the following:

	Yes	No	N/a
4.1.1 the names and presence at the scene of the accident of the client's supervisors (if any) or teachers?	[ ]	[ ]	[ ]
4.1.2 if the client was supervised, the nature and extent of such supervision?	[ ]	[ ]	[ ]
4.1.3 any warning notices, safety training and procedures, safety precautions, protective clothing and oral warnings given to the client?	[ ]	[ ]	[ ]
4.1.4 any previous accidents at the place of work/school, or history of safety complaints (if it seems likely that the client might know these)?	[ ]	[ ]	[ ]
4.1.5 whether the accident was recorded in an accident book?	[ ]	[ ]	[ ]
4.1.6 what happened immediately after the accident (including any things said by the client, fellow employees/students, or the employers/teachers)?	[ ]	[ ]	[ ]
4.1.7 whether, to the knowledge of the client, anything has been changed by the other side as a result of the accident?	[ ]	[ ]	[ ]
4.1.8 if equipment was being operated, a description of the equipment and how it was being used?	[ ]	[ ]	[ ]
4.1.9 in Employment cases where safety/training procedures may be in issue only: N/A [ ]			
4.1.9.1 how long the client had been employed at this place of work?	[ ]	[ ]	[ ]
4.1.9.2 the client's experience of the type of work he or she was currently undertaking?	[ ]	[ ]	[ ]
4.1.9.3 the client's work conditions (hours worked, tasks undertaken etc.)?	[ ]	[ ]	[ ]
4.1.9.4 whether the client is a member of a trades union (and if so whether they have sought its advice).	[ ]	[ ]	[ ]
4.1.9.5 what training was provided by the employer?	[ ]	[ ]	[ ]

	Yes	No	N/a

		Yes	No	N/a
4.1.9.6	whether there is a written contract of employment?	[ ]	[ ]	[ ]

5. Slips, Trips and Falls

N/A [ ]

5.1 Did the file demonstrate that the lawyer had some understanding of all of the following:

		Yes	No	N/a
5.1.1	if the fall was caused by an uneven surface, the dimensions of the hole/obstruction and whether it would be considered dangerous?	[ ]	[ ]	[ ]
5.1.2	any verbal or written warning notices, and (if applicable) when the client was made aware of these?	[ ]	[ ]	[ ]
5.1.3	who did, or might, occupy and (if different) own the property upon which the accident took place?	[ ]	[ ]	[ ]
5.1.4	what happened immediately after the accident; in particular whether any comments were made by people connected with the property on which the accident occurred (e.g. staff or owners of any premises)?	[ ]	[ ]	[ ]
5.1.5	if it seems likely that the client might know this,[6] whether there have been any previous accidents at the site?	[ ]	[ ]	[ ]
5.1.6	if it seems likely that the client might know this, whether or not anything has been changed since the accident to prevent a repeat of the accident?	[ ]	[ ]	[ ]

6. Faulty Goods

N/A [ ]

6.1 Did the file demonstrate that the lawyer had some understanding of all of the following:

		Yes	No	N/a
6.1.1	the clients normal/customary usage of the goods in question and how the goods were being used at the time of the accident?	[ ]	[ ]	[ ]
6.1.2	in what way the goods were or may have been faulty?	[ ]	[ ]	[ ]
6.1.3	who the supplier of the goods was?	[ ]	[ ]	[ ]
6.1.4	when and by whom the goods were purchased?	[ ]	[ ]	[ ]
6.1.5	how much the goods cost?	[ ]	[ ]	[ ]
6.1.6	where, when and by whom the goods were manufactured?	[ ]	[ ]	[ ]
6.1.7	anything said before/during the purchase by any witnesses to the sale (contact names and addresses, or if possible contacts)?	[ ]	[ ]	[ ]
6.1.8	any warnings (written or oral) and when the client became aware of them?	[ ]	[ ]	[ ]
6.1.9	any documentation associated with the product?	[ ]	[ ]	[ ]

15

		Yes	No	N/a
6.1.10	whether the client has contact with the manufacturer retailer, or supplier since the accident? If so, is there detail as to what occurred?	[ ]	[ ]	[ ]
6.1.11	whether the goods are still available for examination?	[ ]	[ ]	[ ]
6.1.12	whether there is an invoice/receipt?	[ ]	[ ]	[ ]

7. Fatal Accident[7]

	N/A	[ ]

7.1 Did the file additionally demonstrate that the lawyer had some understanding of all of the following:

		Yes	No	N/a
7.1.1	date of birth of the deceased?	[ ]	[ ]	[ ]
7.1.2	full name of deceased?	[ ]	[ ]	[ ]
7.1.3	date of death?	[ ]	[ ]	[ ]
7.1.4	address of deceased at date of death?	[ ]	[ ]	[ ]
7.1.5	whether any arrangements have been made to prove the deceased's will (if any) or administer the deceased's estate?	[ ]	[ ]	[ ]
7.1.6	name, address and date of birth of person(s) who will be likely to take out letters of Administration or Grant of Probate?	[ ]	[ ]	[ ]
7.1.7	the date of the accident which caused death or the date of the onset of the disease which caused death?	[ ]	[ ]	[ ]
7.1.8	the legal relationship between the deceased and the client?	[ ]	[ ]	[ ]
7.1.9	the age and relationship of any other dependants of the deceased?	[ ]	[ ]	[ ]
7.1.10	the date and outcome of any inquest?	[ ]	[ ]	[ ]
7.1.11	evidence given at an inquest or prosecution arising out of the fatal accident?	[ ]	[ ]	[ ]
7.1.12	how death was caused?	[ ]	[ ]	[ ]
7.1.13	whether death was instantaneous?	[ ]	[ ]	[ ]

The Client's Injuries

The following criteria apply to all types of personal injury case.

8. Did the file demonstrate that the lawyer had some understanding of all of the following:

		Yes	No	N/a
8.1	the nature and extent of the client's injuries?	[ ]	[ ]	[ ]
8.2	when the injuries became apparent?	[ ]	[ ]	[ ]
8.3	the nature of any treatment, and any time spent in such treatment?	[ ]	[ ]	[ ]
8.4	if the client lost consciousness during the accident, when was this specifically and how long was the client unconscious?	[ ]	[ ]	[ ]

			Yes	No	N/a
8.5		who treated the client (names of the hospital, surgeons and G.P. treating the client)?	[ ]	[ ]	[ ]
8.6		if the client suffered external injuries which are unlikely to give rise to long term scarring, the availability of any photographs of the injuries?	[ ]	[ ]	[ ]
8.7		the current medical status of the client re: injuries, pain, treatment and disablement?	[ ]	[ ]	[ ]
8.8		if the injuries involve continuing treatment, what the prognosis is (e.g. client's views on the future of their own condition as well as any medical opinions the client knows of)?[8]	[ ]	[ ]	[ ]

9. If the injuries have had a significant impact[9] on the client's life, the file should contain further evidence of an understanding of the effects of the accident upon the client's life, in particular:

			Yes	No	N/a
				N/A	[ ]
9.1		if the client was in gainful employment at the time of the accident:	[ ]	[ ]	[ ]
	9.1.1	how much time the client has had off work as a direct result of the injury;	[ ]	[ ]	[ ]
	9.1.2	the employer's name and address;	[ ]	[ ]	[ ]
	9.1.3	what the client's earnings were before the accident (if this is a fatal accident then the deceased's earnings should also be covered);	[ ]	[ ]	[ ]
9.2		where there is evidence of incapacitation:	[ ]	[ ]	[ ]
	9.2.1	the client's current ability to, or prospects for, work;	[ ]	[ ]	[ ]
	9.2.2	restrictions on the client's domestic or social life;	[ ]	[ ]	[ ]
	9.2.3	whether the client has been in contact with the social services and/or claimed any benefits in respect of their injuries;[10]	[ ]	[ ]	[ ]
9.3		where there is evidence of incapacitation and the client was/is in employment, whether the client has or should have been paid Statutory Sick Pay or health insurance by their employer;	[ ]	[ ]	[ ]
9.4		whether the client has received any payment of wages or money in lieu of wages with right of recoupment.	[ ]	[ ]	[ ]
9.5		details of any expenses resulting directly from the accident (special damages) and (if a fatal accident case) from the death of the deceased (e.g. funeral expenses);	[ ]	[ ]	[ ]
9.6		whether the client has suffered from any illnesses/disabilities in the past having a bearing on their current position.	[ ]	[ ]	[ ]

B.   CLIENT COUNSELLING AND ADVICE

The following advice should be given to the client following initial instruction taking and preliminary investigations.

		Yes	No	N/a

10.   Advice given to the client, and recorded on the file (either in attendance notes or in confirmatory letters to the client), should cover the following:

10.1   Who the client may be able to claim against.　　　　[ ]　[ ]　[ ]

10.2   An explanation of the basis of their claim; i.e:

    10.2.1   what they will have to show to enable a claim to be brought;[11]　　[ ]　[ ]　[ ]

    10.2.2   the means by which such a claim can be pursued (negotiation/litigation);　　[ ]　[ ]　[ ]

    10.2.3   an indication of any areas of doubt in proving such a claim, when and how they might be overcome;　　[ ]　[ ]　[ ]

10.3   What the client should be able to claim for; this must cover:[12]

    10.3.1   losses and expenses;　　[ ]　[ ]　[ ]

    10.3.2   any anticipated future losses and expenses;　　[ ]　[ ]　[ ]

    10.3.3   if the client lost time off work, loss of earnings (to date and a future estimate);　　[ ]　[ ]　[ ]

    10.3.4   damages for the injuries themselves, including pain and suffering;　　[ ]　[ ]　[ ]

    10.3.5   (if applicable) bereavement.　　[ ]　[ ]　[ ]

10.4   Where there is evidence of incapacity to the client, was the possibility of welfare benefits for the injuries, disabilities, or financial predicament, and the effect these would have upon any award for damages, considered?　　[ ]　[ ]　[ ]

10.5   Where welfare benefits are being claimed as a result of the client's injuries, was the client advised on the Compensation Recovery Unit's (CRU) claw back provisions?　　[ ]　[ ]　[ ]

10.6   In a claim involving criminal violence, was a claim against the Criminal Injuries Compensation Board considered?　　[ ]　[ ]　[ ]

10.7   Similarly, was the possibility of a criminal compensation order considered?　　[ ]　[ ]　[ ]

10.8   (In Road Traffic cases) if the lawyer has no information on the other side from which they or their insurers can be identified and traced, has the client been advised as to the possibility of an M.I.B. claim?[13]　[ ]　[ ]　[ ]

10.9   Was the limitation period for the action noted in a prominent place upon the file and was this correct?[14]　　[ ]　[ ]　[ ]

10.10   If the case is discontinued, or the case is begun close to or beyond the limitation period, is there an indication that the client was advised of the limitation period?　　[ ]　[ ]　[ ]

Progress of the case

			Yes	No	N/a
11.1	Did the lawyer advise the client how long the client can expect to wait for the claim to be concluded?[15]		[ ]	[ ]	[ ]
11.2	Is there an indication of the steps the lawyer agrees to take in furtherance of the client's claim?		[ ]	[ ]	[ ]
11.3	Is there an indication of the steps the lawyer has asked the client to take (if any) and the time limits within which these should be completed?		[ ]	[ ]	[ ]
11.4	Is the client told when and in what form the next contact will take place?		[ ]	[ ]	[ ]
11.5	Has the lawyer advised the client as to more than one possible course of action from which the client could choose?[16]		[ ]	[ ]	[ ]
11.6	Has the lawyer advised the client of the likely outcome of the case?[17]		[ ]	[ ]	[ ]
11.7	Is there an indication that the client has made an active choice on the lawyers suggested modes of action?		[ ]	[ ]	[ ]
11.8	Has the lawyer noted down the reaction of the client to the decided plan of action (as a minimum, this should include the client's consent to the action going forward)?[18]		[ ]	[ ]	[ ]
11.9	Were any apparent queries from the client dealt with fully, promptly and politely?		[ ]	[ ]	[ ]
11.10	Did the lawyer deal with any evident emotional concerns of the client?		[ ]	[ ]	[ ]
11.11	Any contact with the other side should be explained. In particular, did the lawyer explain when the other side will be contacted and why?		[ ]	[ ]	[ ]
11.12	If it appears likely that the other side will contact the client directly, did the lawyer advise the client as to what they should do in the event that the other side contacted them?		[ ]	[ ]	[ ]
11.13	If the lawyer is not going to represent the client at any hearings, is there an indication that alternative sources of representation or assistance were explained to the client?		[ ]	[ ]	[ ]

Costs

12. Is there an indication of advice given to the client regarding the costs and funding of the case. In particular:

			Yes	No	N/a
12.1	whether or not the client will have to make a contribution to the cost of the case;[19]		[ ]	[ ]	[ ]
12.2	the effects of the statutory charge on any damages received;		[ ]	[ ]	[ ]
12.3	the costs to the client should the case be lost;[20]		[ ]	[ ]	[ ]

		Yes	No	N/a

<table>
<tr><td>12.4</td><td>the nature of revocation and discharge of certificates (if one is awarded);</td><td>[ ]</td><td>[ ]</td><td>[ ]</td></tr>
<tr><td>12.5</td><td>if awarded a full certificate, the duty to report changes of circumstance and address.</td><td>[ ]</td><td>[ ]</td><td>[ ]</td></tr>
<tr><td>12.6</td><td>the limits and extent of Green Form and Full Certificate Funding[21]</td><td>[ ]</td><td>[ ]</td><td>[ ]</td></tr>
</table>

C. PROCEDURAL AND PRACTICAL STEPS

<table>
<tr><td>13.</td><td>Where liability is in doubt and the scene of the accident is relevant, did the lawyer consider arrangements for a site inspection, for photographs to be taken, and a plan drawn?[22]</td><td>[ ]</td><td>[ ]</td><td>[ ]</td></tr>
<tr><td>14.</td><td>If possible, were witnesses contacted and interviewed?</td><td>[ ]</td><td>[ ]</td><td>[ ]</td></tr>
<tr><td>15.</td><td>If the police were involved were they contacted for evidence?</td><td>[ ]</td><td>[ ]</td><td>[ ]</td></tr>
<tr><td>16.</td><td>If liability is not in dispute or if liability is not regarded as a problem, was a doctor contacted for evidence of the client's injuries?</td><td>[ ]</td><td>[ ]</td><td>[ ]</td></tr>
<tr><td>17.</td><td>If liability is not in dispute or if liability is not regarded as a problem, did the lawyer have signed medical authority for the client and was a medical examination and report arranged for the client to attend?</td><td>[ ]</td><td>[ ]</td><td>[ ]</td></tr>
<tr><td>18.</td><td>Did the lawyer attempt to secure contact with the other side informing them of the claim and requesting that they inform their insurers of the claim?</td><td>[ ]</td><td>[ ]</td><td>[ ]</td></tr>
<tr><td>19.</td><td>Did the lawyer write to the client confirming in a comprehensible manner:</td><td></td><td></td><td></td></tr>
<tr><td>19.1</td><td>the basis of the client's claim?</td><td>[ ]</td><td>[ ]</td><td>[ ]</td></tr>
<tr><td>19.2</td><td>an outline of the advice given, including, in particular, areas of uncertainty/difficulty?</td><td>[ ]</td><td>[ ]</td><td>[ ]</td></tr>
<tr><td>19.3</td><td>an estimate of the damages likely to be recoverable (this may be in the form of a range of values and linked to uncertainties in the case)?</td><td>[ ]</td><td>[ ]</td><td>[ ]</td></tr>
<tr><td>20.</td><td>Was the client given an opportunity to read witness statements and reports, and to comment upon these?</td><td>[ ]</td><td>[ ]</td><td>[ ]</td></tr>
<tr><td>21.</td><td>Was the client kept informed of any developments with the other side's insurance company?</td><td>[ ]</td><td>[ ]</td><td>[ ]</td></tr>
<tr><td>22.</td><td>Were letters to the client comprehensible?</td><td>[ ]</td><td>[ ]</td><td>[ ]</td></tr>
<tr><td>23.</td><td>Was the client encouraged to keep written records of the accident and further treatment?</td><td>[ ]</td><td>[ ]</td><td>[ ]</td></tr>
<tr><td>24.</td><td>Was the client encouraged to keep written records of all costs and expenses incurred as a result of injuries and treatment and to keep the solicitor informed?</td><td>[ ]</td><td>[ ]</td><td>[ ]</td></tr>
<tr><td>25.</td><td>For accidents at work where the client has had more than three days off work or longer than 24 hours' hospitalisation, did the lawyer consider seeking a factual statement from the inspector of the Health and Safety Executive (or confirmation that the H.S.E. has not been involved)?[23]</td><td>[ ]</td><td>[ ]</td><td>[ ]</td></tr>
</table>

II Pre-action Stages in Medical Negligence Cases

A. Procedural and Practical Steps

		Yes	No	N/a
26.	Has the solicitor written to the institution at which the negligent treatment was given including the following:	[ ]	[ ]	[ ]
26.1	Clearly identifying the client[24]	[ ]	[ ]	[ ]
26.2	A brief description of what occurred including a general indication of the negligence that is being alleged?	[ ]	[ ]	[ ]
26.3	A request for full medical notes and records?[25]	[ ]	[ ]	[ ]
26.4	Clear direction that the notes and records should be disclosed directly to the lawyer?[26]	[ ]	[ ]	[ ]
26.5	Anticipating points that may be raised e.g. the meeting of reasonable photocopying charges?[27]	[ ]	[ ]	[ ]
26.6	If the institution is not forthcoming with notes were they warned that:	[ ]	[ ]	[ ]
26.6.1	an application for pre- action discovery will be made if the notes are not disclosed?	[ ]	[ ]	[ ]
26.6.2	this will include a claim for costs against them?	[ ]	[ ]	[ ]
26.7	A signed Form of Consent from the client authorising the disclosure of all medical records?	[ ]	[ ]	[ ]
27.	On receipt of the medical notes has the lawyer gone through these with the client?	[ ]	[ ]	[ ]
28.	Has the solicitor sought at least one relevant expert report before issuing proceedings covering both negligence and causation?[28]	[ ]	[ ]	[ ]
29.	Did the letter(s) of request to the expert(s) contain:			
29.1	The name and address of the client?[29]	[ ]	[ ]	[ ]
29.2	The name of the institution or doctor against which the claim may be made?	[ ]	[ ]	[ ]
29.3	A copy of the client's statement/proof of evidence?	[ ]	[ ]	[ ]
29.4	An explanation of what the solicitor requires from the expert, identifying clearly any specific areas to be reported on?	[ ]	[ ]	[ ]
29.5	A confirmation that reasonable fees will be met by the firm?[30]	[ ]	[ ]	[ ]
29.6	If the Legal Aid Board has specified a maximum authority, a statement to that effect?	[ ]	[ ]	[ ]
29.7	A request for details of any reference material used by the expert in compiling the report?	[ ]	[ ]	[ ]

		Yes	No	N/a

29.8   Instructions to keep separate sections of the report relating to the client's present condition and prognosis and those relating to the question of liability and negligence so that the former may be disclosed independently, if necessary?   [ ]   [ ]   [ ]

29.9   If the expert is to obtain the client's medical records, did the solicitor enclose the client's consent to this?   [ ]   [ ]   [ ]

30.   Upon receipt of the expert's report(s) did the solicitor:

30.1   Allow the client to comment on it, or a summary of its conclusions?   [ ]   [ ]   [ ]

30.2   If the report was unfavourable, consider the possibility of seeking a further report and applying for authority to do so from the Legal Aid Board?   [ ]   [ ]   [ ]

30.3   If more than one expert is being retained as a potential witness, has each retained expert seen and commented on the evidence of the other experts?[31]   [ ]   [ ]   [ ]

31.   If the Legal Aid Board refuses authority to obtain a further report(s) where the first was unfavourable, has the solicitor considered with the client the possibility of discharging the certificate, the client independently obtaining a further report and, if this is favourable, applying again for a Legal Aid certificate?[32]   [ ]   [ ]   [ ]

32.   On receipt of the medical notes has the lawyer gone through these with the client?   [ ]   [ ]   [ ]

III   The Start of Proceedings (issuing proceedings/receiving the defence)

Once proceedings have been issued and the defence received from the other side, the following points should have been covered.

This section should not be audited if proceedings have not yet been issued.

A.   STRATEGIC DECISION MAKING

33.   Was quantum estimated to determine court venue?[33]   [ ]   [ ]   [ ]

34.   If the reasonably expected recovery from the case was clearly less than £50000, was the case commenced in the County Court?   [ ]   [ ]   [ ]

35.   In deciding to issue proceedings, were the following matters considered by the lawyer:

35.1   that there is a reasonable prospect of success, or is it apparent that proceedings are necessary to protect the client's position;   [ ]   [ ]   [ ]

35.2   that a settlement is not imminent;[34]   [ ]   [ ]   [ ]

35.3   whether or not the defendant is likely to be able to meet the claim (this can usually be assumed where the defendant is insured, or is backed by a corporation or other institution);   [ ]   [ ]   [ ]

		Yes	No	N/a

35.4	the cost implications for the client;	[ ]	[ ]	[ ]
36.	Where there is more than one potential defendant, was there evidence that the lawyer has considered how many and which of the potential defendants should be issued against?[35]	[ ]	[ ]	[ ]
37.	Where one of the defendants was acting as an employee at the time of the injury, was consideration given to action being taken against the employers?	[ ]	[ ]	[ ]

B. Procedural and Practical Steps

The procedural section is divided into six prevalent types of personal injury case, and a general statement of claim section for other types of personal injury claim. A fatal accidents item (45) could apply alongside any of items 38–44. The remaining items contain procedural criteria applicable to all types of personal injury case.

38. Road Traffic Accidents
N/A [ ]

38.1 In the Statement of Claim in Road Traffic Accident cases have the following been included:[36]

38.1.1	Are the parties clearly identifiable?	[ ]	[ ]	[ ]
38.1.2	Are all the vehicles that were involved in the accident clearly identified?	[ ]	[ ]	[ ]
38.1.3	Is the location of the accident stated?	[ ]	[ ]	[ ]
38.1.4	Have the directions the plaintiff and the defendant were travelling in been defined?	[ ]	[ ]	[ ]
38.1.5	Have the date and (where relevant) the time of the accident been stated?	[ ]	[ ]	[ ]
38.1.6	Is a description of how the accident happened included?[37]	[ ]	[ ]	[ ]
38.1.7	Has the lawyer included specific allegations of how the defendant's negligence caused the accident?[38]	[ ]	[ ]	[ ]
38.1.8	If relevant, a statement that the plaintiff will rely on the conviction of the defendant if any?	[ ]	[ ]	[ ]

39. Accidents at Work
N/A [ ]

39.1 In a Statement of Claim for Accidents at Work have the following points been included/stated:

39.1.1	The identity of the parties and their work relationships?	[ ]	[ ]	[ ]
39.1.2	The plaintiff's job description or job title?	[ ]	[ ]	[ ]

		Yes	No	N/a
39.1.3	The name and address of the plaintiff's place of work (if it was the accident site)?	[ ]	[ ]	[ ]
39.1.4	The nature of the plaintiff's place of work?[39]	[ ]	[ ]	[ ]
39.1.5	The location of the accident?	[ ]	[ ]	[ ]
39.1.6	The date and, where relevant, the time of the accident?	[ ]	[ ]	[ ]
39.1.7	A description of how the accident happened?[40]	[ ]	[ ]	[ ]
39.1.8	Specific allegations of how the defendant's negligence/breach of statutory duty caused the accident?	[ ]	[ ]	[ ]

40. Industrial Deafness or Industrial Disease   N/A   [ ]

40.1 In a Statement of Claim for Industrial Deafness or Industrial Disease have the following points been included/stated:

		Yes	No	N/a
40.1.1	The identity of all relevant employers?	[ ]	[ ]	[ ]
40.1.2	The plaintiff's employment status?	[ ]	[ ]	[ ]
40.1.3	The period(s) during which the deafness or disease are said to have been caused?	[ ]	[ ]	[ ]
40.1.4	The plaintiff's job description?	[ ]	[ ]	[ ]
40.1.5	The name and address of plaintiff's place(s) of work?	[ ]	[ ]	[ ]
40.1.6	The nature of the plaintiff's place of work?	[ ]	[ ]	[ ]
40.1.7	A description of the machinery and/or working conditions the plaintiff worked with and/or in?	[ ]	[ ]	[ ]
40.1.8	Specific allegations of the defendant's negligence and/or breach of statutory duty?	[ ]	[ ]	[ ]
40.1.9	A statement that the defendant's negligence and/or breach of statutory duty caused the deafness and/or disease of the plaintiff?	[ ]	[ ]	[ ]

41. Trips, Slips and Falls   N/A   [ ]

41.1 In the Statement of or Particulars of Claim where the plaintiff tripped, slipped or fell have the following been included/stated:

		Yes	No	N/a
41.1.1	The date and place of the accident?	[ ]	[ ]	[ ]
41.1.2	Details including measurements of the hole, obstruction etc?	[ ]	[ ]	[ ]
41.1.3	A description of what the plaintiff was doing when s/he tripped, slipped or fell on the highway, pavement or elsewhere?	[ ]	[ ]	[ ]
41.1.4	A statement of in what capacity the defendant caused the hole, obstruction or hazard causing the plaintiff to fall, trip or slip?	[ ]	[ ]	[ ]

41.1.5	If a highway authority or other local authority is being sued has the plaintiff made an allegation of breach of statutory duty?	[ ]	[ ]	[ ]
41.1.6	Specific allegations establishing a breach of duty of care and/or statutory duty by the defendant?[41]	[ ]	[ ]	[ ]
41.1.7	Where relevant, a statement that the happening of the said accident is evidence in itself of the negligence of the defendants, their servants or agents?	[ ]	[ ]	[ ]
41.1.8	Are the parties clearly identifiable?	[ ]	[ ]	[ ]

42. Medical Negligence   N/A [ ]

42.1 In the Statement or Particulars of Claim in medical negligence cases have the following been included/stated:

42.1.1	The date and (if known) the time of the negligent treatment (or failure to treat)?	[ ]	[ ]	[ ]
42.1.2	Details of the place at which the negligent treatment was given (or failure to treat)?	[ ]	[ ]	[ ]
42.1.3	A description of the circumstances in which the incident occurred?	[ ]	[ ]	[ ]
42.1.4	An outline of the sequence of events and the parties involved?	[ ]	[ ]	[ ]
42.1.5	Details of the alleged negligence/breach of duty of the defendant?	[ ]	[ ]	[ ]
42.1.6	A concise statement of what the plaintiff has suffered?	[ ]	[ ]	[ ]
42.1.7	Particulars of the injuries sustained as a result of the medical negligence and special damages?	[ ]	[ ]	[ ]
42.1.8	A statement that the medical negligence caused the injuries to the plaintiff?	[ ]	[ ]	[ ]

43. Accidents at School   N/A [ ]

43.1 In a statement of Claim for Accidents at School have the following points been included/stated:

43.1.1	The parties involved in the accident?	[ ]	[ ]	[ ]
43.1.2	How the accident was caused i.e. the events leading up to the accident including the accident itself?	[ ]	[ ]	[ ]
43.1.3	What the client was doing there?	[ ]	[ ]	[ ]
43.1.4	If relevant a statement that not enough safety training and procedures, safety precautions and oral instructions were given?	[ ]	[ ]	[ ]
43.1.5	If relevant a statement that not enough supervision was given?	[ ]	[ ]	[ ]

			Yes	No	N/a

			Yes	No	N/a
43.1.6	The location of the accident?		[ ]	[ ]	[ ]
43.1.7	A statement of the capacity in which the defendant caused or contributed to the accident?		[ ]	[ ]	[ ]
43.1.8	Specific allegations establishing a breach of duty of care and/or statutory duty by the defendant or his servant?		[ ]	[ ]	[ ]

44. Other Accidents

				N/A	[ ]

44.1 In a Statement of Claim for those accidents not covered by the above, have the following points been included/stated:

			Yes	No	N/a
44.1.1	The identity of the parties involved?		[ ]	[ ]	[ ]
44.1.2	An explanation of the events leading up to the incident?		[ ]	[ ]	[ ]
44.1.3	In what capacity the client was at the scene?		[ ]	[ ]	[ ]
44.1.4	The date and (where relevant) time of the incident?		[ ]	[ ]	[ ]
44.1.5	Details of any negligence/breach of duty alleged against the defendant/s?		[ ]	[ ]	[ ]
44.1.6	Details of how the negligence/breach of duty caused the incident?		[ ]	[ ]	[ ]

45. Fatal Accidents

				N/A	[ ]

45.1 In the Statement or Particulars of Claim in fatal accident cases have the following been included/stated:[42]

			Yes	No	N/a
45.1.1	Date of death: not usually instantaneous?		[ ]	[ ]	[ ]
45.1.2	Details of the plaintiff describing his/her relationship to the deceased?		[ ]	[ ]	[ ]
45.1.3	Details of other dependants of the deceased (if any)?		[ ]	[ ]	[ ]
45.1.4	Details of the Grant of Probate/Letters of Administration?		[ ]	[ ]	[ ]
45.1.5	A description of the circumstances in which the death occurred?[43]		[ ]	[ ]	[ ]
45.1.6	A summary of the events leading up to the death?		[ ]	[ ]	[ ]
45.1.7	Details of any pre death pain and suffering?		[ ]	[ ]	[ ]

46.	In cases where proceedings are issued against an employer as a result of an employee's negligence does the Statement of Claim cover vicarious liability?[44]	[ ]	[ ]	[ ]
47.	Where a schedule of special damages is served with the statement of claim were the following issues covered:[45]		N/A	[ ]
47.1	Losses and expenses to date;	[ ]	[ ]	[ ]

			Yes	No	N/a
	47.2	Estimated future losses and expenses;	[ ]	[ ]	[ ]
	47.3	Where the client was employed, or in business, at the time of the accident, loss of earnings or profits to date;	[ ]	[ ]	[ ]
	47.4	Estimated future loss of earnings or profits;	[ ]	[ ]	[ ]
	47.5	Where the client was employed at the time of the injury, loss of mobility in the labour market and loss of earning capacity;[46]	[ ]	[ ]	[ ]
	47.6	Loss of pension rights (if any);	[ ]	[ ]	[ ]
	47.7	Medical expenses (if any);	[ ]	[ ]	[ ]
	47.8	The costs of care, attention, accommodation (if any).	[ ]	[ ]	[ ]
	47.9	Any other pecuniary losses or expenses.	[ ]	[ ]	[ ]
48.		Where the lawyer decides not to serve a schedule of special damages and/or a medical report with the statement of claim:[47]		**N/A**	[ ]
	48.1	Were the defendant's solicitors contacted to ask if they would consent to the service of the Statement of Claim without a medical report and special damages claim?	[ ]	[ ]	[ ]
	48.2	If the defendant's solicitors do object, did the plaintiff's lawyer seek an order under Ord.18 R.12 (1)(b) dispensing with the requirements to serve medical reports and/or a schedule of damages or seeking an extension of time for the service of these documents.	[ ]	[ ]	[ ]
49.		Did the medical report and/or statement of claim (if one is served) contain the following details:		**N/A**	[ ]
	49.1	The plaintiff's date of birth?	[ ]	[ ]	[ ]
	49.2	A description of the nature and extent of the injuries sustained, pain and disability suffered?	[ ]	[ ]	[ ]
	49.3	The immediate after-effects of these injuries?	[ ]	[ ]	[ ]
	49.4	The lasting after-effects of these injuries?[48]	[ ]	[ ]	[ ]
	49.5	The nature of any treatment and time spent in such treatment?	[ ]	[ ]	[ ]
	49.6	The prognosis for the client's condition?	[ ]	[ ]	[ ]
50.		If the injuries had a significant impact on the client's life, does the medical report and/or statement of claim include a description of the loss of amenities, i.e:		**N/A**	[ ]
	50.1	Incapacitation/restrictions on the client's domestic and social life?	[ ]	[ ]	[ ]
	50.2	Incapacitation/restrictions on the client's ability to work?	[ ]	[ ]	[ ]
	50.3	Loss of earning capacity?	[ ]	[ ]	[ ]
51.		If the case is to be issued in the High Court, did the lawyer certify on the writ that the claim is worth more than £50 000?	[ ]	[ ]	[ ]

	Yes	No	N/a

52. In County Court cases, unless the claim is clearly less than £5000, did the particulars of claim state that the claim is in excess of £5000?[49]   [ ] [ ] [ ]

53. If the claim is clearly less than £3000, do the particulars of claim limit the value of the claim to £3000?   [ ] [ ] [ ]

54. Does the particulars/statement of claim contain a pleading for interest?   [ ] [ ] [ ]

55. Where a relevant prosecution and conviction followed the accident, were the following included:[50]   [ ] [ ] [ ]

    55.1   the offence(s);   [ ] [ ] [ ]

    55.2   the court; and   [ ] [ ] [ ]

    55.3   the date of the conviction?   [ ] [ ] [ ]

56. If a claim is being made for provisional damages[51], are these pleaded in the statement/particulars of claim?   [ ] [ ] [ ]

57. In cases where the defendant was uninsured/untraced whilst driving, was the M.I.B. notified formally within seven days of the issue of proceedings?   [ ] [ ] [ ]

58. Was notice of commencement of proceedings sent to the insurers before or within 7 days of commencement of proceedings referring to s.152 of the Road Traffic Act 1988.   [ ] [ ] [ ]

59. Where the defendant was untraced, was an application made to the MIB (Motor Insurers Bureau) within 3 years of the accident?   [ ] [ ] [ ]

The Defence

60. On Receipt of the Defence there are a number of points which the lawyer should consider:

    60.1   If the defence alleges that the Limitation Act 1980 bars the plaintiff's claim, has the lawyer considered why the claim is not statute barred or why the plaintiff seeks the exercise of the court's discretion under s.33 of the Limitation Act 1980?   [ ] [ ] [ ]

    60.2   In the High Court, if there is a counterclaim from the defendant, has the plaintiff's lawyer responded to it by drafting a defence to the counterclaim?[52]   [ ] [ ] [ ]

    60.3   If there is an allegation of contributory negligence, has the lawyer considered whether any further evidence is necessary in order to refute the allegation?   [ ] [ ] [ ]

    60.4   Has the lawyer considered making a Request for Further and Better Particulars?   [ ] [ ] [ ]

    60.5   If liability is admitted, has the lawyer considered an application for Summary Judgement and/or interim damages?   [ ] [ ] [ ]

C. CLIENT COUNSELLING AND ADVICE

		Yes	No	N/a
61.	Before the issuing of the proceedings did the lawyer contact the client and advise them on the effect of issuing proceedings in terms of:[53]			
61.1	level of damages to be gained	[ ]	[ ]	[ ]
61.2	length of time to be taken	[ ]	[ ]	[ ]
61.3	likely costs to the client	[ ]	[ ]	[ ]
61.4	likelihood of success	[ ]	[ ]	[ ]
61.5	explaining any other reasons for issuing proceedings which exist in this particular case[54]	[ ]	[ ]	[ ]
62.	If the lawyer advised the client against issuing proceedings, have reasons been given for that advice?	[ ]	[ ]	[ ]
63.	If the client insists that the lawyer issue proceedings, in spite of the lawyer's own advice to the client against issuing proceedings:	[ ]	[ ]	[ ]
63.1	has the Legal Aid Board been informed of this disagreement?[55]	[ ]	[ ]	[ ]
63.2	has the client been asked to sign a written confirmation of their request to issue proceedings?	[ ]	[ ]	[ ]
64.	If the client resists suing against the advice of the lawyer was the client advised that the lawyer will apply to the Legal Aid Board to discharge the certificate and was the client asked to withdraw their instructions?	[ ]	[ ]	[ ]

65. On Receipt of the Defence

		Yes	No	N/a
66.	Did the lawyer give the client a clear explanation of the defence?[56]	[ ]	[ ]	[ ]
67.	Was the client given an opportunity to comment on the defence?	[ ]	[ ]	[ ]
68.	Where the defence contains a counterclaim, was this explained to the client?	[ ]	[ ]	[ ]
69.	Where there were any allegations of contributory negligence:	[ ]	[ ]	[ ]
69.1	were these explained to the client?	[ ]	[ ]	[ ]
69.2	was the client given the opportunity to comment on the allegations of contributory negligence?	[ ]	[ ]	[ ]

IV Payments into Court

The following criteria apply whenever the Plaintiff's solicitor receives notice of a payment into court.

A. STRATEGIC DECISION MAKING

		Yes	No	N/a
70.	Has the lawyer made an up to date evaluation of the strength of the case in terms of:	**N/A** [ ]		
70.1	liability	[ ]	[ ]	[ ]
70.2	general damages (upper and lower values)	[ ]	[ ]	[ ]

			Yes	No	N/a
70.3	special damages		[ ]	[ ]	[ ]
70.4	the costs of further action		[ ]	[ ]	[ ]
70.5	any allegations of contributory negligence?		[ ]	[ ]	[ ]

71. If the client has been claiming benefits as a result of the injuries received, has the lawyer taken into account in the evaluation of damages the statutory deductions for welfare benefits?[57]   [ ]   [ ]   [ ]

72. On receipt of a copy CRU[58] certificate, did the lawyer check with the client as to whether the figure for deductible benefit was correct?[59]   [ ]   [ ]   [ ]

B. PROCEDURAL AND PRACTICAL STEPS

73. Has the lawyer acknowledged safe receipt of the Notice of Payment Into Court within three days?[60]   [ ]   [ ]   [ ]

74. Where the payment in is accepted within 21 days of receipt of the notice of payment in, and where the plaintiff is neither a minor nor a person under a disability:[61]   **N/A**   [ ]

     74.1 was the defendant notified of the acceptance within 21 days of receipt of the notice?   [ ]   [ ]   [ ]

     74.2 was the court contacted confirming acceptance within 21 days of receipt of the notice?   [ ]   [ ]   [ ]

75. If payment in is to be accepted for a plaintiff who is a minor or is under any other disability has a summons been issued seeking court approval of the settlement?[62]   [ ]   [ ]   [ ]

76. If the client rejected the payment in although the lawyer and/or counsel deemed it reasonable and recommended acceptance, is there evidence of immediate notification to the Legal Aid Board, covering the following points:[63]   **N/A**   [ ]

     76.1 why the payment in was rejected;   [ ]   [ ]   [ ]

     76.2 why the payment in was made by the defendant;   [ ]   [ ]   [ ]

     76.3 why the payment in was quantified at that amount by the defendant;[64]   [ ]   [ ]   [ ]

     76.4 if counsel's opinion was sought on the payment in, was this included with the notification to the Board?   [ ]   [ ]   [ ]

77. Where the payment in is accepted longer than 21 days after receipt of payment in: [ ]   [ ]   [ ]

     77.1 was the consent of the defendant to late acceptance sought?   [ ]   [ ]   [ ]

     77.2 have steps been taken to obtain an Order/Summons for payment out and interest?   [ ]   [ ]   [ ]

     77.3 were costs also dealt with?   [ ]   [ ]   [ ]

C. CLIENT COUNSELLING AND ADVICE

		Yes	No	N/a

78. Is there evidence of clear advice being given to the client regarding the payment in, covering:

78.1 the consequences of acceptance;   [ ] [ ] [ ]

78.2 where there is more than one defendant, the consequences of acceptance on the claim in relation to the remaining defendants?   [ ] [ ] [ ]

78.3 the possible consequences of rejection, in particular:

78.3.1 that if the amount of damages they are eventually awarded is not more than the amount paid into court, the client will bear costs incurred by the defendant after the payment into court?   [ ] [ ] [ ]

78.3.2 an outline of what such costs are likely to be?   [ ] [ ] [ ]

78.3.3 that such costs would be deducted from any damages received by the client?[65]   [ ] [ ] [ ]

78.3.4 that the Legal Aid Board must be informed of unreasonable refusals to accept payments in and the circumstances in which this may lead to discharge of the certificate?   [ ] [ ] [ ]

78.4 whether the payment is reasonable having regard to current upper and lower assessments of quantum and liability, etc.;   [ ] [ ] [ ]

78.5 whether acceptance or rejection is recommended.   [ ] [ ] [ ]

79. If payment in is accepted is the client advised as to what must now be done and how long it is likely to take before the client receives any money?[66]   [ ] [ ] [ ]

V Settlement of the Case

The following criteria apply where a settlement is agreed between plaintiff and defendant either before or after the issue of proceedings. This may occur without any payment into court but it may also occur after a payment into court. However, the criteria do not apply where a payment in is simply accepted.

A. STRATEGIC DECISION MAKING

80. Has the lawyer made an up to date evaluation of the strength of the case in terms of:

80.1 liability   [ ] [ ] [ ]

80.2 general damages (upper and lower values)   [ ] [ ] [ ]

80.3 special damages   [ ] [ ] [ ]

80.4 the costs of pursuing the case further   [ ] [ ] [ ]

81. Has the lawyer taken into account any allegations of contributory negligence?   [ ] [ ] [ ]

82. Did the settlement cover the following issues:[67]

82.1 how much is being accepted in full and final settlement?   [ ] [ ] [N/a]

			Yes	No	N/a
82.2	whether or not it takes into account interim payments made (if any)?		[ ]	[ ]	[ ]
82.3	the payment out of money in court (if any)?		[ ]	[ ]	[ ]
82.4	the time limit within which payment should be made to the client's lawyer?		[ ]	[ ]	[ ]
82.5	interest on money in court (if any)?		[ ]	[ ]	[ ]
82.6	interest accruing on late payment?		[ ]	[ ]	[ ]
82.7	whether or not costs are agreed?		[ ]	[ ]	[ ]
82.8	was it evident that the lawyer had considered (where relevant) any monies which will have to be deducted from the client's settlement?[68]		[ ]	[ ]	[ ]

B. PROCEDURAL AND PRACTICAL STEPS

83. Has the fee earner written to the Legal Aid Board:[69]

		Yes	No	N/a
83.1	confirming the settlement?	[ ]	[ ]	[ ]
83.2	notifying it of the agreement on costs (if there is agreement)?	[ ]	[ ]	[ ]
83.3	stating profit costs?	[ ]	[ ]	[ ]
83.4	stating counsel's fees?	[ ]	[ ]	[ ]
83.5	stating agreed disbursements?	[ ]	[ ]	[ ]

84. Where negotiation on costs is not continuing in cases which settle after proceedings have been issued and if agreement could not be reached on costs, has a bill of costs been drawn up and lodged with the court's taxing office within three months of the settlement?[70] [71]   [ ] [ ] [ ]

85. In cases which settle after proceedings have been issued and if costs were not agreed, has an order been sought containing a clause allowing the plaintiff's costs to be taxed.[72]   [ ] [ ] [ ]

86. If proceedings have not commenced at the time of the agreement, has the Area Office assessed the costs and/or confirmed that the case had been closed?[73]   [ ] [ ] [ ]

87. On completion of the settlement, has the Legal Aid Certificate been discharged?[74]   [ ] [ ] [ ]

C. CLIENT COUNSELLING AND ADVICE

88. Had the client been kept adequately informed of all negotiations?[75]   [ ] [ ] [ ]

89. Were the client's instructions sought on all offers made?[76]   [ ] [ ] [ ]

90. Was the client advised on the settlement, i.e.:

		Yes	No	N/a
90.1	the consequences of acceptance	[ ]	[ ]	[ ]

		Yes	No	N/a

90.2   the possible consequences of rejection, in particular:

90.2.1   what they are likely to achieve if the settlement is refused;   [ ]   [ ]   [ ]

90.2.2   that the Legal Aid Board must be informed of any refusal of a reasonable offer and the circumstances in which this may lead to discharge of the certificate.   [ ]   [ ]   [ ]

90.2.3   whether the settlement is reasonable having regard to a current upper and lower assessments of quantum and liability, etc.;   [ ]   [ ]   [ ]

90.2.4   whether acceptance or rejection is recommended.   [ ]   [ ]   [ ]

Welfare Benefits

91.   If the client is claiming loss of earnings, is it clear from the file whether or not the client is receiving, or has been in receipt of welfare benefits at any time since the injury occurred and which benefit, if any, these were?[77]   [ ]   [ ]   [ ]

92.   Where benefits have been received as a result of the client's injuries,   [ ]   [ ]   [ ]

92.1   has the solicitor informed the client of the fact that the D.S.S. has a claim on compensation payments for damages in personal injury actions if damages paid by the defendant are above £2500 for personal injuries and of the defendant's right to deduct half the relevant benefits if the damages are lower than that?[78]   [ ]   [ ]   [ ]

92.2   did the plaintiff's lawyer apply to the CRU (Compensation Recovery Unit) for benefit information relevant to the client (if no copy certificate has been received following the defendant's application to the CRU)?[79]   [ ]   [ ]   [ ]

92.3   if a CRU certificate has been received, has the lawyer consulted the client, to ensure it is correct?[80]   [ ]   [ ]   [ ]

92.4   if there is likely to be a deduction for welfare benefit payments has the lawyer advised the client as to the size of this deduction?   [ ]   [ ]   [ ]

92.5   if the client has been claiming benefits as a result of the injuries received, has the lawyer taken into account in their evaluation of damages the statutory deductions for welfare benefits?[81]   [ ]   [ ]   [ ]

VI Going to Trial

A. STRATEGIC DECISION MAKING

93.   Has the lawyer checked any limitation on the Legal Aid Certificate?   [ ]   [ ]   [ ]

94.   Has an up to date assessment of general damages been made (upper and lower valuations)?   [ ]   [ ]   [ ]

95.   Has an up to date assessment of special damages been made?   [ ]   [ ]   [ ]

96.   Has an up to date medical report been obtained?   [ ]   [ ]   [ ]

		Yes	No	N/a

97. Has the lawyer considered with the client the pros and cons of proceeding to trial in the light of: [ ] [ ] [ ]

    97.1   the level of current offer (if any) being made by the defendant; [ ] [ ] [ ]

    97.2   the amount of money currently paid into court (if any); [ ] [ ] [ ]

    97.3   the extra costs that will be incurred; [ ] [ ] [ ]

    97.4   the potential distress and inconvenience that could be caused to the client; [ ] [ ] [ ]

    97.5   the risks of litigation generally. [ ] [ ] [ ]

B. PROCEDURAL AND PRACTICAL STEPS

98. Has a summary of the case been prepared prior to trial (where Counsel is instructed this will take the form of a brief to Counsel) covering the following points:[82] [83] [ ] [ ] [ ]

    98.1   an outline of how the accident occurred; [ ] [ ] [ ]

    98.2   what the principal issues are; [ ] [ ] [ ]

    98.3   where the dispute(s) on liability lie; [ ] [ ] [ ]

    98.4   what evidence is relevant to the issues, and in particular, what will be available at court; [ ] [ ] [ ]

    98.5   a description of the injuries sustained by the client; [ ] [ ] [ ]

    98.6   a description of the client's current physical position and the prognosis; [ ] [ ] [ ]

    98.7   a summary of expert evidence regarding injuries covering: [ ] [ ] [ ]

        98.7.1 which experts each side is using; [ ] [ ] [ ]

        98.7.2 whether any evidence is agreed; [ ] [ ] [ ]

        98.7.3 an evaluation of the conflicts/weaknesses in the expert evidence. [ ] [ ] [ ]

    98.8   a summary of how financial losses are calculated (unless the method of calculation is self evident); [ ] [ ] [ ]

    98.9   a summary of which financial losses are agreed; [ ] [ ] [ ]

    98.10   a summary of how non-agreed losses will be proved; [ ] [ ] [ ]

    98.11   where there is a claim for future losses, an explanation of the figure proposed for this and suggested multipliers; [ ] [ ] [ ]

    98.12   where there is a claim for future loss of earning capacity, explanations of how this figure is arrived at and the evidence available to support such a claim; [ ] [ ] [ ]

		Yes	No	N/a

		Yes	No	N/a
98.13	an estimation of quantum for each individual head of the claim as well as an overall total figure;	[ ]	[ ]	[ ]
98.14	a summary of negotiations, all offers and all payments in;	[ ]	[ ]	[ ]
98.15	The position regarding exchange of witness statements?	[ ]	[ ]	[ ]
99.	Was a pre-trial conference arranged before the trial between the client and the person who is to represent them?[84]	[ ]	[ ]	[ ]
100.	Are all experts, witnesses and counsel's clerk or the person who is to represent the client at trial (if counsel is not to be instructed to represent) informed of time, date and place of trial as soon as the date is known?	[ ]	[ ]	[ ]
101.	Are all witnesses given an opportunity to read their statements/proofs of evidence prior to trial?[85]	[ ]	[ ]	[ ]

Evidence

		Yes	No	N/a
102.	Were the client's experts given an opportunity to comment on the defendant's expert reports as and when these were received by the lawyer?	[ ]	[ ]	[ ]
103.	If there is any witness who cannot attend court, has a notice been served under the Civil Evidence Act?	[ ]	[ ]	[ ]
104.	Have any photographs, plans, videos or films which are to be used been sent to the other side (if possible) at least ten days before the trial?[86]	[ ]	[ ]	[ ]
105.	Were all expert reports which are to be relied upon sent to the court at least two clear days before the trial (7 days clear in the County Court) or in accordance with the Directions made in the case?	[ ]	[ ]	[ ]
106.	If the other side have not agreed any relevant photographs and/or plans:	[ ]	[ ]	[ ]
106.1	has the solicitor issued a subpoena/witness summons to the makers to prove them formally?	[ ]	[ ]	[ ]
106.2	has the other side been notified and informed that they will bear these costs?	[ ]	[ ]	[ ]
107.	Have all reluctant witnesses and witnesses who are likely to need formal authority to come to court been made the subject of a subpoena/witness summons?	[ ]	[ ]	[ ]
108.	Has conduct money/expenses been tendered for all witnesses?	[ ]	[ ]	[ ]

C. CLIENT COUNSELLING AND ADVICE

		Yes	No	N/a
109.	Was the client advised of the possible outcomes of the trial, in terms of:			
109.1	what will happen if they lose;	[ ]	[ ]	[ ]
109.2	what will happen if they win;	[ ]	[ ]	[ ]
109.3	what the costs position will be;	[ ]	[ ]	[ ]

				Yes	No	N/a

109.4   what level of damages (upper and lower limits) the client can expect from a successful trial;   [ ]   [ ]   [ ]

109.5   if contributory negligence is alleged, the likely effect of this upon any damages award.   [ ]   [ ]   [ ]

110.   Was the client advised on the process of the trial, in particular:

110.1   how long the trial is expected to last;   [ ]   [ ]   [ ]

110.2   an outline of the issues that will be raised;   [ ]   [ ]   [ ]

110.3   how the client will be expected to participate in the proceedings;   [ ]   [ ]   [ ]

TRANSFER OF FILES AND COMPLAINTS

These criteria are considered throughout the file on all cases.

111.   If the file is to be transferred to another office, department or fee earner: **N/A**   [ ]

111.1   is there evidence (letter/attendance note) of explanation to the client of the transfer?[87]   [ ]   [ ]   [ ]

111.2   was the client given the name of the person taking over the case?   [ ]   [ ]   [ ]

111.3   was the client asked for acknowledgement/approval of the transfer?   [ ]   [ ]   [ ]

112.   Where the client makes a complaint, did the lawyer: **N/A**   [ ]

112.1   Respond to it immediately?   [ ]   [ ]   [ ]

112.2   Advise the client who else they can contact in the firm to consider the complaint?   [ ]   [ ]   [ ]

112.3   If the problem is solved to the client's satisfaction, was the solution confirmed in writing?   [ ]   [ ]   [ ]

112.4   If the problem is not solved to the client's satisfaction, were they referred to the Solicitors' Complaints Bureau?   [ ]   [ ]   [ ]

Personal Injury—Notes to the Criteria

1. Particular reference was had to: *A Practical Approach to Legal Advice and Drafting* by Susan Blake (3rd ed, Blackstone Press); *Personal Injury Litigation* by John Pritchard (6th ed, Longman); *Client Interviewing for Lawyers* by Avrom Sherr (Sweet & Maxwell 1986); *Personal Injury Practice* by Hendy, Day and Buchan (LAG 1992); and Lewis, CJ: *Medical Negligence: A Practical Guide* (Tolley, 1992)

2. This criterion will be satisfied either by knowledge of the number or by having sought (unsuccessfully) the national insurance number of the client.

3. Certain types of personal injury case may be caused by exposure to a risk over a period of time, e.g. industrial deafness and vibration whitefinger cases.

4. Certain types of personal injury case may be caused by exposure to a risk over a period of time, e.g. industrial deafness and vibration whitefinger cases.

5. This section relates to any vehicle that is involved in an accident. If, for example, a bus is one of the vehicles, then the solicitor must still ascertain whereabouts in the bus the client was sitting etc. and explain why no seat belt was worn (e.g. because none was fitted).

6. e.g. Because the client is familiar with the area where the fall occurred.

7. These criteria are derived in particular from Pritchard pp.215–216.

8. The client's view will be an important indicator of the effect of the injuries on the client, but practitioners will not be expected to form firm views on prognosis until receipt of appropriate medical reports.

9. Significant impact will be a question of common sense taking into account all circumstances. Significant means serious or lasting not merely transient or uncomfortable. The fact that the victim may have had a modest amount of time off work or been incapacitated for a short while does not necessarily mean that the injuries were significant. Incapacitation and incapacity bear the same meaning.

10. Such benefits may include income support, housing benefit, council tax benefit, statutory sick pay, sickness benefit, invalidity benefit, disability living allowance and disability working allowance.

11. This might cover the broad principles of negligence (breach of duty, causation, etc.).

12. The following criteria are taken from Pritchard p 32. In the early stages of a case the advice may be general in nature. It is not suggested, at this stage, that figures (in pounds) be attached to each of the heads

13. Full civil legal aid will not be given for untraced driver claims involving the Motor Insurers' Bureau.

14. This is generally three years from the time of the accident, although the limitation period for accidents injuring a minor does not start to run until the minor is eighteen years of age. For aircraft accidents there is a two year limitation period only. Also for accidents occurring during the course of sea voyages between U.K. ports and foreign ports, the limitation is two years. The limitation period does not begin to run until the client had knowledge of the injury or of the defendant's negligence (see, e.g. Pritchard, p.195). If it is not possible to note the precise limitation period, a note of this uncertainty must be made on the file giving an indication of the extent of such uncertainty. A warning should be given that the limitation period may be different for accidents in foreign countries.

15. This will be satisfied by a broad indication of how long the claim will take or when the lawyer is likely to be in a firmer position to predict the conclusion of a case.

16. See, e.g. Binder and Price: *Legal Interviewing and Counselling: A Client-Centred Approach*. [West (1977)], especially pp.147–155; also Sherr (1986) on the literature on vigilant and non-vigilant

decision making. Such an approach is central to the client having some say in the handling of their case and providing informed consent to action taken on their behalf. This is still consistent with the lawyer also advising the client of which course of action is *most* advisable.

17. This will be satisfied by a broad indication of the likely outcome or when the lawyer is likely to be in a firmer position to predict outcome.

18. See Sherr, op. cit., pp. 100–102.

19. Green Forms signed after 12 April 1993 will not be subject to a contribution but Full Certificates may be. Advice on contribution may be given on receipt of the offer of full legal aid.

20. Such advice may need to be in broad terms at the start of a case, rather than providing specific ideas as to the precise pound value of costs.

21. In an untraced driver case, the MIB will normally meet the solicitor's costs (in a fixed amount) the Green Form would only be a fall back option.

22. Liability will always be in doubt until the case is settled, particularly at this stage, unless, for example, there is already an admission of liability from the insurers, in which case this question can be ignored. It is not enough for the lawyer to indicate that he or she considers that liability is clear cut–it may not prove to be so.

23. See, Hendy et al, op.cit., p.36. Consideration may also need to be given to non-party discovery later in the case.

24. e.g. By name, time of involvement with institution, hospital number, etc., as appropriate.

25. Including any investigational notes.

26. Pritchard, J: The proposed defendant will probably agree to the release of medical notes and records, but probably offer that they will be forwarded direct to the plaintiff's medical experts. The disadvantage of this is that the notes and records cannot be made available to the plaintiff's solicitor, nor the plaintiff. See also, Lewis, C.J: *Medical Negligence: A Practical Guide*, "Never accept disclosure to a nominated expert only".

27. Pritchard, J., p.205

28. The lawyer may wish to avoid the use of the word 'negligence'. Lewis suggests that, "the word 'negligence' should be avoided because it can put an expert off as it has a condemnatory ring to it." Lewis, op.cit., p.105. The auditor is looking for instructions covering both breach of duty and causation.

29. This is necessary, for example, to enable the expert to arrange a direct appointment with the client.

30. i.e. Such fees as are allowed on legal aid taxation. The full fee will not be payable until after taxation, but an interim payment on account will be sought from the Legal Aid Board.

31. Here, retained experts are experts the lawyer is considering using in disclosed reports and/or trial.

32. Pritchard, p.208

33. Personal Injury actions of a value of less than £50,000 must be issued in the County Court, if they are issued in the High Court the claim should include a certificate of value that the case exceeds £50,000. Similarly there are differing fees for different value claims in the County Court.

34. If there is any doubt about whether or not a settlement is imminent and if there are reasonable prospects of success, the lawyer should issue proceedings, see, Hendy et al, p.77. See also, Hazel Genn, *Hard Bargaining*.

35. Hendy et al stated that it is generally wisest to sue against the defendant against whom liability is clearest. If proceedings are taken to protect the plaintiff's position, then all potential defendants should be issued against. Hendy et al, op.cit., pp.78–79. Practitioners have advised that in circumstances of doubt, all defendants need to be issued against.

36. These points would need to be satisfied whether the solicitor or Counsel drafted the statement of claim.

37. It is not good practice to provide a full narrative description of the accident. The description should be kept as short as possible, with the wording concentrated on allegations of negligence.

38. e.g. An allegation that the defendant drove too fast; an allegation that the defendant failed to accord precedence to the plaintiff; an allegation that the defendant failed to keep any proper lookout; an allegation that the defendant failed to warn the plaintiff in time, adequately or, at all, of the movement of the defendant's vehicle; an allegation that the defendant drove into the plaintiff and/or failed to stop, slow down (or accelerate), swerve, or so to control or manage the defendant's vehicle so as to avoid the accident; an allegation that the defendant failed to steer a safe course; an allegation that the defendant failed to maintain proper control of the vehicle that he/she was driving, or lost control of the vehicle.

39. e.g. Was it an office or a factory?

40. This should concentrate on allegations of negligence and breach of duty.

41. e.g. An allegation that the defendant caused or permitted the hazard to exist; an allegation that the defendant failed to remove the particular hazard; an allegation that the defendant failed to heed the presence of the hazard; an allegation that the defendant failed to fence or guard the hazard; an allegation that the defendant failed to warn of the presence of the hazard; an allegation that the defendant failed to ensure that the highway or pavement was safe for pedestrians.

42. This will be in addition to any of the above types of accident which apply, e.g. a fatal accident caused by a road traffic accident would need to cover both the question on the road traffic accident particulars of claim and the fatal accident questions.

43. This should concentrate on allegations of negligence/breach of duty.

44. e.g. By ensuring that the Statement of Claim states that the employee responsible for the injury was acting as the defendant's servant or agent.

45. In High Court cases the Statement of Claim is usually served after the writ. It should not be regarded as lack of competence to have issued proceedings without *full* details of pension and earnings loss.

46. In cases of maximum severity it may not be appropriate to serve a schedule of special damages or a medical report but the court's leave must be obtained.

47. This information could be in the Statement of Claim, or the Schedule of Special Damages. A compliance will be recorded if it is in either document.

48. i.e. Permanent and semi-permanent after-effects of the injuries. The medical report may not be able to cover the lasting effects of the injuries at this stage, nor the client's prognosis (see 49.6)). Nonetheless there should be some indication that these have been considered.

49. These limits on County Court cases apply to cases issued after 30.11.92.

50. This is only relevant where the offence is relevant to an issue of negligence, e.g. a conviction for driving without insurance would *not* be relevant.

51. "A provisional damage claim may be appropriate where there is a chance that, in the future, the plaintiff will suffer some serious deterioration in his/her physical or mental condition." Hendy et al, op.cit., p.108.

52. If this is within the scope of the certificate.

53. Whilst it may not be possible for the lawyer to be specific on precise values for all of these factors, an outline of these issues must be given to the client at this stage.

54. Such as the need to issue protective proceedings.

55. Reg 67(1)(a) and 67 (2) Civil Legal Aid (General) Regulations 1989.

56. It would be satisfactory for the lawyer to provide a summary of the defence for the client to comment on.

57. See, for example, Hendy et al, pp.53–56 for a discussion of claw-back of welfare benefits.

58. The Compensation Recovery Unit.

59. Hendy et al, p.55, e.g. benefit should not be deducted if its payment is unrelated to the injury.

60. Osborne, Craig, p.134. RSC. Ord. 22. Weekend days are *not* included in the assessment of three days.

61. A Mental Health Act patient.

62. Pritchard, J., p.171: "If an infant plaintiff wants to accept money paid into court, a summons will still have to be issued. The infant cannot simply withdraw the money from court. The usual procedure applies: issue a summons asking for the proposed terms of settlement (including payment out of the money in court)to be approved. There is no need to serve the usual notice of acceptance of payment in on the other side,because a summons will have to be issued to accept the money..."

63. See, Hendy et al, p.68. See also, Reg. 70, *Civil Legal Aid (General) Regulations 1989*.

64. It will not always be evident why the defendant made a payment in at this amount, but the lawyer should have some understanding as to why a particular amount was chosen.

65. Through the operation of the statutory charge.

66. In the High Court, the plaintiff's solicitor must take immediate steps to take the money out of court. In the County Court, the plaintiff's solicitor should diarise acceptance and seek to ensure the money is promptly sent.

67. See, for example, Pritchard, pp.161–164.

68. e.g. Welfare Benefits to be deducted by the C.R.U. or money to be repaid to an employer under a contractual duty at the successful conclusion of a claim.

69. This is usually on a standard form.

70. If costs cannot be agreed, then they must be taxed within 3 months of settlement. This criterion will normally be "not applicable" in closed cases where costs will already have been decided one way or the other. By definition the case will not be closed until costs are resolved.

71. It is common to obtain a Consent Order to extend the fine and this could be an alternative to complying with the three months.

72. Under Reg 107; Civil Legal Aid (General) Regulations 1989.

73. Reg. 105, Civil Legal Aid (General) Regulations, 1980—The Area Committee must assess the costs if proceedings have not yet been commenced and there has been no subsequent change of solicitor or counsel. See also, *Law Society Gazette*, 26 April 1989, p.41.

74. Where a final claim is received or there is no claim on the fund, the area offices informally discharge the legal aid certificate- i.e. there is no Notice of Discharge.

75. *Civil Litigation—A Guide To Good Practice*. This need not extend to every single telephone call made, e.g. where the client has given the lawyer general authority to negotiate, but any specific offers should be put to the client.

76. *Civil Litigation—A Guide To Good Practice*

77. Relevant benefits for these purposes include Statutory Sick Pay, Unemployment Benefit, Severe Disablement Allowance, retirement allowance, invalidity benefit, reduced earnings allowance, disability living allowance, income support, sickness benefit, attendance allowance, family credit and industrial injuries benefits.

78. Damages in this context includes general damages, special damages and future losses. An amount equivalent to the welfare benefits paid by the DSS to the client is remitted by the defendant to the Compensation Recovery Unit.

79. The plaintiff's lawyer may do this so that he/she can accurately assess the sum that should be deducted by the defendant before making any payment. In addition it enables the plaintiff to evaluate correctly any settlement offer.

80. Hendy et al, p.55, e.g. benefit should not be deducted if payment is unrelated to the injury.

81. See, for example, Hendy et al, pp.53–56 for a discussion of claw-back of welfare benefits. Claw-back applies to claims after 1.1.89.

82. See, Hendy et al, p.184–187.

83. If no summary is prepared, many of these points may be covered in the statement of claim and the medical report. There must, however, be evidence of any necessary updating in the summary of the case prepared for trial.

84. Hendy et al, p.187: "A Pre-trial conference with the client is of the greatest value and should be arranged in every case. Only in the very simplest and most straightforward of case can the pre-trial conference be left to the morning of the trial. A conference the night before has little advantage."

85. Signed witness statements should be obtained from all witnesses as

    a. if witness statements are to be exchanged, the Practice Rules require the statement to be signed.

    b. if the witness is asked to sign the statement, it will reduce the problem of failing to come up to proof in the witness box.

    c. The Civil Evidence Act provides that a signed witness statement can be used if a witness dies before trial.

86. Although it is not clear whether the plaintiff is obliged to seek such agreement at least ten days before trial, Hendy et al state that: "it is better practice to disclose at least ten days before trial."

87. The Guide To The Professional Conduct Of Solicitors (1993, Law Society), Ch 13, p.278, 13.02, 2.

Chapter Two:
Matrimonial/Family

This chapter sets out transaction criteria in the matrimonial/family category. The criteria are based on a review of legal aid files and relevant literature, including the Solicitors Family Law Association Code of Practice and the Additional Guidelines of the Law Society Family Law Committee, May 1991.

The work covers green form and fully certificated work. Individual lawyers must consider when further work should be carried out under a full certificate and apply at the appropriate stage.

The first set of criteria cover a number of proceedings in relationship breakdown. The latter part of the chapter sets out criteria dealing with work done under the green form, or completed under an emergency certificate, for cases where a spouse or cohabitee has been suffering violence or harassment from the other party to a relationship.

Advising on the Breakdown of a Relationship

The criteria cover proceedings between married and unmarried couples in the following types of proceedings:

- Legal procedures for the breakdown itself (marriage only);

- The housing and financial difficulties of relationship breakdown;

- Section 8 orders for any children affected by the relationship breakdown.

These are **preceded** by a general initial instructions and investigation section covering elements common to all three of the above types of case.

Within each of the three major types of transaction criteria, the following stages will be considered according to the circumstances of each case.

I.   Initial Instructions and Investigations

II.   Settlements

III. Proceedings

IV.   Settlement of Disputes/ Consent Orders

V.   Hearings of the Disputes

The following quality issues are considered as appropriate within the above stages:

- Getting Information from the Client

- Strategic Decision Making

- Client Counselling and Advice

- Procedural and Practical Steps

- Transfer of Files and Complaints

Transfer of Files and Complaints (questions 176–177) are considered throughout the file and are applicable to all cases.

Violence against the Client

The criteria covering cases up to full certificate are followed by a section dealing with work done under the green form or completed under an emergency certificate for cases where a spouse or cohabitee has been suffering violence or harassment from the other party to a relationship.

The criteria are split into three sub-headings, all of which must be satisfied.

I.   Getting Information from the Client

II.   Advising on this Information

III. Further Investigation, Research, and Action

Outcome Measures

The Board is interested in exploring the relationship between the outcome of cases, their cost, compliance levels with the transaction criteria, and other franchise requirements. Although there will inevitably be differences on individual cases, it may be possible to define a statistical relationship between outcomes, cost and levels of compliance which will allow effective comparison between firms to be made. Draft outcome measures for Personal Injury, Matrimonial/Family and Crime are contained in chapter 10.

1 Initial Instructions and Investigation (General)

These criteria should be present in all three types of family cases covered by this document.

A. GETTING INFORMATION FROM THE CLIENT

		Yes	No	N/a
1.	Does the file show:			
1.1	the client's full name?	[ ]	[ ]	[ ]
1.2	the full name of the client's former partner?	[ ]	[ ]	[ ]
1.3	the client's official address?	[ ]	[ ]	[ ]
1.4	the client's contact address and telephone number?	[ ]	[ ]	[ ]
1.5	the other party's current address (if possible)?	[ ]	[ ]	[ ]
1.6	if applicable, the name and address of the other party's solicitors?	[ ]	[ ]	[ ]
1.7	the dates of birth (or age) of both parties?	[ ]	[ ]	[ ]
1.8	whether the client is married or not?	[ ]	[ ]	[ ]
1.9	(if the client is unmarried or has only been married a short time) when the relationship began?	[ ]	[ ]	[ ]
1.10	the date of any marriage?	[ ]	[ ]	[ ]
1.11	the place where the marriage took place?	[ ]	[ ]	[ ]
1.12	the full names and dates of birth of each child, if any?[1]	[ ]	[ ]	[ ]
1.13	the natural parents of each child?	[ ]	[ ]	[ ]
1.14	where and with whom the children reside?	[ ]	[ ]	[ ]
1.15	whether there are any court orders in relation to any of the children?	[ ]	[ ]	[ ]
2.	Does the file show some understanding of:			
2.1	the nature of any problems in the relationship, in particular:			
2.1.1	what caused them, when they began and how they have persisted?	[ ]	[ ]	[ ]
2.1.2	if the problem involves the behaviour of one or other of the parties, does the lawyer know if violence was used or threatened?	[ ]	[ ]	[ ]
2.2	whether either party is forming or has formed a relationship with another person?	[ ]	[ ]	[ ]
2.3	if so,:		N/A	[ ]

				Yes	No	N/a

2.3.1 the name and (if possible) address of that person?   [ ]   [ ]   [ ]

2.3.2 whether they intend to cohabit with that person?   [ ]   [ ]   [ ]

2.4   whether there are any care/court proceedings concerning the relationship and/or children currently or in the past, and if so the nature and outcome of these?   [ ]   [ ]   [ ]

2.5   whether either party and any of the children suffer from any physical or mental illness/disability and, if so, what?   [ ]   [ ]   [ ]

2.6   whether or not the parties have had any previous marriages or relationships which have resulted in any children and, if so, where the children live and how old they are?   [ ]   [ ]   [ ]

3.   Where it seems likely that residence and/or contact will be contested and the child(ren) are presently resident with the client, has the lawyer asked the client if there is any reason to fear abduction of the child(ren) by the other party?   [ ]   [ ]   [ ]

Initial Agreement

4.   Does the file show whether the parties have reached any agreement on financial matters and (if applicable) the child(ren)?   [ ]   [ ]   [ ]

5.   If there is such an agreement, does the file show some understanding of: **N/A**   [ ]

5.1   whether it is in writing?   [ ]   [ ]   [ ]

5.2   the client's attitude to that agreement?   [ ]   [ ]   [ ]

B. CLIENT COUNSELLING AND ADVICE

These criteria apply to all three major sections of work covered by the transaction criteria (i.e. divorce, finance and children) unless the text specifically indicates otherwise.

Progress of the case

6.1   Is there an indication of the steps the lawyer has agreed to take and have they been communicated to the client?   [ ]   [ ]   [ ]

6.2   Is there an indication of the steps the lawyer has asked the client to take?   [ ]   [ ]   [ ]

6.3   Is the client told when and in what form the next contact with the lawyer will take place?[2]   [ ]   [ ]   [ ]

6.4   Has the lawyer advised the client as to alternative courses of action from which the client could choose?[3]   [ ]   [ ]   [ ]

6.5   Is there an indication that the client made an active choice on the lawyer's suggested modes of action?   [ ]   [ ]   [ ]

6.6   Has the lawyer noted down the reaction of the client to the decided plan of action (as a minimum, this should include the client's consent to the action going forward)?   [ ]   [ ]   [ ]

				Yes	No	N/a

			Yes	No	N/a
6.7	Were any apparent queries from the client dealt with fully, promptly and politely?		[ ]	[ ]	[ ]
6.8	Did the lawyer deal with any evident emotional concerns of the client?		[ ]	[ ]	[ ]
6.9	Did the lawyer explain any contact with the other side? In particular, when they will be contacted and why?		[ ]	[ ]	[ ]
6.10	If it appears likely that the other side will contact the client directly and that this would cause the client concern, was the client advised as to what they should do in the event that the other side does contact them?		[ ]	[ ]	[ ]
6.11	If the lawyer considers that Counsel's opinion is required at any point in the case has the lawyer advised the client of that and sought the client's consent to obtain Counsel's opinion?		[ ]	[ ]	[ ]
6.12	Was Counsel's opinion explained to and discussed with the client as and when it was received?		[ ]	[ ]	[ ]
6.13	Was the client kept informed of the outcome and effect of any interim hearings?		[ ]	[ ]	[ ]

Initial Agreement

			Yes	No	N/a
7.	If there is initial agreement on financial or children matters, has the lawyer:			**N/A**	[ ]
7.1	noted the suggested terms of the agreement?		[ ]	[ ]	[ ]
7.2	advised the client on whether the agreement is in their best interests (and the interests of any children)?		[ ]	[ ]	[ ]
7.3	with financial agreements, considered whether there has been adequate disclosure?		[ ]	[ ]	[ ]
7.4	with financial agreements, advised the client of the importance of full disclosure?		[ ]	[ ]	[ ]

Costs And Funding Of The Case

			Yes	No	N/a
8.	Is there an indication of advice given to the client regarding the costs and funding of the case? In particular:				
8.1	the availability of green form/ABWOR/civil legal aid;		[ ]	[ ]	[ ]
8.2	the limits and extent of green form funding;		[ ]	[ ]	[ ]
8.3	whether or not the client will have to make a contribution to the case and the duration of contributions;		[ ]	[ ]	[ ]
8.4	the likely level of costs to the client;[4]		[ ]	[ ]	[ ]
8.5	when payment of costs is likely to be required;		[ ]	[ ]	[ ]

			Yes	No	N/a

8.6 the nature and consequences of revocation and discharge of certificates (if one is granted);   [ ]   [ ]   [ ]

8.7 where there is a full certificate, the duty to report changes of circumstance and address;[5]   [ ]   [ ]   [ ]

9. Unless there is no possibility of financial matters being in dispute, was the client advised in writing as to the operation of the solicitor's (green form) and statutory charge: **N/A**   [ ]

9.1 on any lump sum payments from the other side?   [ ]   [ ]   [ ]

9.2 on the financial share in, and occupation of, any house?   [ ]   [ ]   [ ]

9.3 on any other valuable, disputed property (e.g. pensions) from the relationship?   [ ]   [ ]   [ ]

9.4 on the possible adjournment of the charge and interest payable?   [ ]   [ ]   [ ]

Contacting The Other Side (The First Letter)

10. If the other party is contacted directly by the lawyer, and it is unclear whether or not they are legally represented, are they advised to seek legal advice?[6]   [ ]   [ ]   [ ]

Mediation, Conciliation and Negotiation

It is to be noted that in some cases there are no facilities for mediation, particularly financial mediation. In these areas such issues would be considered not applicable. In cases where there may be some dispute or negotiation over issues involving children and/or finance, the following criteria apply:

11. Has the lawyer considered advising the client on the nature of mediation and/or conciliation?   [ ]   [ ]   [ ]

12. Has the lawyer advised the client of the advantages/disadvantages of negotiating a settlement?[7]   [ ]   [ ]   [ ]

13. Before advising the client on whether or not to use mediation and/or conciliation does the lawyer have an understanding of the following:[8]

13.1 how the client feels about negotiating with the former spouse?   [ ]   [ ]   [ ]

13.2 any specific problems the client foresees about such negotiations?   [ ]   [ ]   [ ]

14. Where mediation/conciliation is advised, has the lawyer explained the role of any independent agencies[9] assisting in the mediation/ conciliation process and where/how to contact them?   [ ]   [ ]   [ ]

Urgent Steps

15. If the former shared home is owner occupied and house is in joint names, did the lawyer consider with the client the option of severing the joint tenancy?   [ ]   [ ]   [ ]

16. If the former shared home is owner occupied and is in the other party's sole name, did the lawyer consider with the client whether to: **N/A**   [ ]

			Yes	No	N/a

16.1 register a Class F Land Charge/pending land action (unregistered land only)? [ ] [ ] [ ]

16.2 lodge a Notice/Caution at the Land Registry (registered land only)?[10] [ ] [ ] [ ]

17. If the other side appears likely to seek to remove financial assets out of the jurisdiction or otherwise dissipate assets, was the client advised on the possibility of a section 37 or similar injunction?[11] [ ] [ ] [ ]

18. Has the client been advised of the need to sever/limit any joint financial liabilities/accounts (e.g. joint bank accounts, credit cards and supplies of utilities)? [ ] [ ] [ ]

19. Where the other spouse/partner is the sole tenant of rented accommodation, did the lawyer consider the danger of unilateral termination of the tenancy by them and (if applicable) the need to protect the client's interests in the former home? [ ] [ ] [ ]

20. Has the lawyer advised the client of the need to write a will/new will? [ ] [ ] [ ]

Danger of Abduction

21. Where there was an indication that the client may remove a child from the jurisdiction of the court did the lawyer advise the client that this may be a criminal offence and of the court's power to order return of children pursuant to the Child Abduction and Custody Act?[12] [ ] [ ] [ ]

22. If there was a real and imminent risk of a child being removed illegally from the jurisdiction by the other party, did the lawyer; **N/A** [ ]

22.1 seek an appropriate order?[13] [ ] [ ] [ ]

22.2 alert the police to the risk? [ ] [ ] [ ]

22.3 take steps to implement the port alert system? [ ] [ ] [ ]

22.4 notify the Home Office not to issue a passport for the child without leave of court or consent of the other party? [ ] [ ] [ ]

22.5 consider applying for an existing passport to be surrendered? [ ] [ ] [ ]

23. If the whereabouts of a child is not known has the lawyer considered with the client asking the court to order a person to reveal the whereabouts?[14] [ ] [ ] [ ]

Severing a Joint Tenancy

24. If a decision to sever a joint tenancy is made: **N/A** [ ]

24.1 where the title to the land is unregistered, did the lawyer obtain the deeds from the mortgagee to endorse notice of severance on the conveyance? [ ] [ ] [ ]

		Yes	No	N/a
24.2	where title to the land is registered, did the lawyer register a joint proprietorship restriction at the HM Land Registry?	[ ]	[ ]	[ ]
24.3	did the lawyer send notice of severance to the other party?	[ ]	[ ]	[ ]
24.4	did the lawyer send notice of severance to the mortgagee?	[ ]	[ ]	[ ]

2 Legal Procedures for the Breakdown Itself (Marriage only)

These criteria apply only to clients who are married and are considering judicial separation or divorce from their spouse, or clients who are the subject of divorce or judicial separation proceedings. They do not apply to nullity. Unless the text of criteria indicates that they relate to divorce only then the criteria apply to either divorce or judicial separation.

I. Initial Instructions and Investigations

A. GETTING INFORMATION FROM THE CLIENT

			Yes	No	N/a
25.	Does the file show some understanding of the current position of both parties to the relationship? In particular:				
	25.1	whether the client is currently living with the other party, and if not, how long the parties have been living apart?	[ ]	[ ]	[ ]
	25.2	if the client has ever separated from the other party in the past and divorce/judicial[15] separation on the basis of desertion or separation is being considered, does the file show:		N/A	[ ]
		25.2.1 how long this period (or these periods) were?	[ ]	[ ]	[ ]
		25.2.2 when the last separation ended?	[ ]	[ ]	[ ]
		25.2.3 if the parties are currently living apart, whether or not this period has been interrupted by any periods of cohabitation?	[ ]	[ ]	[ ]
	25.3	if the parties are still living in the same accommodation, does the file show some understanding of the nature of the continuing relationship?[16] In particular:		N/A	[ ]
		25.3.1 whether or not the two parties are sharing a room;	[ ]	[ ]	[ ]
		25.3.2 whether or not the two parties are having sexual relations;	[ ]	[ ]	[ ]
		25.3.3 whether either party is carrying out domestic or other tasks for the other party;	[ ]	[ ]	[ ]
		25.3.4 the financial arrangements between the parties;	[ ]	[ ]	[ ]
	25.4	whether the other side has contacted a lawyer or started proceedings for divorce or judicial separation and if so relevant dates and court details;	[ ]	[ ]	[ ]
26.	Does the lawyer have some understanding of the parties' attitudes to the future of the relationship? In particular:				
	26.1	whether the client wishes to attempt or has attempted reconciliation;	[ ]	[ ]	[ ]
	26.2	whether the client wants a divorce, or judicial separation;[17]	[ ]	[ ]	[ ]
	26.3	what the other party's attitudes are likely to be to the client's wishes for the future of the relationship;	[ ]	[ ]	[ ]

	Yes	No	N/a

26.4   if the other party has instituted divorce or separation proceedings and the client has received the petition, does the lawyer have an understanding of the client's views on the fact(s) set out in the petition?   [ ]   [ ]   [ ]

B.   CLIENT COUNSELLING AND ADVICE

The applicability of many of the questions will depend upon the grounds for any proposed divorce/judicial separation and the parties' attitudes to pursuing proceedings.[18], [19]

27.   Did the lawyer give an indication of how long proceedings would be likely to take, including (in divorce cases) an explanation of decree nisi and decree absolute?   [ ]   [ ]   [ ]

28.   Was the client advised that proceedings can be stopped at any time up until decree of judicial separation/(divorce) decree absolute?   [ ]   [ ]   [ ]

29.   If it is apparent that the other party may attempt to defend divorce proceedings/judicial separation, did the lawyer consider with the client how this might affect the cost and progress of the client's case?   [ ]   [ ]   [ ]

30.   If the client is considering seeking divorce or judicial separation (or cross-petitioning for divorce), did the lawyer advise the client as to the different possibilities for taking proceedings? In particular, the advice should cover the following points: N/A   [ ]

30.1   if the client is considering reconciliation, has the lawyer considered with the client as to how prospects for reconciliation will affect any proceedings?   [ ]   [ ]   [ ]

30.2   if the marriage is less than a year old was the client informed that a divorce cannot be granted within a year of marriage, although judicial separation/nullity maybe available?   [ ]   [ ]   [ ]

30.3   If the client is still living in the same accommodation as the other party, has the lawyer advised the client on separating from the other party?[20]   [ ]   [ ]   [ ]

30.4   Adultery   N/A   [ ]

30.4.1   If a client is advised a divorce could proceed because of the other party's adultery and the client is finding it intolerable to live with the other party, does the file show some understanding of:

30.4.1.1   the evidence for claiming there has been adultery?   [ ]   [ ]   [ ]

30.4.1.2   with whom adultery has been committed?   [ ]   [ ]   [ ]

30.4.1.3   whether the client wishes to name the person(s) with whom adultery has been committed.   [ ]   [ ]   [ ]

30.5   Behaviour   N/A   [ ]

30.5.1   if the client is advised that a divorce/judicial separation could proceed on the basis of the other party's behaviour:

			Yes	No	N/a

30.5.1.1   did the lawyer consider whether there is evidence of behaviour of the other party which could be thought unreasonable[21] so that the client cannot be expected to live with respondent?   [ ]   [ ]   [ ]

30.5.1.2   did the lawyer consider with the client whether or not to warn the other party of the petition's grounds and/or agree its contents?   [ ]   [ ]   [ ]

30.6   Desertion   N/A   [ ]

30.6.1   if a client is advised a divorce/judicial separation could proceed because of the other party's desertion:

30.6.1.1   if the parties are living in the same building, is there some consideration as to whether or not the parties are living apart and is it concluded that they are?   [ ]   [ ]   [ ]

30.6.1.2   if the period of living apart is less than two years, has the lawyer considered how long remains before the two year period will be complete?   [ ]   [ ]   [ ]

30.6.1.3   did the lawyer consider whether or not the client consented to the separation?   [ ]   [ ]   [ ]

30.6.1.4   if the parties have lived together for any time during the period of desertion, this must total less than six months, does it?   [ ]   [ ]   [ ]

30.7   Two Years Separation   N/A   [ ]

30.7.1   if a client is advised a divorce/judicial separation could proceed because of 2 years separation:

30.7.1.1   where the parties are living in the same building, is there some consideration as to whether or not the parties have been living apart, and how it is to be demonstrated to the court that they have been living apart?   [ ]   [ ]   [ ]

30.7.1.2   if the period of living apart is less than two years, has the lawyer considered how long remains before the two year period will be complete?   [ ]   [ ]   [ ]

30.7.1.3   did the lawyer consider whether the other party would consent to divorce?   [ ]   [ ]   [ ]

30.7.1.4   if the parties have lived together for a period or periods during their separation, this must total less than six months. Does it?   [ ]   [ ]   [ ]

		Yes	No	N/a

30.8   Five years separation ······ N/A [ ]

30.8.1   if a client is advised a divorce/judicial separation could proceed because of 5 years separation:

    30.8.1.1   if the parties are living in the same building, is there some consideration as to whether or not the parties have been living apart, and how it is to be demonstrated to the court that they have been living apart? [ ] [ ] [ ]

    30.8.1.2   if the period of living apart is less than five years, has the lawyer considered how long remains before the five year period will be complete? [ ] [ ] [ ]

    30.8.1.3   if the parties have lived together for a period or periods during their 5 year period of separation this must total less than six months. Does it? [ ] [ ] [ ]

    30.8.1.4   has the lawyer considered the possibility of the responsdent pleading a hardship defence?[22] [ ] [ ] [ ]

Responding to Possible Divorce/Judicial Separation Proceedings

31.   Where the client has reason to believe the other party has or will issue divorce proceedings or proceedings for judicial separation, have the following points been covered?

    31.1   if client wishes to defend the divorce/judicial separation, has the lawyer advised the client as to possible defences and the cost/funding consequences of defending? [ ] [ ] [ ]

    31.2   if and when the petition becomes available, has the lawyer considered with the client whether or not any of the allegations should be disputed or changes in the allegation made and if so the costs implications of doing so?[23] [ ] [ ] [ ]

C.   PROCEDURAL AND PRACTICAL STEPS

32.   Where the lawyer is acting on behalf of the petitioner: ······ N/A [ ]

    32.1   If the client wishes to pursue divorce/judicial separation proceedings:

        32.1.1   was a draft petition drawn up and the client given an opportunity to read and amend this? [ ] [ ] [ ]

        32.1.2   where there are children under 16 or under the age of 18 and in full time education or undergoing training for a trade or a profession: [ ] [ ] [ ]

            32.1.2.1   was a draft statement of arrangements drawn up and the client given an opportunity to read and amend this? [ ] [ ] [ ]

            32.1.2.2   unless there is a dispute as to arrangements for the children, did the lawyer attempt to agree the statement of arrangements between both parties?[24] [ ] [ ] [ ]

			Yes	No	N/a

32.1.2.3 and, if the parties agreed the arrangements for the children, did the lawyer attempt to obtain the signatures of both parties on the Statement of Arrangements for Children?   [ ]   [ ]   [ ]

33.   Was the client given an opportunity to consider the substance of any documents/letters containing allegations or denials on the substance of the divorce/judicial separation (if there are any)?[25]   [ ]   [ ]   [ ]

Proof And Acknowledgement of Service

34.   *Where the lawyer is advising/acting on behalf of the **petitioner**:*   **N/A**   [ ]

   34.1   Was the client informed in writing, as and when the following occur:

      34.1.1 the petition has been lodged;   [ ]   [ ]   [ ]

      34.1.2 once service of petition has been acknowledged?   [ ]   [ ]   [ ]

   34.2   If the other side is reluctant to acknowledge service of the petition, has the petitioner's lawyer considered other methods of service?[26]   [ ]   [ ]   [ ]

   34.3   If applicable, has the lawyer collected the necessary information to enable personal service?[27]   [ ]   [ ]   [ ]

35.   *Where the lawyer is advising/acting on behalf of the **respondent**:*   **N/A**   [ ]

   35.1   Has the lawyer explained to the client the procedure that follows Acknowledgement of Service?   [ ]   [ ]   [ ]

Request for Directions and Affidavit in Support

36.   Where the lawyer is advising/acting on behalf of the petitioner: **N/A**   [ ]

   36.1   Has the lawyer given the client an opportunity to read and amend the affidavit in support of petition before it is sworn?   [ ]   [ ]   [ ]

37. Decree Nisi   **N/A**   [ ]

(Divorce only) Where the lawyer is advising/acting on behalf of the petitioner or respondent:

38.   Was the client informed when the decree nisi will be pronounced (once this date is available)?   [ ]   [ ]   [ ]

39.   Has the client been advised as to the effect of a decree nisi?[28]   [ ]   [ ]   [ ]

40.   Where financial matters are in dispute and a petition is being sought only on the basis of separation (2 or 5 years), was the client advised of the possibility of either party seeking a postponement of decree absolute (under S.10 MCA 1973) pending consideration of financial matters?   [ ]   [ ]   [ ]

41. Decree Absolute   N/A   [ ]

*(Divorce only) Where the lawyer is advising/acting on behalf of the petitioner **or** respondent*

42.   Has the client been advised that the petitioner may apply for decree absolute
       six weeks after decree nisi?   [ ] [ ] [ ]

43.   Where the lawyer is advising/acting on behalf of the respondent has the client
       been informed that the client may apply for decree absolute three months
       after the petitioner may first have applied should the petitioner fail to apply? [ ] [ ] [ ]

44.   Has the lawyer sent the client the original decree absolute? [ ] [ ] [ ]

45.   Has the lawyer advised the client of the effect of the decree absolute?[29] [ ] [ ] [ ]

46.   If the client is the Petitioner and the petition contains no prayer for ancillary
       relief, or the client is the Respondent, has the client been advised of the
       consequences of remarriage upon the client's ability to make application to
       the Court to resolve financial issues arising from the marriage? [ ] [ ] [ ]

47.   Has the client been advised of the consequences of remarriage upon wills
       made before remarriage?   [ ] [ ] [ ]

3   Housing and Financial Difficulties of Relationship Breakdown

These criteria apply where financial matters are or have been a significant issue between the parties. It applies to couples who are or have been married and unmarried couples where children of the relationship have been living with the couple.

I   Initial Instructions and Investigations

This section covers the information which would be expected as a precursor to negotiation on financial matters. It would not all necessarily be gained at a first interview.

A.   GETTING INFORMATION FROM THE CLIENT

			Yes	No	N/a
48.		Does the file show some understanding of the financial position of the client? In particular:			
	48.1	where the client is working:		N/A	[ ]
		48.1.1 the client's occupation(s)?	[ ]	[ ]	[ ]
		48.1.2 details of employer(s) and place(s) of work?	[ ]	[ ]	[ ]
		48.1.3 whether the client works part-time?[30]	[ ]	[ ]	[ ]
		48.1.4 the size and stability of the client's income (from all sources)?	[ ]	[ ]	[ ]
		48.1.5 if the client has children living with them, whether or not the client is in receipt of Family Credit and, if so, to what value, from what date and when the application will next be reviewed?	[ ]	[ ]	[ ]
	48.2	where the client is not working full time, whether or not the client is in receipt of:		N/A	[ ]
		48.2.1 income support?	[ ]	[ ]	[ ]
		48.2.2 (if the client is owner occupier) whether it includes mortgage interest?	[ ]	[ ]	[ ]
		48.2.3 (if the client is in rented accommodation) housing benefit?	[ ]	[ ]	[ ]
		48.2.4 the size of payments under these benefits?	[ ]	[ ]	[ ]
	48.3	the client's and (if possible) other party's income support or national insurance number?	[ ]	[ ]	[ ]
	48.4	whether or not the client is in receipt of:			
		48.4.1 one parent benefit?	[ ]	[ ]	[ ]

			Yes	No	N/a
	48.4.2	child benefit?	[ ]	[ ]	[ ]
48.5		the making of, or agreements to make, any payments between the parties and what such payments are for;	[ ]	[ ]	[ ]
48.6		if the client has been married before or has had children with another partner, does the former spouse/partner make (or receive) any payments to (or from) the client;	[ ]	[ ]	[ ]
48.7		if payments are made, whether they are made voluntarily or under order?	[ ]	[ ]	[ ]
48.8		the size and nature of any payments from other people (if any), and the relationship with the client of any such people;	[ ]	[ ]	[ ]
48.9		whether or not the client has any savings and/or capital (including pensions) other than the former home, and (if applicable) the details and amount of such capital;	[ ]	[ ]	[ ]
48.10		if the client is not working or is working only part-time, does the lawyer have an understanding of the client's ability/prospects for work?	[ ]	[ ]	[ ]
48.11		whether the client has any joint accounts or credit cards with the other party?[31]	[ ]	[ ]	[ ]
48.12		whether either party has any debts?	[ ]	[ ]	[ ]
48.13		if either party has debts:[32]			
	48.13.1	the names of creditors?	[ ]	[ ]	[ ]
	48.13.2	the amount?	[ ]	[ ]	[ ]
	48.13.3	whether it is secured (or not) and if so, on what?	[ ]	[ ]	[ ]
	48.13.4	whether it is a joint debt?	[ ]	[ ]	[ ]
	48.13.5	for what the debt(s) were incurred?	[ ]	[ ]	[ ]

49. Does the file show some understanding of the financial position of the other party? In particular:

		Yes	No	N/a
49.1	the size of the other party's income;	[ ]	[ ]	[ ]
49.2	whether or not the other party is in receipt of welfare benefits;	[ ]	[ ]	[ ]
49.3	whether the other party is in receipt of any money from the client, or the client has agreed to make any such payments;	[ ]	[ ]	[ ]
49.4	where the other party has been married before or has had children with another partner, does that previous spouse/partner make or receive any payments as a result (and their approximate size, if applicable);	[ ]	[ ]	[ ]
49.5	the size of any payments from or to other people (if there are any);	[ ]	[ ]	[ ]
49.6	whether the other party is currently living with another person (including any children);	[ ]	[ ]	[ ]

		Yes	No	N/a

49.7   if the other party is not working or is working only part-time, does the lawyer have an understanding of the other party's ability/ prospects for work?   [ ]   [ ]   [ ]

50.   Does the file show some understanding about the ownership of any shared residence of the client and the other party? In particular:

50.1   whether the residence was owner occupied or rented?   [ ]   [ ]   [ ]

50.2   if the residence was *owner occupied*, does the lawyer know, or attempt to find out: **N/A**   [ ]

50.2.1   in whose name(s) the property was purchased?   [ ]   [ ]   [ ]

50.2.2   in whose names(s) the property is now?   [ ]   [ ]   [ ]

50.2.3   if it is in joint names, whether the beneficial interest is held as a joint tenancy or a tenancy in common?   [ ]   [ ]   [ ]

50.2.4   date of purchase?   [ ]   [ ]   [ ]

50.2.5   purchase price?   [ ]   [ ]   [ ]

50.2.6   who provided the initial capital?   [ ]   [ ]   [ ]

50.2.7   the size of any mortgage?   [ ]   [ ]   [ ]

50.2.8   the identity of the lender?   [ ]   [ ]   [ ]

50.2.9   the type of mortgage?[33]   [ ]   [ ]   [ ]

50.2.10   if it is an endowment mortgage, the details of the linked policies and their maturity date?   [ ]   [ ]   [ ]

50.2.11   the present (approximate) value of equity in the property?   [ ]   [ ]   [ ]

50.2.12   the size of monthly mortgage repayments?[34]   [ ]   [ ]   [ ]

50.2.13   how mortgage payments are/were met?   [ ]   [ ]   [ ]

50.2.14   whether there are any mortgage payment arrears?   [ ]   [ ]   [ ]

50.2.15   whether any agreement has been reached about repayments with the lender?   [ ]   [ ]   [ ]

50.2.16   whether there is any further borrowing (in addition to a first mortgage) against the house (and if so how much is outstanding)?   [ ]   [ ]   [ ]

50.2.17   if there is a second creditor/mortgagee, who the creditor/ mortgagee is?   [ ]   [ ]   [ ]

50.2.18   if the client did not take out the loan, whether the loan or any extension of the loan was obtained with the client's knowledge and/or agreement?   [ ]   [ ]   [ ]

50.2.19   if the client did not agree to the loan, whether the client was in occupation of the property at the time?   [ ]   [ ]   [ ]

			Yes	No	N/a
	50.2.20	whether there are any possession proceedings pending?	[ ]	[ ]	[ ]
50.3		if the residence was *rented*, does the lawyer know, or attempt to find out;		N/A	[ ]
	50.3.1	in whose name the tenancy was taken out?	[ ]	[ ]	[ ]
	50.3.2	the type of tenancy?[35]	[ ]	[ ]	[ ]
	50.3.3	the name of the landlord?	[ ]	[ ]	[ ]
	50.3.4	the landlord's address?	[ ]	[ ]	[ ]
	50.3.5	the address of the rented accommodation?	[ ]	[ ]	[ ]
	50.3.6	the size of monthly/weekly rent repayments?	[ ]	[ ]	[ ]
	50.3.7	whether there are any rent arrears?	[ ]	[ ]	[ ]
51.		Where either party has a pension/insurance policy, does the file show some understanding of:		N/A	[ ]
51.1		the value of the pension/policy?[36]	[ ]	[ ]	[ ]
51.2		on what event(s) the pension/policy's value is realised?	[ ]	[ ]	[ ]
51.3		whether they can be charged, assigned or otherwise produce immediate funds?[37]	[ ]	[ ]	[ ]
51.4		in relation to any assurance/insurance policies:		N/A	[ ]
	51.4.1	the type of policy	[ ]	[ ]	[ ]
	51.4.2	the name of the company	[ ]	[ ]	[ ]
	51.4.3	policy number	[ ]	[ ]	[ ]
	51.4.4	the beneficiary's name	[ ]	[ ]	[ ]
	51.4.5	whether the policy is written in trust	[ ]	[ ]	[ ]
51.5		in relation to any pensions:		N/A	[ ]
	51.5.1	the size of current contributions by either spouse	[ ]	[ ]	[ ]
	51.5.2	details of the pension scheme	[ ]	[ ]	[ ]
52.		If there is any other property[38] (including business assets, if any) of either party which could be of value and in dispute, does the lawyer show some understanding of:		N/A	[ ]
52.1		the value of such property?	[ ]	[ ]	[ ]
52.2		in whose name the property was purchased?	[ ]	[ ]	[ ]
52.3		the contributions of both parties' to the purchase price?	[ ]	[ ]	[ ]

		Yes	No	N/a

52.4   any outstanding borrowing against such property? [ ] [ ] [ ]

53.   Does the file show some understanding of the needs, obligations and responsibilities of the client?[39] In particular, the size (per month or week) of, and who (if anyone) is making the following payments:

53.1   rent or mortgage? [ ] [ ] [ ]

53.2   council tax/community charge?[40] [ ] [ ] [ ]

53.3   utility costs (fuel and water)? [ ] [ ] [ ]

53.4   housekeeping and other household expenses? [ ] [ ] [ ]

53.5   payments on any outstanding debts (if applicable)? [ ] [ ] [ ]

53.6   cost of childminding (if applicable)? [ ] [ ] [ ]

54.   If the parties are or were married and if the children are not the natural children of both parties did the lawyer consider whether they are 'children of the family', taking into account: **N/A** [ ]

54.1   how long the child(ren) has been living with the non-natural parent? [ ] [ ] [ ]

54.2   the attitude towards and treatment of the child(ren) by the non-natural parent? [ ] [ ] [ ]

54.3   whether the non-natural parent helps support the child(ren)? [ ] [ ] [ ]

B. STRATEGIC DECISION MAKING

General Points

55.   Has the lawyer made calculations of both parties' total income and outgoings (per week or per month) based on the figures and information obtained from the client and the other spouse? [ ] [ ] [ ]

56.   If the lawyer makes any applications, has the timing of making any applications been considered by the lawyer and discussed with the client? [ ] [ ] [ ]

Maintenance for the children

The application of the Child Support Act: where the Child Support Agency[41] has jurisdiction, the courts have no power to make, vary or revive any maintenance order in relation to the child. From *5 April 1993* parties have to apply to the Agency for an assessment where there is a family breakdown or where no existing arrangement for the support of children has been made. There are however circumstances where orders will still have to be made under the jurisdiction of the court. From 5 April 1993 the courts will *retain* jurisdiction only in the following circumstances:

i)   Where the maximum assessment which can be made under the Child Support Act has been made, and the person with care of the child seeks more maintenance for the child.[42]

ii)   Where there are 17- to 19- year- olds who are not in full- time education and where there are young persons aged 19 or over who are in full- time education.

iii)   Where there are step- children.

iv)   Where lump sum and property adjustment orders for children are sought.

v)   Where the child is disabled.

vi)   Where any party or the child is not habitually resident in the UK.

vii) Where a child is or has been married.

viii) Where school fees are sought.

ix)   Where there is agreement for child maintenance made under section 8(5) of the Child Support Act.[43]

		Yes	No	N/a
57.	If any of the above circumstances (i) to (ix) apply has the lawyer considered whether any children will not be subject to a Child Support Agency assessment?	[ ]	[ ]	[ ]

Orders Not Made Under the Child Support Act

The following criteria apply to cases where the court made an order in relation to contested applications for child maintenance prior to 5 April 1993 or where such orders will be applied for (after 5 April 1993) under the jurisdiction of the court under one of the above exceptions.[44] They do not apply where only nominal orders are sought.

58.	Has the lawyer considered the following factors[45] before applying for an order in respect of a child:	**N/A** [ ]		
	58.1 The financial needs of the child?	[ ]	[ ]	[ ]
	58.2 Earning capacity/financial resources of the child, if any?	[ ]	[ ]	[ ]
	58.3 The child's income, if any?	[ ]	[ ]	[ ]
	58.4 The child's expected education and training?	[ ]	[ ]	[ ]
	58.5 The parties' income and/or earning capacity?	[ ]	[ ]	[ ]
	58.6 The parties' present and future financial needs and responsibilities?	[ ]	[ ]	[ ]
	58.7 The parties' standard of living prior to the marriage breakdown?	[ ]	[ ]	[ ]
	58.8 If applicable, any physical or mental disabilities of the parties or the child(ren)?	[ ]	[ ]	[ ]
59.	Where the lawyer sought a financial order in the interest of a child against a party who is not the parent of that child, did the lawyer consider the following factors:	**N/A** [ ]		
	59.1 What responsibility that party took for the child's maintenance?	[ ]	[ ]	[ ]
	59.2 How long that party took responsibility for the child's maintenance?	[ ]	[ ]	[ ]
	59.3 If that party maintained the child, did he know that it was not his own child?	[ ]	[ ]	[ ]
	59.4 Whether that third party is obliged to maintain someone else?	[ ]	[ ]	[ ]

		Yes	No	N/a

60. Has the lawyer made a Child Support Act calculation?   [ ]   [ ]   [ ]

Maintenance Assessments Under the Child Support Act

61. Where the Child Support Agency assessment is to be made the following criteria apply: **N/A** [ ]

     61.1   Where the client is going to be the absent parent does the file show some understanding of: **N/A** [ ]

         61.1.1   what the child's maintenance requirement is?[46]   [ ]   [ ]   [ ]

         61.1.2   the parent's net income?   [ ]   [ ]   [ ]

         61.1.3   the parent's exempt income?[47]   [ ]   [ ]   [ ]

         61.1.4   the parent's assessable income?[48]   [ ]   [ ]   [ ]

         61.1.5   the parent's protected income?   [ ]   [ ]   [ ]

Maintenance between Married Partners

The following criteria apply to parties that are or have been married where maintenance payments between the adult parties is in issue.

62. Where parties are/were married has the lawyer considered, as far as is known, the following factors before applying for an order?[49]   **N/A** [ ]

     62.1   the client's and other party's income?   [ ]   [ ]   [ ]

     62.2   the client's and other party's earning capacity (present and future)?   [ ]   [ ]   [ ]

     62.3   the client's and other party's other financial resources?   [ ]   [ ]   [ ]

     62.4   present and future financial requirements, obligations and responsibilities of the parties?[50]   [ ]   [ ]   [ ]

     62.5   the parties' standard of living prior to the breakdown of the marriage?   [ ]   [ ]   [ ]

     62.6   the duration of the marriage?   [ ]   [ ]   [ ]

     62.7   age of the parties?   [ ]   [ ]   [ ]

     62.8   the conduct of the parties?   [ ]   [ ]   [ ]

     62.9   the parties' contribution to the welfare of the family (both present and future)?[51]   [ ]   [ ]   [ ]

     62.10   if applicable, any physical or mental disability of the parties?   [ ]   [ ]   [ ]

     62.11   if applicable, any benefit lost by reason of dissolution of the marriage?[52]   [ ]   [ ]   [ ]

     62.12   the likely costs of the case (e.g. to be deducted under the statutory charge)?   [ ]   [ ]   [ ]

The Former Home

	Yes	No	N/a

63. Where the former home was owner occupied[53], has the lawyer considered the following before making an application for an order in relation to the home: **N/A**   [ ]

    63.1   what rights the client had, if any, in the ownership of the home?   [ ] [ ] [ ]

    63.2   unless the client does not wish to reside in the former home, the likelihood of the client being able to secure/ maintain their occupation in the former home?   [ ] [ ] [ ]

    63.3   whether either or both parties will want to or need to sell the former matrimonial home?   [ ] [ ] [ ]

64. If the client is likely to retain an interest in the property has the lawyer considered the most appropriate way the client will retain an interest in the property?[54]   [ ] [ ] [ ]

C. CLIENT COUNSELLING AND ADVICE

General Points

65. Has the lawyer considered what kind of financial settlement the client has in mind?   [ ] [ ] [ ]

66. Has the lawyer explained the possible options the client has with regard to a financial settlement?   [ ] [ ] [ ]

67. Where there seems a likelihood that financial matters could be contested did the lawyer consider with the client the possibility of negotiation, conciliation, and taking court proceedings over financial matters?[55]   [ ] [ ] [ ]

68. In such a consideration was the effect of the costs (e.g. by the statutory charge and contributions (if any)) born in mind?   [ ] [ ] [ ]

69. Did the lawyer advise the client how long the case is likely to take?   [ ] [ ] [ ]

70. Did the lawyer indicate the likely outcome of the case?[56]   [ ] [ ] [ ]

71. Was the client informed of the substance of all offers for settlement in financial matters?   [ ] [ ] [ ]

72. Where the client is not receiving financial support from the other party and, it appears, is likely to be entitled to such support, has the lawyer considered with the client the possibility of making an application for an interim order?   [ ] [ ] [ ]

Maintenance for the children

Where an order will be made under the jurisdiction of the court:

73. Was the client advised of the possibility of maintenance payments for the children, for or against the client?   [ ] [ ] [ ]

Where a Child Support Agency assessment will be made:

74. Has the lawyer advised the client that the parent not living with the child(ren) will have to make periodical payments of maintenance of such amount as determined by the Child Support Agency under the statutory formula?   [ ] [ ] [ ]

	Yes	No	N/a

75. Has the lawyer explained to the client that the level of child maintenance is non- negotiable under the formula? [ ] [ ] [ ]

76. Has the lawyer explained that the level of child support will be reviewed annually? [ ] [ ] [ ]

77. If either lawyer or client is dissatisfied with a CSA assessment, has the lawyer advised the client of the right to appeal and time limits for appeal?[57] [ ] [ ] [ ]

Maintenance between Partners

78. Was the client advised of the possibility of maintenance payments for or against them? [ ] [ ] [ ]

The Former Home

79. Did the lawyer advise the client:

    79.1 if the former home was owner occupied, as to the future ownership and occupation of the former home of both parties? [ ] [ ] [ ]

    79.2 where the parties live in rented accommodation: **N/A** [ ]

        79.2.1 whether the tenancy should be put in the client's sole name (where the accommodation is in the other party's name)? [ ] [ ] [ ]

        79.2.2 the effect of any rent arrears (if any) on this? [ ] [ ] [ ]

    79.3 if the client is considering leaving the former home voluntarily, the dangers of voluntarily vacating rented accommodation?[58] [ ] [ ] [ ]

80. Where the client is living in temporary accommodation, did the lawyer advise the client on contacting the local authority in an attempt to expedite a housing application or contact local housing associations? [ ] [ ] [ ]

Other Capital/Property

81. If there is any other contested property (e.g. pensions) which could be of value, has the lawyer advised the client as to the client's rights to any such property? [ ] [ ] [ ]

Welfare Benefits

82. Did the lawyer consider the client's entitlement to welfare benefits?[59] In particular: **N/A** [ ]

    82.1 if the client is working less than 16 hours a week has the lawyer advised the client as to the possibility of claiming income support?[60] [ ] [ ] [ ]

    82.2 if the client is working less than 16 hours, and it seems possible, from the above advice, that income support will be available, has the lawyer advised the client as to help they might receive with housing costs? In particular: [ ] [ ] [ ]

	Yes	No	N/a

82.2.1   if they live in rented accommodation, that they should be able to claim for some or all of their rent;   [ ]   [ ]   [ ]

82.2.2   if they live in owner occupied accommodation, that they will only be able to claim for the interest on any mortgage payments;   [ ]   [ ]   [ ]

82.2.3   if they live in owner occupied accommodation, that claims for mortgage interest payments for the first sixteen weeks of an income support claim may be reduced;   [ ]   [ ]   [ ]

82.3   If the client is working less than 16 hours per week and is still living in the same accommodation as the other party and is not claiming income support separately from the other party, has the lawyer advised as to any effects on the client's entitlement to income support of separating from the other party?[61]   [ ]   [ ]   [ ]

82.4   if the client is in paid work for 16 hours or more per week, and has at least one child under the age of 16 (or under 19 and in full time education) was the client advised of the possibility of claiming Family Credit (if they are not already doing so)?   [ ]   [ ]   [ ]

82.5   if the client is on Income Support and without sufficient resources to meet the immediate short- term needs of themselves or their family has the lawyer advised the client of the availability of a crisis and/or budgeting loan?[62]   [ ]   [ ]   [ ]

82.6   where the client is caring for children, has the lawyer advised on additional child benefits?[63]   [ ]   [ ]   [ ]

Council Tax/Community Charge (Poll Tax)

83.   Did the lawyer consider the position of the Council Tax (or the Community Charge between April 1st. 1990 and April 1st. 1993.) with the client? In particular:[64]

83.1   (Community Charge only) if the separation was before April 1st 1993, was the client advised to notify the local authority of the separation from their spouse?   [ ]   [ ]   [ ]

83.2   (Community Charge only) if the separation was before April 1st 1993, was the client advised that each member of a former couple is separately liable for the community charge?   [ ]   [ ]   [ ]

83.3   if not already doing so, was the client advised on the possibility of claiming Council Tax reductions (or Community Charge benefit separately if prior to April 1st.1993.)?[65]   [ ]   [ ]   [ ]

II   Proceedings

A.   GETTING INFORMATION / OBTAINING EVIDENCE[66]

The Home

84.   Where the matrimonial home is owner occupied and is going to be part of a financial settlement, has the lawyer:[67]   Yes   No   N/a

84.1   sought to arrange a joint valuation with the other side or where a joint valuation has not been sought, has the lawyer arranged exchange of valuations of the property or agreed a valuation based on one valuer's report?   [ ]   [ ]   [ ]

Other Capital

		Yes	No	N/a
85.	Where other valuable assets/capital (including pensions and insurance policies) are subject to dispute, did the lawyer seek documentary evidence of their value?	[ ]	[ ]	[ ]

The Client's Income/Outgoings

		Yes	No	N/a
86.	Has the lawyer sought documentary evidence to substantiate *each doubtful or contested aspect* of the client's income?[68]	[ ]	[ ]	[ ]
87.	Has the lawyer sought the following documentary evidence to substantiate *each doubtful or contested aspect* of the client's outgoings?[69]	[ ]	[ ]	[ ]

The Other Side's Income/Outgoings

Where applicable, did the lawyer seek the following evidence from the other side to substantiate claims made by the other side, ie:

		Yes	No	N/a
88.	Has the lawyer sought documentary evidence to substantiate *each doubtful or contested aspect* of the other party's income?	[ ]	[ ]	[ ]
89.	Has the lawyer sought documentary evidence to substantiate *each doubtful or contested aspect* of the other party's outgoings?	[ ]	[ ]	[ ]

B. CLIENT COUNSELLING AND ADVICE

		Yes	No	N/a
90.	Where the client is not forthcoming with documentation relating to the client's financial position has the lawyer explained to the client that a failure to make full disclosure may put the client at risk on costs?[70]	[ ]	[ ]	[ ]
91.	Has the lawyer checked the replies to any Rule 2.63 (formerly Rule 77(4)) questionnaire(s) and other documents relating to the other side's income, outgoings and capital and discussed this with the client?	[ ]	[ ]	[ ]
92.	Where there is an exchange of affidavits has the client been given an opportunity to comment on affidavits (or a summary thereof) from the other side?	[ ]	[ ]	[ ]

C. PROCEDURAL AND PRACTICAL STEPS

		Yes	No	N/a
93.	Where the lawyer is not satisfied that the other spouse has fully disclosed all relevant information did the lawyer consider preparing a Rule 2.63 questionnaire and discuss any draft with the client?	[ ]	[ ]	[ ]
94.	Where the former home is a tenancy and the lawyer has advised the client to put the tenancy in the sole name of the client, were attempts made to have the tenancy put in the client's name?[71]	[ ]	[ ]	[ ]

Affidavits in Support of Ancillary Relief Applications:

N/A [ ]

		Yes	No	N/a
95.	Has the lawyer calculated all income and outgoings consistently (i.e. in one of either monthly or weekly figures)?[72]	[ ]	[ ]	[ ]
96.	Where the other party does not file an affidavit has the lawyer considered making an application for:			

		Yes	No	N/a
96.1	an interim order for the other party to file an affidavit?	[ ]	[ ]	[ ]
96.2	if that is not successful, for penal notice to be endorsed?[73]	[ ]	[ ]	[ ]

III Calderbank Letters[74] and Open Offers[75]

The following stage applies where a Calderbank letter or an 'open offer' is received or made by the lawyer from the other side. A Calderbank letter can be recognised by being marked as "without prejudice save as to costs" and/or ending with words such as "although this letter is without prejudice to the issues, our client reserves the right to refer to the question of costs if so advised in accordance with the principles in Calderbank v Calderbank".[76]

		Yes	No	N/a
97.	Prior to having made or after having received a Calderbank and/or open offer has the lawyer:		**N/A**	[ ]
97.1	advised the client of the costs dangers in refusing to offer or accept a reasonable compromise?[77]	[ ]	[ ]	[ ]
97.2	considered whether full disclosure of relevant financial and other circumstances has been obtained from the other party?	[ ]	[ ]	[ ]
97.3	if making an offer, considered whether there is enough time before the court hearing for the other party to consider the offer and to respond to it?[78]	[ ]	[ ]	[ ]
97.4	if making an offer, provided the client with an opportunity to read and agree a draft of the letter?	[ ]	[ ]	[ ]
98.	In relation to a Calderbank letter, are all matters already agreed between the parties clearly stated, as such?	[ ]	[ ]	[ ]
99.	If an open offer/Calderbank letter is received, did the lawyer advise the client in writing as to whether or not to accept it or make a counter offer?	[ ]	[ ]	[ ]
100.	If the client rejects an open offer/Calderbank letter and the lawyer clearly views such rejection as unreasonable, did the lawyer advise the client that they are obliged to report the matter to the Legal Aid Board and that legal aid may be withdrawn as a result?	[ ]	[ ]	[ ]

IV Settlement of Disputes/ Consent Order   N/A [ ]

These criteria apply where the spouses have negotiated a settlement and sought a consent order or come to a written agreement in relation to Child Support Act Cases.[79]

A. STRATEGIC DECISION MAKING

		Yes	No	N/a
101.	Has the solicitor considered whether all relevant information has been obtained from the other spouse before advising the client as to whether or not a proposed settlement is acceptable?	[ ]	[ ]	[ ]
102.	Has the lawyer considered with the client:			
102.1	if the client is on welfare benefit, the future welfare benefit consequences?	[ ]	[ ]	[ ]

	Yes	No	N/a

102.2   what the client will receive as a consequence of the consent order?   [ ]   [ ]   [ ]

102.3   what liabilities the client will have under the order, if any?[80]   [ ]   [ ]   [ ]

102.4   the tax consequences, if any?   [ ]   [ ]   [ ]

B. CLIENT COUNSELLING AND ADVICE

103. Has the lawyer considered with the client whether the other spouse has made full disclosure?   [ ]   [ ]   [ ]

104. Has the lawyer advised the client as to whether or not to settle on the terms being suggested?   [ ]   [ ]   [ ]

105. Has the lawyer given the client a firm indication of the amount of costs (if any) to be deducted under the statutory charge?   [ ]   [ ]   [ ]

106. Was the client given an opportunity to read and comment upon any draft consent orders?[81]   [ ]   [ ]   [ ]

107. Was the consent order explained to the client either in an attendance or in a letter in clear and accurate language?[82]   [ ]   [ ]   [ ]

108. Was the consent order signed by the client?   [ ]   [ ]   [ ]

C. PROCEDURAL AND PRACTICAL STEPS

Statement of Information[83]

109. Has the solicitor ensured that the details of the client's capital and net income are shown as being correct at the date of the Statement of Information?[84]   [ ]   [ ]   [ ]

110. Does the Statement of Information include the following information:

110.1   a summary of the approximate amount or value of the capital resources of each party if any?[85]   [ ]   [ ]   [ ]

110.2   a summary of the approximate amount or value of net income and resources of each party?   [ ]   [ ]   [ ]

110.3   the net equity in any property of the parties?   [ ]   [ ]   [ ]

110.4   details of what arrangements are intended for the accommodation of each of the parties and any minor child(ren) of the family?   [ ]   [ ]   [ ]

110.5   the plans of either spouse to remarry or cohabit?   [ ]   [ ]   [ ]

110.6   where applicable, whether or not any and every mortgagee of the property has been served with notice of application for an order providing for a transfer of property?   [ ]   [ ]   [ ]

111. Did the client confirm the details included in the form before submission to the court?   [ ]   [ ]   [ ]

V Preparation for Final Hearings of Financial Dispute

This stage applies to cases which proceed to a full/final hearing of the dispute.

		Yes	No	N/a

A. STRATEGIC DECISION MAKING

112. Has the lawyer considered with the client the option of proceeding to trial in the light of:

		Yes	No	N/a
112.1	the level of current offers (if any) being made by the other party	[ ]	[ ]	[ ]
112.2	Calderbank letters, if any?	[ ]	[ ]	[ ]
112.3	the extra costs that will be incurred?	[ ]	[ ]	[ ]
112.4	the potential distress and inconvenience that could be caused to the client?	[ ]	[ ]	[ ]

B. CLIENT COUNSELLING AND ADVICE

113. Has the lawyer considered with the client whether the other spouse has made full disclosure? [ ] [ ] [ ]

114. Was the client advised of the possible outcomes of the hearing, in terms of:

		Yes	No	N/a
114.1	what is likely to happen if the case turns out unfavourably for the client?	[ ]	[ ]	[ ]
114.2	what is likely to happen if the case turns out favourably for the client?	[ ]	[ ]	[ ]
114.3	what the costs position is likely to be?	[ ]	[ ]	[ ]

115. Was the client advised on the process of the final hearing, in particular:

		Yes	No	N/a
115.1	the type and format of the hearing?[86]	[ ]	[ ]	[ ]
115.2	how long the hearing is expected to last?	[ ]	[ ]	[ ]
115.3	an outline of the issues that will be raised?	[ ]	[ ]	[ ]
115.4	how the client will be expected to participate in the proceedings?	[ ]	[ ]	[ ]
115.5	an outline of the procedure and what the client should expect from any cross-examination?	[ ]	[ ]	[ ]

116. If the lawyer does or considers using Counsel, was the client advised of the advantages and disadvantages of using Counsel, in particular in relation to costs? [ ] [ ] [ ]

117. If Counsel was used, did the lawyer consider with the client whether to arrange a pre-trial conference before the date of the hearing between the client and Counsel? [ ] [ ] [ ]

C.   PROCEDURAL AND PRACTICAL STEPS

Prior to the hearing

		Yes	No	N/a
118.	Where the other party refused to produce documentation relevant to the proceedings did the lawyer seek an order that the other party produce specific documentation?	[ ]	[ ]	[ ]

119. Has a summary of the case been prepared prior to the final hearing (where Counsel is instructed this will take the form of a brief to Counsel) covering the following points:

		Yes	No	N/a
119.1	a chronology of events in the marriage?	[ ]	[ ]	[ ]
119.2	facts that are agreed and accepted?	[ ]	[ ]	[ ]
119.3	the main issues that are going to be heard?	[ ]	[ ]	[ ]

120. Did the lawyer prepare for submission to the court:

		Yes	No	N/a
120.1	an estimate of costs covering the costs already incurred and an estimate of expected costs of the hearing?[87]	[ ]	[ ]	[ ]
120.2	a chronology of material facts?	[ ]	[ ]	[ ]

After the hearing

121. Did the lawyer explain the effects of any order or settlement in terms of:[88]

		Yes	No	N/a
121.1	capital assets/home (if any)	[ ]	[ ]	[ ]
121.2	periodical payments for the client and children (including potential variations and Child Support Agency assessments)	[ ]	[ ]	[ ]
121.3	costs/the statutory charge	[ ]	[ ]	[ ]

122. Where applicable, did the lawyer advise what the client could do:

		Yes	No	N/a
122.1	if the client's financial circumstances change?	[ ]	[ ]	[ ]
122.2	if there are problems of non payment of maintenance?	[ ]	[ ]	[ ]

		Yes	No	N/a
123.	Did the lawyer advise the client as to the prospects of appeal by either side?	[ ]	[ ]	[ ]
124.	Did the lawyer explain the taxation process to the client, including the client's rights to make representations as to the amount of costs.	[ ]	[ ]	[ ]

4 Residence and Contact for any Children Affected by the Relationship

This section need only be considered where arrangements for residence/contact of children affected by the relationship under s.8 of the Children Act 1989 are not agreed. It covers both married and unmarried couples. It does not cover grandparents.

I Initial Instructions and Investigations

A. GETTING INFORMATION FROM THE CLIENT

125. Does the file show some understanding of the circumstances of any child(ren) affected by the parties' relationship, in particular:

		Yes	No	N/a
125.1	the full names, sex and dates of birth of each child;	[ ]	[ ]	[ ]
125.2	the names and addresses of the natural parents of each child;	[ ]	[ ]	[ ]
125.3	where and with whom the children reside;	[ ]	[ ]	[ ]
125.4	the existence of any maintenance orders or payments for any of the child(ren) and who they are against/in favour of;	[ ]	[ ]	[ ]
125.5	the state of health, including disabilities, of any children;	[ ]	[ ]	[ ]
125.6	if the child(ren) are of school age, where they go to school and whether fee paying or state. If fee paying, whether this is a viable proposition in the future and (if applicable) any special educational needs;	[ ]	[ ]	[ ]
125.7	where there is a difference between the parties on religion or nationality, whether or not the child(ren) are being brought up in any strong religious faith or national identity and which nationality or nationalities the child(ren) hold;	[ ]	[ ]	[ ]
125.8	if a change of residence is being suggested, and if any of the children are of school age, does the lawyer know if this would involve a change of school?	[ ]	[ ]	[ ]
125.9	when either party is proposing that the child(ren) be moved from the former family home, does the lawyer know:	N/A		[ ]
125.9.1	the nature of accommodation where it is proposed the child(ren) will live (i.e. is the accommodation shared, how much room there is)?	[ ]	[ ]	[ ]
125.9.2	how permanent these arrangements are?	[ ]	[ ]	[ ]
125.10	the degree of understanding/maturity of the children;	[ ]	[ ]	[ ]
125.11	the existence of other children in the family unit or extended family;	[ ]	[ ]	[ ]
125.12	existing contact arrangements and how they are working;	[ ]	[ ]	[ ]

	Yes	No	N/a

126. Where the client does not currently have the children living with them, does the file show some understanding of the following: **N/A** [ ]

    126.1   what kind of residence/contact the client has in mind for the children?   [ ]   [ ]   [ ]

    126.2   what kind of residence/contact agreement the client would find acceptable?   [ ]   [ ]   [ ]

    126.3   the other party's attitude to the client's wishes to visiting the child(ren) or having them to visit?   [ ]   [ ]   [ ]

    126.4   whether any third party has alternative proposals for residence contact;   [ ]   [ ]   [ ]

127. Does the file show some understanding of the likely/perceived effects on the children of current and (if different) proposed arrangements for the children?   [ ]   [ ]   [ ]

128. Unless the child(ren) are very young (pre-school age), does the lawyer have some understanding of the child(ren)'s views as to the current/proposed arrangements for contact/residence?[89]   [ ]   [ ]   [ ]

129. If either party is working and wishes to have the child(ren) living with them, does the lawyer know what arrangements may be made for the care of the child(ren) during workdays and school holidays?   [ ]   [ ]   [ ]

130. Where either party is not the natural parent of any of the children, and where residence and/or contact could be at issue does the file show some understanding of the attitudes of the non-natural parents to the children? In particular: **N/A** [ ]

    130.1   how long has the child (or children) been living with the non-natural parent;   [ ]   [ ]   [ ]

    130.2   the attitude towards, and treatment of, the child by the non-natural parent;   [ ]   [ ]   [ ]

    130.3   whether the non-natural parent helps support the child financially;   [ ]   [ ]   [ ]

131. Where the child(ren) have had contact with the Social Services or other welfare organisations (e.g. NSPCC), does the lawyer have details of the reasons for the contact and (if possible) the identity of the social workers involved?   [ ]   [ ]   [ ]

B.   STRATEGIC DECISION MAKING

132. In considering issues of residence, contact or other section 8 orders, in particular:

    132.1   unless the children are very young (pre- school age), the wishes and feelings of the child concerned (considered in the light of the child's age and understanding)?[90]   [ ]   [ ]   [ ]

    132.2   the child's physical, emotional and education needs?[91]   [ ]   [ ]   [ ]

    132.3   the current residence of the child(ren) and any other accommodation available for the child(ren) to live in and any other people living in any such accommodation?   [ ]   [ ]   [ ]

132.4   (if the client works) arrangements for care of child(ren) during working hours and holidays?

[ ]   [ ]   [ ]

132.5   if a change in circumstances is being suggested the likely effect on the child of any such change?

[ ]   [ ]   [ ]

132.6   the child's age, sex, background and any other characteristics of the child which the court will consider relevant?[92]

[ ]   [ ]   [ ]

132.7   any harm which the child has suffered or is at risk of suffering?[93]

[ ]   [ ]   [ ]

132.8   how capable each of the child's parents, and any other person[94] in relation to whom the court considers the question to be relevant, is of meeting the child(ren)'s needs?

[ ]   [ ]   [ ]

132.9   if a separation of siblings is suggested the effect on the children?

[ ]   [ ]   [ ]

133.   In considering the possibility of contact visits, either for the client or by the other party, were the following points considered:

133.1   both parties' attitudes to visits?

[ ]   [ ]   [ ]

133.2   unless the children are very young (pre- school age), the child(ren)'s attitudes to such visits?[95]

[ ]   [ ]   [ ]

133.3   when the client would like such visits to take place?

[ ]   [ ]   [ ]

133.4   which aspects of the arrangements are likely to be agreed with the other party and which are likely to cause disagreement?[96]

[ ]   [ ]   [ ]

133.5   arrangements for the collection and return of the children?

[ ]   [ ]   [ ]

133.6   current arrangements for residence and contact to take place before formal arrangements can be made;

[ ]   [ ]   [ ]

134.   In negotiating the residence/contact issues of the parties' relationship break-down, has the lawyer considered the following;

N/A   [ ]

134.1   the time scale within which the issue is likely to be resolved?[97]

[ ]   [ ]   [ ]

134.2   in considering or making offers on issues of residence/ contact, has the lawyer considered the parties' express wishes and needs in deciding how practical the offer is?

[ ]   [ ]   [ ]

134.3   any other services that might be available?[98]

[ ]   [ ]   [ ]

Unmarried Fathers

135.   Where the client is an unmarried father seeking parental responsibility,[99] has the lawyer considered:

N/A   [ ]

135.1   seeking written agreement from the mother of the child?

[ ]   [ ]   [ ]

135.2   how the client can show the court that it is in the child's best interests for the father to have parental responsibility?

[ ]   [ ]   [ ]

Interim Orders

		Yes	No	N/a
136.	Where the parties cannot agree about current arrangements for residence or contact has the lawyer considered applying for an interim order?[100]	[ ]	[ ]	[ ]
137.	If an interim order is in force, has the lawyer sought a copy of the order(s)?	[ ]	[ ]	[ ]

Specific Issues/Prohibited Steps

		Yes	No	N/a
138.	Where the client is particularly concerned with the conduct of the other party towards the child(ren) has the lawyer considered seeking a prohibited steps or specific issue order?[101]	[ ]	[ ]	[ ]

Variation of Interim Orders

		Yes	No	N/a
139.	Where the other party seeks or has obtained an interim order and either party wants the terms of the order varied or discharged has the lawyer considered whether the circumstances of the client and the child have changed since the making of the order?	[ ]	[ ]	[ ]

C. CLIENT COUNSELLING AND ADVICE

		Yes	No	N/a
140.	Has the client been informed about other agencies such as family conciliation or mediation before taking proceedings under the Children Act?	[ ]	[ ]	[ ]
141.	Has the lawyer advised the client on the need to consider whether making an order would be better for the child than making no order at all?[102]	[ ]	[ ]	[ ]
142.	Has the lawyer advised the client that the court's paramount consideration in deciding any question concerning a child's upbringing is the welfare of the child?[103]	[ ]	[ ]	[ ]
143.	Has the solicitor advised the client of the importance of attempting to co-operate in order to preserve a role for the absent parent in parenting?[104]	[ ]	[ ]	[ ]
144.	Did the lawyer advise the client generally about parental responsibility?[105]	[ ]	[ ]	[ ]
145.	Unless the client is an unmarried father without parental responsibility, did the lawyer advise the client on the likely practical significance of the continuing parental responsibility of both parents?	[ ]	[ ]	[ ]
146.	Were the client's views on any proposed options from the other side for contact and residence sought?	[ ]	[ ]	[ ]
147.	Did the lawyer advise the client of how long it is likely to be before residence/contact issues are resolved?[106]	[ ]	[ ]	[ ]
148.	Where a Welfare Officer's report was prepared:			
148.1	did the client get the opportunity to read it or comment on it?	[ ]	[ ]	[ ]
148.2	was the client warned that its contents are confidential and should not be disclosed to anyone else?	[ ]	[ ]	[ ]
148.3	was the client advised of its likely effect?	[ ]	[ ]	[ ]

Unmarried Fathers

		Yes	No	N/a
149.	Where the client is an unmarried father of a child and the client was not married to the mother of the child at the time of the birth of the child, did the lawyer advise:		N/A	[ ]
149.1	whether the client should apply for parental responsibility?[107]	[ ]	[ ]	[ ]
149.2	if the client is advised to apply, was he advised how to achieve parental responsibility?[108]	[ ]	[ ]	[ ]
150.	If the client is a father who has acquired parental responsibility by written agreement with the mother, has the agreement been registered/lodged at the Principal Registry of the Family Division?	[ ]	[ ]	[ ]

Interim Orders

		Yes	No	N/a
151.	If the lawyer has advised the client to seek an interim order:		N/A	[ ]
151.1	has the lawyer clearly stated the reasons for doing so?	[ ]	[ ]	[ ]
151.2	has the lawyer explained the procedure for obtaining an interim order to the client?	[ ]	[ ]	[ ]
152.	If contact is taking place between the parties and the children and there are problems with the contact visits, did the lawyer advise the client as what to do?	[ ]	[ ]	[ ]

II SETTLEMENTS

These criteria apply where the parties have negotiated an agreement on residence/contact issues without necessarily obtaining a consent order.

A. STRATEGIC DECISION MAKING

		Yes	No	N/a
153.	Did the lawyer, prior to drafting the agreement, consider:			
153.1	the child(ren)'s best interests?	[ ]	[ ]	[ ]
153.2	unless the child(ren) are very young (pre-school age), the child(ren)'s wishes?	[ ]	[ ]	[ ]
153.3	the other party's or parties' wishes?	[ ]	[ ]	[ ]
153.4	the practicalities of the arrangements?	[ ]	[ ]	[ ]

B. CLIENT COUNSELLING AND ADVICE

		Yes	No	N/a
154.	Was the client given an opportunity to read and amend the draft agreement/ consent order, if any?	[ ]	[ ]	[ ]
155.	Was the client advised on:			
155.1	the consequences of the agreement?	[ ]	[ ]	[ ]
155.2	what to do if there are problems?	[ ]	[ ]	[ ]

C PROCEDURAL AND PRACTICAL STEPS	Yes	No	N/a

156. Where a consent order is to be sought, has the lawyer ensured that a consent notice of application for an order as agreed was endorsed by both parties prior to sending it to court?   [ ] [ ] [ ]

157. Where a settlement was reached following an application but prior to the hearing did the lawyer inform the court thereof?   [ ] [ ] [ ]

III. Proceedings

This stage applies where proceedings are started under s.8 of the Children Act.

A. CLIENT COUNSELLING AND ADVICE

158. Where a directions hearing takes place, was the client informed: **N/A** [ ]

     158.1   when and where any directions hearings are taking place?   [ ] [ ] [ ]

     158.2   of the purpose of any directions hearings?   [ ] [ ] [ ]

     158.3   whether or not the client and child(ren) needed to attend?   [ ] [ ] [ ]

     158.4   of the outcome of the directions hearing (including the nature/ effect of the directions given)?   [ ] [ ] [ ]

159. Was the client advised of the costs implication of starting proceedings?   [ ] [ ] [ ]

B. PROCEDURAL AND PRACTICAL STEPS

160. If there has been any involvement of Social Services or other Welfare Agencies in the affairs of either party and the child(ren), did the lawyer attempt to contact them?   [ ] [ ] [ ]

161. Where a Section 8 order was obtained ex parte, did the applicant's lawyer serve a copy of the order respectively on each party and on any person who has the actual care of the child and who had such care immediately prior to the making of the order?   [ ] [ ] [ ]

162. Where the lawyer is acting for the applicant in an application for a section 8 order: **N/A** [ ]

     162.1   Where the client was not the petitioner or respondent to divorce proceedings, was Form CHA 10 completed?   [ ] [ ] [ ]

     162.2   Where the client was petitioner or respondent in divorce proceedings, was Form CHA 10(D) completed?   [ ] [ ] [ ]

     162.3   Has the lawyer ensured that all respondents[109] have been given the following:

         162.3.1   written notice of the date, time and place of the hearing or directions appointment fixed?   [ ] [ ] [ ]

     162.4   Has the lawyer filed a statement before the directions hearing that service of a copy of the application has been effected on each of the respondents?   [ ] [ ] [ ]

163. Where the lawyer is acting on behalf of the respondent was the respondent's answer to the s.8 application (CHA 10A) filed and served within 14 days of service of the application?   [ ]   [ ]   [ ]

164. Has the lawyer ensured that all Directions have been complied with including any need to alert the Court Welfare Officer of their required attendance at Court?   [ ]   [ ]   [ ]

165. If there are any public law proceedings in relation to the client's case, has the lawyer obtained details of these?   [ ]   [ ]   [ ]

IV HEARINGS OF THE DISPUTES

The following criteria should be completed if there are any court hearings the client attended. If there is a full hearing the criteria should be applied to that hearing.

A. CLIENT COUNSELLING AND ADVICE

166. Did the lawyer inform the client of the date, place and time of the hearing?   [ ]   [ ]   [ ]

167. Has the lawyer explained to the client the necessity of attending court?[110]   [ ]   [ ]   [ ]

168. Has the lawyer explained to the client what will happen at the hearing, in particular:

    168.1   whether the hearing will be held in Chambers or in private at the magistrates' court?   [ ]   [ ]   [ ]

    168.2   the nature of the proceedings and how the client will be expected to participate (e.g. how evidence is given)?   [ ]   [ ]   [ ]

    168.3   how long it will last?   [ ]   [ ]   [ ]

169. Has the lawyer considered with the client the desirability of bringing the children to court and how their views, if appropriate, can be made known to the court?   [ ]   [ ]   [ ]

B. PROCEDURAL AND PRACTICAL STEPS

170. If any oral evidence is to be adduced at the hearing has the lawyer: N/A [ ]

    170.1   filed and served on the parties, any welfare officer and any guardian ad litem, written statements of the substance of the oral evidence to be adduced?[111]   [ ]   [ ]   [ ]

    170.2   ensured that each statement is signed and dated?   [ ]   [ ]   [ ]

    170.3   ensured that each statement contains a declaration that the maker of the statement believes it to be true and understands that it may be placed before the court?   [ ]   [ ]   [ ]

171. If there are other documents[112] on which it is intended to rely, have these been filed and served as specifically directed by the Court, or in the absence of specific direction, before the hearing or appointment?   [ ]   [ ]   [ ]

	Yes	No	N/a

172. If any filed and served documents need to be amended, has the solicitor requested leave in writing? [ ] [ ] [ ]

173. If a child needs to be medically or psychiatrically examined, has the solicitor applied for leave and served the application on all parties and if there is one, the guardian ad litem?[113] [ ] [ ] [ ]

C. POST HEARING PROCEDURAL AND PRACTICAL STEPS   N/A [ ]

174. Did the lawyer explain the effects of any order or settlement in terms of:

    174.1 where the child(ren) will reside [ ] [ ] [ ]

    174.2 the periods of contact the child(ren) will have with the client or the other side [ ] [ ] [ ]

    174.3 the effect of a residence order on changing surname? [ ] [ ] [ ]

    174.4 the effect of a residence order on the ability of either parent to remove the child from England and Wales? [ ] [ ] [ ]

175. Was the client invited, in writing, to contact the lawyer should there be any future difficulties with arrangements concerning the child(ren)? [ ] [ ] [ ]

Transfer of Files and Complaints

176. If the file was transferred from the main file-handler to another office, department or case worker: N/A [ ]

    176.1 Is there evidence (letter/attendance note) of explanation to the client of the transfer?[114] [ ] [ ] [ ]

    176.2 Was the client given the name and status of the person taking over the case?[115] [ ] [ ] [ ]

    176.3 Was the client asked for acknowledgement/approval of the transfer? [ ] [ ] [ ]

177. Where the client makes a complaint, did the lawyer: N/A [ ]

    177.1 respond to it immediately? [ ] [ ] [ ]

    177.2 advise the client who else they can contact in the firm to consider the complaint? [ ] [ ] [ ]

    177.3 if the problem is not solved to the client's satisfaction, were they referred to the Solicitors' Complaints Bureau? [ ] [ ] [ ]

Violence Against the Client (Green Form/Emergency Only)

I GETTING INFORMATION FROM THE CLIENT

	General Information	Yes	No	N/a
1.	Has the lawyer recorded:			
1.1	the client's full name?	[ ]	[ ]	[ ]
1.2	the client's address and telephone number?	[ ]	[ ]	[ ]
1.3	the client's date of birth?	[ ]	[ ]	[ ]

Details of incidents

		Yes	No	N/a
2.	Does the lawyer have some understanding of:			
2.1	the behaviour that the client is worried by?	[ ]	[ ]	[ ]
2.2	when such behaviour began?	[ ]	[ ]	[ ]
2.3	when and what all recent occurrences were?	[ ]	[ ]	[ ]
2.4	when and what the more serious occurrences were?	[ ]	[ ]	[ ]
2.5	the existence of any witnesses to the incidents?	[ ]	[ ]	[ ]
2.6	whether the client objects to the lawyer contacting the witnesses?	[ ]	[ ]	[ ]
2.7	the clients explanation of the incidents, including the client's own behaviour?	[ ]	[ ]	[ ]
3.	Does the lawyer know whether the police have been called to any of the incidents?	[ ]	[ ]	[ ]
4.	If the police have been called, does the lawyer have an understanding of:	**N/A**		[ ]
4.1	the date of the incident when the police were called?	[ ]	[ ]	[ ]
4.2	the place of the incident?	[ ]	[ ]	[ ]
4.3	any available information that can help identify the police officers (e.g. their names, numbers or police station)?	[ ]	[ ]	[ ]
4.4	the outcome of the police visit?	[ ]	[ ]	[ ]
5.	Does the lawyer know whether the other side has any criminal convictions for violent behaviour?	[ ]	[ ]	[ ]
6.	Does the lawyer know whether the client or the client's children have had any contact with the medical services as a result of any injuries sustained?	[ ]	[ ]	[ ]
7.	If so, does the lawyer have information that can identify the medical personnel, or hospitals, involved?	[ ]	[ ]	[ ]
8.	Does the lawyer know whether the client or the client's children have had any contact with the Social Services or other welfare organisations?	[ ]	[ ]	[ ]

	Yes	No	N/a

9. If so, does the lawyer have information that can identify the social worker, authority, or organisation involved? [ ]　[ ]　[ ]

10. If the client has any children living with her or him:　　　　N/A　[ ]

    10.1 does the lawyer know if the client has any worries about the children because of the other party's behaviour? [ ]　[ ]　[ ]

    10.2 if so, does the lawyer know the nature of these worries? [ ]　[ ]　[ ]

    10.3 does the lawyer know who the natural parents of the children are? [ ]　[ ]　[ ]

    10.4 does the lawyer know their client's view of the children's attitudes towards the behaviour of the other party? [ ]　[ ]　[ ]

11. Does the lawyer know whether there were any legal proceedings with regard to the parties relationship/behaviour, whether there are any existing injunctions, and/or whether any legal proceedings are pending? [ ]　[ ]　[ ]

12. If so, does the lawyer know whether the client did/does have legal aid with regard to any of these proceedings? [ ]　[ ]　[ ]

Status of parties' relationship

13. Does the lawyer know whether the parties are married or not? [ ]　[ ]　[ ]

14. Does the lawyer know whether the parties are or were living in the same accommodation? [ ]　[ ]　[ ]

15. Does the lawyer have some understanding of the nature of the parties' relationship at the time of the incidents complained of, in particular whether or not they were living together? [ ]　[ ]　[ ]

16. Does the lawyer have some understanding of the client's views and feelings on the current and future relationship with the other party? [ ]　[ ]　[ ]

17. Does the lawyer have some understanding of the client's views and feelings on the future arrangements for the children, in particular:　　N/A　[ ]

    17.1 does the client want to look after the children? [ ]　[ ]　[ ]

    17.2 if so, is it known what the proposed arrangements for looking after the children are? in particular, details of where the children will live, care when the client is at work, etc. [ ]　[ ]　[ ]

    17.3 is it known how the client views contact with the children by the other side? [ ]　[ ]　[ ]

    17.4 if the client does not wish the other side to have contact, does the lawyer know the reasons for this view? [ ]　[ ]　[ ]

Residences

18. Does the lawyer know where the client is living currently and for how long they have lived there? [ ]　[ ]　[ ]

19. If the client is not living at his or her normal address, does the lawyer know if the client wishes to keep this address confidential? [ ]　[ ]　[ ]

	Yes	No	N/a

20. If the client was, or is, living with the other party, does the lawyer know:

20.1 whether the house is rented or owner occupied?   [ ]   [ ]   [ ]

20.2 in whose name(s) the house is held?   [ ]   [ ]   [ ]

20.3 whether or not the client has any legal interest in the property (this is assumed if the couple are married)?   [ ]   [ ]   [ ]

20.4 unless there is no suggestion that the client has any interest in the former shared residence, whether or not the payments on the property are still being paid?   [ ]   [ ]   [ ]

Client finances

21 Does the Lawyer have an understanding of the financial position of the client? In particular:

21.1 how many hours the client works[116] and the size of the client's income (if any);   [ ]   [ ]   [ ]

21.2 the size of any benefit payments to the client, i.e.;   N/A   [ ]

21.2.1 income support   [ ]   [ ]   [ ]

21.2.2 one parent benefit   [ ]   [ ]   [ ]

21.2.3 child benefit   [ ]   [ ]   [ ]

21.2.4 housing benefit   [ ]   [ ]   [ ]

II ADVISING ON THIS INFORMATION

22. Where there is evidence of violence or threatened violence or harassment, was the client advised as to the possibility of taking court action to prevent the other party behaving in such a way?   [ ]   [ ]   [ ]

23. Furthermore, did the lawyer ensure that the client's view was sought on the effectiveness of such an approach. In particular was the client advised:

23.1 as to the nature, availability and effect of a non-molestation injunction/protection order?   [ ]   [ ]   [ ]

23.2 as to the nature, availability and effect of an ouster injunction/exclusion order?   [ ]   [ ]   [ ]

23.3 where the client is not currently living in the house that had been shared, as to the availability of an order to ensure that s/he would be permitted in the previously shared address?   [ ]   [ ]   [ ]

24. Where there is evidence of a real and immediate danger of serious injury to the client[117] was the client advised of the possibility of making an immediate ex parte application to the court?   [ ]   [ ]   [ ]

25. Where the client has suffered actual bodily harm and is likely to be subject to bodily harm again, was the client advised to apply for a power of arrest to be attached to any injunctions sought? Furthermore, did the lawyer ensure that the client's view were sought on the effectiveness of this action?   [ ]   [ ]   [ ]

			Yes	No	N/a

26. Where the client was living with the other party in owner occupied accommodation, was the client advised as to the possibility of protecting their interest in that property to prevent resale or further mortgaging of the property? [ ] [ ] [ ]

27. If the client is living with the other party, does the lawyer consider the possibility of alternative accommodation, including local authority housing, for the client? [ ] [ ] [ ]

28. Where the client is living in temporary accommodation, was the client advised of the possibility of obtaining local authority housing? [ ] [ ] [ ]

29. If the client is working less than 16 hours a week, has the lawyer advised the client as to the possibility of claiming income support as a single (separated) person? [ ] [ ] [ ]

30. If the client is working less than 16 hours, and it seems possible that income support will be available, has the lawyer advised the client as to help they might receive with housing costs: [ ] [ ] [ ]

31. If the client is working less than 16 hours per week and is still living in the same accommodation as the other party, did the lawyer advise as to any effects on the client's entitlement to income support of separating from the other party?[118] [ ] [ ] [ ]

32. If the client is in paid work for more than 16 hours per week, and has at least one child under the age of 16 (or under 19 and in full time education) has the lawyer advised the client of the availability of Family Credit? [ ] [ ] [ ]

33. Did the lawyer consider the position of the Community Charge[119] with the client? In particular:

33.1 was the client advised on notifying the local authority of the separation from their spouse (if and when this occurs)? [ ] [ ] [ ]

33.2 was the client advised on the possibility of claiming Community Charge benefit? [ ] [ ] [ ]

Progress of the case

34.1 Did the lawyer advise the client of how long the case is likely to take? [ ] [ ] [ ]

34.2 Is there an indication of the steps that the lawyer has agreed to take and have these been advised to the client? [ ] [ ] [ ]

34.3 Is there an indication of the steps the lawyer has asked the client to take? [ ] [ ] [ ]

34.4 Is the client told when and in what form the next contact will take place? [ ] [ ] [ ]

34.5 Has the lawyer advised the client as to more than one possible course of action? [ ] [ ] [ ]

34.6 Did the lawyer indicate the likely outcome of the case? [ ] [ ] [ ]

34.7 Is there an indication that the client made an active choice on the lawyer's suggested mode of action? [ ] [ ] [ ]

		Yes	No	N/a

		Yes	No	N/a
34.8	Has the lawyer noted down the reaction of the client to the decided plan of action (as a minimum, this should include the client's consent to the action going forward)?	[ ]	[ ]	[ ]
34.9	If the lawyer is not going to represent the client at any hearings, is there an indication that alternative sources of representation or assistance were explained to the client?	[ ]	[ ]	[ ]
34.10	Were any apparent queries from the client dealt with fully, promptly and politely?	[ ]	[ ]	[ ]
34.11	Did the lawyer deal with any emotional concerns of the client?	[ ]	[ ]	[ ]
34.12	Did the lawyer explain any contact with the other side? In particular, when the other side will be contacted and why?	[ ]	[ ]	[ ]
34.13	Did the lawyer advise the client as to what to do if contacted by the other side?	[ ]	[ ]	[ ]

Costs and Funding of the Case

		Yes	No	N/a
35.	Is it apparent that the client has been advised regarding the costs and funding of the case? In particular:			
35.1	the availability of green form/ABWOR/civil legal aid	[ ]	[ ]	[ ]
35.2	the limits and extent of green form funding.	[ ]	[ ]	[ ]
35.3	whether or not the client will have to make a contribution to the case;	[ ]	[ ]	[ ]
35.4	the effects of the solicitor's and statutory charge on any damages received (if these are being claimed);	[ ]	[ ]	[ ]
35.5	the costs to the client should the case be lost;	[ ]	[ ]	[ ]
35.6	the nature and consequences of revocation and discharge of certificates (if a certificate is granted);	[ ]	[ ]	[ ]
35.7	the duty to report changes of circumstance and address;	[ ]	[ ]	[ ]

III FURTHER INVESTIGATION, RESEARCH AND ACTION

Action Before Proceedings

		Yes	No	N/a
36.	If the client agrees, did the lawyer attempt to contact and interview any witnesses to the incidents?	[ ]	[ ]	[ ]
37.	If the client agrees, did the lawyer contact the client's local police force:		N/A	[ ]
37.1	stating who they act for, and the nature of any proceedings?	[ ]	[ ]	[ ]
37.2	if the client has had previous contact with the police, requesting information on any complaints/prosecutions?	[ ]	[ ]	[ ]
37.3	requesting that the client's future complaints be taken seriously?	[ ]	[ ]	[ ]

			Yes	No	N/a

38.1 Unless the application was ex parte, did the solicitor arrange for personal service of applications against the other side? [ ] [ ] [ ]

38.2 Where an ex parte order was granted, did the solicitor arrange for personal service of the order against the other side? [ ] [ ] [ ]

39. Where service is to be made, has the lawyer asked for any available photographs of the other party? [ ] [ ] [ ]

40. Did such arrangements include the person serving the documents having a description of the other side and/or a photograph (if available)? [ ] [ ] [ ]

41. Furthermore, did such arrangements include a description of the other side's place and hours of work, as well as likely addresses at which the other side could be reached? [ ] [ ] [ ]

42. Did the lawyer ensure there was an affidavit of service, or if service could not be made, was an application for substituted service made? [ ] [ ] [ ]

43. Where the former home was owner-occupied as a matrimonial home, and unless it is clear the client has no interest in the former home, did the lawyer check ownership rights and register either a charge or a notice? [ ] [ ] [ ]

44. If the home was joint owned (and if registered land), did the lawyer consider severing the tenancy between the parties by writing to the other party and also writing to the Land Registry? [ ] [ ] [ ]

Proceedings

45. Has the lawyer advised the client as to which form of proceedings and which court provides the most appropriate course of action in the client's case? [ ] [ ] [ ]

46. *Where proceedings are begun under the DVMPA 1976:*[120]   **N/A** [ ]

46.1 is there evidence that the client has suffered violence, threats of violence or repeated acts of harassment? [ ] [ ] [ ]

46.2 were the parties living together as husband and wife at the time of the incidents complained of? [ ] [ ] [ ]

46.3 if the client believes the children are also in danger, has protection of them been also sought? [ ] [ ] [ ]

47. *Where proceedings are begun under the MCA 1973:*[121]   **N/A** [ ]

47.1 is there evidence that the client has suffered violence, threats of violence or repeated acts of harassment? [ ] [ ] [ ]

47.2 is there a marriage in existence between the parties? [ ] [ ] [ ]

47.3 has a petition for divorce or judicial separation been filed or an undertaking to file a petition given (and decree absolute not yet granted)? [ ] [ ] [ ]

47.4 if the client believes the children are also in danger, has protection of them also been sought? [ ] [ ] [ ]

		Yes	No	N/a

48. *Where proceedings are begun under the DPMCA 1978 in the magistrates court:*[122]   **N/A**   [   ]

48.1   is there evidence that the client or any children of the family have suffered violence or threats of violence?   [   ]   [   ]   [   ]

     48.2   is there a marriage in existence between the parties?   [   ]   [   ]   [   ]

     48.3   if the client believes the children are also in danger has protection of them been sought also?   [   ]   [   ]   [   ]

     48.4   is there evidence that an order is necessary for the protection of client or child?   [   ]   [   ]   [   ]

     48.5   is there evidence that an order would be better for the welfare of any children involved?   [   ]   [   ]   [   ]

49. If an injunction is sought in the County Court to restrain assault, battery and/ or trespass: **N/A**   [   ]

     49.1   were the parties living apart at the time of the incidents?   [   ]   [   ]   [   ]

     49.2   was there no marriage in subsistence between the parties?   [   ]   [   ]   [   ]

     49.3   was an application for damages included in the application?[123]   [   ]   [   ]   [   ]

50. If the application is also to oust or exclude the other party, is there some evidence that other lesser forms of injunction are inadequate?   [   ]   [   ]   [   ]

51. If an application is to be made ex parte: **N/A**   [   ]

     51.1   is there evidence of a real and immediate danger of serious injury to the client?[124]   [   ]   [   ]   [   ]

     51.2   (unless an ancillary injunction is sought under wardship) is the application supported by an affidavit?   [   ]   [   ]   [   ]

     51.3   is there a date on the application upon which the ex parte order expires (the return date)?   [   ]   [   ]   [   ]

52. If a power of arrest is sought: **N/A**   [   ]

     52.1   is there evidence of actual bodily harm?   [   ]   [   ]   [   ]

     52.2   is there evidence that the client was likely to be subject to actual bodily harm again?   [   ]   [   ]   [   ]

     52.3   were the client's local police contacted if this application was successful?   [   ]   [   ]   [   ]

Outcomes

53. If the client wishes to withdraw proceedings, did the lawyer speak directly to the client as to the effects of any withdrawal or reconciliation with the other party?   [   ]   [   ]   [   ]

		Yes	No	N/a
54.	If the litigation is resolved by undertakings, are the nature and effect of the undertakings explained to the client?	[ ]	[ ]	[ ]
55.	If an injunction or court order is granted, is the nature and effect of the other side breaching such an order explained to the client?	[ ]	[ ]	[ ]
56.	If a power of arrest is attached to any order, is the nature and effect of the other side breaching such an order explained to the client?	[ ]	[ ]	[ ]
57.	Is the client advised, in writing, of what to do in the event that the other side resumes threats, violence or harassment?	[ ]	[ ]	[ ]
58.	Are ex parte applications made within twenty four hours of the decision of lawyer and client to proceed with an ex parte order?	[ ]	[ ]	[ ]
59.	Are other applications issued within two days of a decision to proceed with an injunction?	[ ]	[ ]	[ ]
60.	Where a power of arrest is granted, did the lawyer serve the police station with a copy of the order?	[ ]	[ ]	[ ]

Matrimonial/Family—Notes to the Criteria

1.   This includes all children of the parties' marriage/cohabitation and children within either parties' household.

2.   This may be in an agreed time or after an agreed time.

3.   Advice of this nature may well not be applicable under a Green Form only divorce.

4.   This will be satisfied by an indication in broad terms of the rate of charging and a broad estimate of likely cost.

5.   This can encompass changes in the personal circumstances of the client and changes in the case itself.

6.   Solicitors Family Law Association Code of Practice, para. 4.2.

7.   A negotiated settlement may well reduce costs if it prevents unnecessary proceedings. The Court of Appeal has stressed the importance of responding to negotiation in *Gojkovic No.2* (1992) 1 All ER 267.

8.   Most mediation is child-centred at present but may also focus on 'comprehensive mediation' of financial and children issues.

9.   e.g. Mediation/conciliation services and/or marriage guidance services, if appropriate.

10. A caution can only be lodged at the Land Registry if the client is petitioner and a divorce has been commenced, or if the client is a respondent to a petition and has commenced her application for ancillary relief.

11. S.37 Matrimonial Causes Act 1973.

12. Solicitors Family Law Association Code of Practice 6.5.

13. e.g. A residence or prohibited steps order.

14. Family Law Reform Act 1986 s.33

15. This refers to previous periods of separation, i.e. not the instant one.

16. These criteria will not necessarily be relevant where there is *continuing* adultery and/or behaviour and proceedings are to go ahead on either adultery or behaviour. In such circumstances they will not be audited.

17. The lawyer may also wish to consider a separation agreement.

18. e.g. if a petition was to be sought solely on the basis of the other party's adultery, 30.5–30.8 would not apply.

19. "Petitions" include both divorce and judicial separation unless stated to the contrary.

20. If separation is not practical, this advice should cover advice on living separately under the same roof

21. 'Unreasonable' here is not meant to denote a legal term of art. Failure to reach competence will only be said to have occurred when there is obviously no evidence upon which to base a claim that the respondent's behaviour was unreasonable.

22. S.5 MCA 1973. It is a defence to a s.1(2)(e) petition if the respondent can show that the dissolution of the marriage will result in grave financial or other hardship and in all the circumstances it would be wrong to dissolve the marriage.

23. Sometimes a petition will cite exaggerated facts which the respondent may want to change into something less severe.

24. r. 2.2, Family Proceedings Rules 1991.

25. The lawyer may be guided by the SFLA Code of Practice, para. 1.5 "The Solicitor should also have regard to the impact of correspondence on the other party when writing a letter of which a copy may be sent to that party and should also consider carefully the impact of correspondence on his own client before sending copies of letters to the client."

26. Other methods of service include bailiff service, personal service by an enquiry agent or solicitor, substituted service, an order for deemed service or service via the D.S.S.

27. e.g. A description/photograph of the other party, place of work, and other addresses and times at which other party could be served.

28. e.g. Regarding rights of occupation, pension rights, state pension contributions, maintenance pending suit, etc, and inability to remarry.

29. e.g. On freedom to remarry, effect on pension provisions (if any), etc.

30. If this is clearly above 16 hours per week then there is no need for an exact figure of hours worked.

31. Other than joint mortgage accounts which are dealt with at 50 post.

32. This could include business loans and charges against property, other than joint mortgages which are dealt with at 50 post.

33. e.g. Is it a repayment or an endowment mortgage, is there a collateral life policy, etc.

34. Including any arrears and insurance/endowment premiums in relation to the mortgage.

35. e.g. Is it a secure/assured/protected tenancy

36. e.g. This maybe the surrender value or the value of the endowment fund.

37. See, p.153: Hodson & Dunmall, *The Business of Family Law*.

38. This may include items such as a car, household items, and jewellery.

39. See, s.25(2)(b) of the Matrimonial Causes Act 1973.

40. Council Tax commenced 1st April 1993.

41. The Child Support Agency is the administrative body responsible for the implementation of the Child Support Act 1991.

42. s.8(6)

43. s.8.(5): 'The Lord Chancellor or in relation to Scotland the Lord Advocate may by order provide that, in such circumstances as may be specified by the order, this section shall not prevent a court from exercising any power which it has to make a maintenance order in relation to a child if:

   a. a written agreement (whether or not enforceable) provides for the making, or securing, by an absent parent of the child of periodical payments to or for the benefit of the child; and,

   b. the maintenance order which the court makes is, in all material respects, in the same terms as that agreement.

44. "From April 1993 to April 1996, the Agency will also take on income support, family credit and disability working allowance cases, whether there is a court order or agreement in force or not. Where a court order or maintenance agreement is in force, the parties may not apply for child support maintenance until April 1996." Martha Street, Money and Family Breakdown, The Practitioner's guide to benefits and child support, Ch.18, p.379.

45. Before the court makes orders for the benefit of a child of the family the court will take the factors cited into account.

46. The maintenance requirement is a notional minimum amount necessary for the maintenance of the qualifying child(ren). This includes the personal allowance for each qualifying child and person with care (where a qualifying child is under 16), family premium if applicable less child benefit (but not one parent benefit) for each qualifying child. See *Martha Street, Money and Family Breakdown*, (Legal Action Group 1993), p.412.

47. Exempt income is equivalent to income support personal allowance for those of 25 or over and the personal allowance for each natural or adoptive child who is living with him or her plus, if applicable, the family premium, lone parent or disability premiums and reasonable housing costs. See *Martha Street; Money and Family Breakdown*, (Legal Action Group, 1993), p.410.

48. The assessable income is a parent's net income less exempt income and is the income from which child support maintenance is paid.

49. Before the Court makes an Order for the parties the Court will take into account the factors listed in ss.25(1)-(4)and 25A MCA 1973.

50. These could include among others, financial obligations due to re-marriage and existing obligations arising from a previous marriage.

51. This can include assisting in the family business, looking after the children, cleaning the matrimonial home.

52. This can include loss of pension, private health care, and insurance rights.

53. Ingleby R, Solicitors and Divorce, Ch.6, p.75.

54. For example, transferring the property into joint names (if not already so), stipulating circumstances when the property will be sold, agreeing proportions of the sale price, or registering a charge for a fixed sum or a charge for a proportion of the proceeds of sale. See guideline 8.5 of the Additional Guidelines of the Law Society Family Law Committee.

55. The lawyer may wish to be guided by the Solicitors Family Law Association Code of Practice, para. 1.1.

56. This will be satisfied by an indication in broad terms of the possible outcome.

57. Appeal to a child support appeal tribunal lies within 28 days of notice being given of a review of a child support officer's decision, or a refusal to review. See, Street, op.cit., p.394 et seq for further details.

58. e.g. The possibility of being deemed intentionally homeless.

59. If the client has been given welfare benefits advice on a separate file, the auditor will need to consider this second file.

60. i.e. Where the client is looking after any children, e.g. the family premium, single parent premium and dependent children's allowance.

61. If the client and the other party are living under the same roof but separately, the client may be able to claim income support.

62. A budgeting loan is discretionary and could for example be available for essential household items, essential home repairs and removal charges if it is essential for the client to move to suitable accommodation. After 6 months the client may also be eligible for Social Fund grants and loans.

These loans may be made only if the client gets income support and has done so for the last 26 weeks or if s/he has suffered an emergency or disaster. If these circumstances do not apply, this question will be not applicable.

63. e.g. help from the Local Authority with the cost of things like school meals, travel to school and school clothing.

64. Criteria 83.1 and 83.2 will not apply where it is evident that the client was already being treated as separate from the other party by the local authority.

65. Under the Council Tax help may be given to clients who are single occupiers, who were exempt under the Community Charge, who are disabled—where property has been altered to provide for their special needs, and for their special requirements, who are on low incomes.

Council Tax reductions may include; Council Tax Benefit, Transitional Relief, Second Audit Rebate and Status Discounts.

66. Clout,I, *The Matrimonial Solicitor, A guide to good practice,* p.67: "You are in no position to make proper judgment about the likely outcome of the case without quite detailed financial information." Evidence usually takes the form of documentation but where there is no such documentary evidence, the lawyer may have to arrange for affidavits.

67. Additional Guidelines of the Law Society Family Law Committee para.6.3 cited in Hodson & Dunmall, *The Business of Family Law*, p.307 : "Where possible, property valuations should be obtained from a valuer jointly instructed by both parties. Where each party instructs a valuer, reports should be exchanged and if necessary the valuers should meet in an attempt to resolve differences. If possible a valuation obtained by one party should be agreed by the other party. In any event only one valuer should be instructed by each party (see *E v E* (1990) 2 FLR 233)." It is important to time the valuation appropriately. Too early a valuation could prove worthless and waste costs.

68. The auditor should look at the facts of the case and establish whether the necessary evidence has been sought, for example, bank statements for the last 12 months, salary pay-slips, child benefit books, and proof of other state benefits, and any other documents which are proof of amounts of money which the client receives.

69. For example, bank statements, passbooks for Building Society or Post Office Accounts, Pension Contributions, insurance contributions, tax, electricity bills, gas bills, telephone bills, water rate charges, H.P. agreements, loan agreements, rent-books, and any other documents which are proof of amounts of money which the client has to pay regularly which can include car tax, clothes and shoes, medical expenses, travel costs, and food bills.

70. *W v. W* (1989) 153 Justice of the Peace Journal 769.

71. e.g. By a transfer of property order, if appropriate; by application under the MHA 1973; or by mutual agreement between spouse and landlord.

72. Hodson with Dunmall, *The Business of Family Law,*(Family Law 1992), p.268.

73. If it may be appropriate to apply for penal notice to be endorsed immediately.

74. Both parties are under a duty to make Calderbank offers where appropriate and take real and meaningful part in negotiations (Moorish v Moorish [1984] Fam 26). Also see, Additional Guidelines of the Law Society Family Law Committee, guideline 7.1. "It is arguable that in cases where both sides are legally aided Calderbank letters have no place because an order for costs from one party to the other is highly unlikely. This argument has lost some of its force since the provision for interest on the

statutory charge came into effect, but it is worth bearing in mind", p.75 Clout I, *The Matrimonial Solicitor, A guide to good practice*, Family Law, Jordan & Sons Ltd 1992.

75. Open offers are offers made which are *not* 'without prejudice' and can be as, or more, useful than Calderbank letters. They can also be used in conjunction with Calderbank letters. Hodson & Dunmall, *The Business of Family Law, p.89*, Family Law, Jordan & Sons 1992.

76. Hodson & Dunmall, op.cit., p.89.

77. Hodson & Dunmall, op.cit., p.87.

78. It has been held that 10 days before a hearing is not enough time to consider a Calderbank letter. *Gojkovic v Gojkovic (No 2)* [1991] 2 FLR 233.

79. Under the Child Support Act 1991, s.9., written agreements can be entered into but such agreements cannot purport to restrict the right to use the Child Support Agency. See, Street, op.cit., p.377.

80. For example, the clients position with regard to future mortgage payments, council tax, and possible repairs to the property, as well as tax implications. See guideline 8.4 of the Additional Guidelines of the Law Society Family Law Committee.

81. As a minimum, it should be clear from the file whether the lawyer explained the effect of any Consent Order.

82. See guideline 8.8 of the Additional Guidelines of the Law Society Family Law Committee.

83. This is also known as the Rule 2.61 statement (formerly Rule 76A).

84. The lawyer should have up to date valuations of any property and information as to the client's net income and outgoings before completing the Statement of Information. See Additional Guidelines of the Law Society Family Law Committee, Drafting Consent Orders guideline 8.1.

85. All capital resources should be included.

86. e.g. A private hearing in chambers.

87. *Practice Direction (Ancillary Relief: Costs Estimate)* [1988] 2 ALL ER 63.

88. e.g. The irreversibility of lump sum/property orders.

89. The lawyer is not required to talk directly with the child(ren). An understanding gained from the client or other source will be acceptable. Such other sources might include (if appropriate) school teachers, health visitors, child-minders or relatives of the parties/children.

90. This is relevant unless the child is very young (pre-school age). The lawyer is not required to talk directly with the child(ren).

91. The following could for example be considered: the ability to provide a home for the child(ren), the importance a parent places on academic achievement, punctuality, tidiness, giving assistance in the household, the amount a child should spend watching television, and the need for continuity of the child(ren)'s existing arrangements. See S.M. Cretney, *Elements of Family Law*, pp.263–266, Sweet & Maxwell 1992.

92. The lawyer may have considered among other things; the cultural and religious background of the child(ren), and how the child(ren)'s age and sex may affect their needs.

93. Normally this would not apply, except in circumstances where some harm is alleged (e.g. a violent parent, sexual abuse, or neglect).

94. i.e. Any other person likely to be involved in the care of the child(ren).

95. The lawyer is not required to talk directly with the child(ren).

96. Gwynn Davis, points out that, "technical legal advice always comes in partisan wrapping, so failing to cater for those couples who *can* agree": Partisans and Mediators, Oxford University Press (1988).

97. S.1(2) C.A.,1989 states that delay in resolving an issue is regarded as being likely to prejudice the child's welfare.

98. e.g. Conciliation services, services for young people.

99. e.g. By seeking a residence order.

100. Black & Bridge: *A practical approach to Family Law*, p.333, Blackstone Press 1992.

101. A prohibited steps or specific issue order could be obtained where there is a dispute as to the child(ren)'s education, determining whether the child(ren) can be taken abroad, preventing a parent seeing the child(ren).

102. This is the principle of non-intervention introduced under the Children Act, 1989. It is for the Court to decide whether or not it would be better to make an order. It should only do so if it is considered to be in the best interests of the child.

103. Solicitors Family Law Association's Code Of Practice, para 6.1.

104. Solicitors Family Law Association's Code Of Practice, para 6.2:"The solicitor should aim to promote co-operation between parents in decisions concerning the child, both by formal arrangements (such as orders[that used to be made] for joint custody), by practical arrangements (such as shared involvement in school events) and by consultation on important questions."

105. In particular this might cover the following aspects; that under the Children Act both parents continue to have parental responsibility after the divorce or if unmarried, that the mother will have parental responsibility in absence of an order or a contact; and on the effect of orders for residence/contact on parental responsibility. The relevant Children Act forms set out clearly relevant aspects of this. Evidence that the client has read and signed this form will be indicative of compliance.

106. This does not require a precise figure in (say) months, but the lawyer should give some indication of how long a case is likely to take.

107. A father will not have parental responsibility where the father was not married to the mother at the time of the birth of the child, unless the child was subsequently legitimised. A child can be legitimised where the father subsequently marries the mother of the child, or where the child is adopted by the husband of the mother of the child, that is not the natural father of the child.

108. The client could apply for a parental responsibility order or enter into a parental responsibility agreement.

109. As defined in column (iv) of Schedule 2 to the Family Proceedings Rules,1991 (Rule 4(3)) Harris, PM and Scanlan, DE, 'The Children Act 1989 A Procedural Handbook' 1991, Butterworths.

110. If no one appears at the appointed time and place for a directions appointment or a hearing, the court may refuse the application. Harris, P.M. and Scanlan, D.E., op.cit., p.98.

111. A specific direction will be required to enable this.

112. Including experts' reports.

113. Unless the clerk or court directs otherwise.

114. The Guide To The Professional Conduct Of Solicitors (1993, Law Society), Ch 13, p.278, 13.02, 2.

115. The family practitioner is often out at court and there must be others at hand with knowledge of the case. This should be explained to the client so that s/he does not feel that the case is being passed between fee earners with no obvious file handler. Hodson, D. with Dunmall, L. 'The Business of Family Law' 1992, Family Law.

116. If this is clearly above 24 hours per week, then there is no need for an exact figure of hours worked.

117. Practice Direction (1978) 1 All ER 919 LAG Emergency Procedures Handbook, p 29.

118. If the client and the other party are living under the same roof but separately, the client may be able to claim income support.

119. Community Charge applied between 1st April 1990 and 1st April 1993. Unless some of the period covered by the lawyer's advice falls within this period, all parts of this question are not applicable.

120. Domestic Violence and Matrimonial Proceedings Act 1976.

121. Matrimonial Causes Act 1973.

122. Domestic Proceedings and Matrimonial Causes Act 1978.

123. This application need not be proceeded with but an application is essential if an injunction is to be awarded in such circumstances.

124. Practice Direction [1978] 2 All ER 919. LAG Emergency Procedures Handbook; p29

Chapter Three:
Criminal

The criteria in this chapter cover work carried out for defendants at the police station (duty and own solicitor work) and at all other stages of the criminal process when funded by the Legal Aid Board, except for duty solicitor work in the magistrates court. Aspects of a case which are dealt with summarily and successfully (e.g. an immediate, successful bail application where a lawyer does not have recourse to prior preparation or a need to make notes of summary action) are also excluded from any assessment.

Five sets of quality issues are addressed. These are:

- Getting Information from the Client

- Strategic Decision Making

- The Handling Of Procedural Steps And Preparation

- Client Counselling and Advice

- Transfer of Files And Complaints

The first four of these are considered at a number of specific stages throughout the file:

I   First Interview At The Police Station

II   Taking Instructions Outside The Police Station

III   Initial Applications (Legal Aid And Bail)

IV   Preparatory Work

V   Mode Of Trial Procedure And Committal

VI   Brief to Counsel

VII   Magistrates' Court Trial / Crown Court Trial

VIII   Sentencing

Transfer of Files and Complaints (see section IX) are considered throughout the file and are applicable to all cases.

Many transaction criteria for criminal work undertaken by lawyers under the green form Advice and Assistance scheme also apply to legal services rendered under the Advice at Police Stations scheme, the Duty Solicitor scheme, and to work carried out under a full criminal legal aid certificate. Thus transaction criteria developed for criminal work under the green form scheme[1] are incorporated into this set of transaction criteria.

Outcome Measures

The Board is interested in exploring the relationship between the outcome of cases, their cost, compliance levels with the transaction criteria, and other franchise requirements. Although there will inevitably be differences on individual cases, it may be possible to define a statistical relationship between outcomes, cost and levels of compliance which will allow effective comparison between firms to be made. Draft outcome measures for Personal Injury, Matrimonial/Family and Crime are contained in chapter 10.

I First Interview at the Police Station

These criteria apply to all cases where a lawyer advises the client at the police station.

A. GETTING INFORMATION FROM THE CLIENT
Initial Steps

			Yes	No	N/a
1.		If one or more of the following applied did the lawyer attend the police station?[2]		**N/A**	[ ]
	1.1	there is to be an interview;	[ ]	[ ]	[ ]
	1.2	there are to be identification procedures;	[ ]	[ ]	[ ]
	1.3	there is a complaint of serious police misconduct;	[ ]	[ ]	[ ]
	1.4	the suspect is a juvenile or person at risk;	[ ]	[ ]	[ ]
	1.5	appropriate advice cannot be given with sufficient confidentiality over the telephone;	[ ]	[ ]	[ ]
	1.6	necessary representation in continued detention or bail cannot be made over the telephone.	[ ]	[ ]	[ ]
2.		If the lawyer did not attend the client at the police station		**N/A**	[ ]
	2.1	did the solicitor give advice over the telephone directly to the client?	[ ]	[ ]	[ ]
	2.2	was a reason given on the record for not attending the police station?	[ ]	[ ]	[ ]
3.		Does the record show a note of the following:[3]			
	3.1	the client's name?	[ ]	[ ]	[ ]
	3.2	the client's address?[4]	[ ]	[ ]	[ ]
	3.3	the client's daytime or contact telephone number, if any?[5]	[ ]	[ ]	[ ]
	3.4	the client's nightime or contact telephone number, if different from the daytime number?	[ ]	[ ]	[ ]
	3.5	if the client is likely to continue to be detained, the telephone number of an adult (e.g. fiancee/parent) who can be contacted?[6]	[ ]	[ ]	[ ]
	3.6	the client's date of birth/age?	[ ]	[ ]	[ ]
	3.7	if the client is a juvenile or mentally handicapped, the name and address of an appropriate adult?[7]	[ ]	[ ]	[ ]
	3.8	the client's custody number (if they have been arrested)?	[ ]	[ ]	[ ]

		Yes	No	N/a

4. Does the file show from what source the instructions were accepted?   [ ] [ ] [ ]

5. If the case was a duty solicitor case passed to the duty solicitor by the telephone referral service, did the file show: **N/A** [ ]

    5.1   what time the call was made to the police station?   [ ] [ ] [ ]

    5.2   who the solicitor spoke to?   [ ] [ ] [ ]

    5.3   if the solicitor spoke to the client, what advice was given?   [ ] [ ] [ ]

6. If the lawyer is attending as Duty Solicitor does the lawyer have the name of the client's own solicitor (if they have one)?   [ ] [ ] [ ]

7. Does the file show:

    7.1   whether or not the client's attendance at the police station was voluntary or whether they had been arrested?[8]   [ ] [ ] [ ]

    7.2   what has taken place so far[9], since the client's arrival at the police station?   [ ] [ ] [ ]

    7.3   when the client was arrested?[10]   [ ] [ ] [ ]

    7.4   when detention was authorised?[10]   [ ] [ ] [ ]

    7.5   whether there has been any questioning by the police prior to the lawyer's attendance at the police station?[11]   [ ] [ ] [ ]

8. Did the lawyer attempt to obtain or see a copy of the custody record?[10]   [ ] [ ] [ ]

9. Did the lawyer obtain details of the allegation?   [ ] [ ] [ ]

10. Has the lawyer attempted to obtain information from the police in the case (e.g. an outline of the evidence against the client)?[12]   [ ] [ ] [ ]

11. Does the file show some understanding of the information gathered from the police, if any?   [ ] [ ] [ ]

12. Where the lawyer has sent a representative is it clear from the file, whether or not the suspect and police were informed, or aware, of the representative's status?[13]   [ ] [ ] [ ]

13. Where the lawyer attends at the request of a third party, did the lawyer: **N/A** [ ]

    13.1   note the name, address and relationship to the client of the third party?   [ ] [ ] [ ]

    13.2   confirm the client's acceptance of instructions?   [ ] [ ] [ ]

Refusal of Access

14. If access to the police station was refused, does the file show some understanding of:[14]   **N/A** [ ]

    14.1   the circumstances of refusal?   [ ] [ ] [ ]

		Yes	No	N/a
14.2	whether denial of access has been questioned?	[ ]	[ ]	[ ]
14.3	what further action has been taken?	[ ]	[ ]	[ ]

Initial Interview with the Client

15. To enable bail representations to be made in the police station, does the lawyer have information on the following:[10]   **N/A** [ ]

		Yes	No	N/a
15.1	the client's occupation?	[ ]	[ ]	[ ]
15.2	the client's marital status?	[ ]	[ ]	[ ]
15.3	where there are dependants, the relationship of these to the client?	[ ]	[ ]	[ ]

16. Does the file show:

		Yes	No	N/a
16.1	details[15] of any Probation Officer or Social Worker, where one is involved with the client?	[ ]	[ ]	[ ]
16.2	whether the client is already the subject of a bail or other court orders?	[ ]	[ ]	[ ]

Instructions on the Alleged Offence(s)

17. Does the file show some understanding of the following:

		Yes	No	N/a
17.1	brief instructions from the client on the events of the alleged offence (or what the client was doing at the time of the alleged offence if the client has an alibi);[16]	[ ]	[ ]	[ ]
17.2	whether the client made any statement or confession to the police or other witnesses, and if so, what was said;	[ ]	[ ]	[ ]
17.3	where the client has spoken to the police prior to the client's arrival in the police station, whether the police have made any written record of comments by the client other than when interviewed in the police station?	[ ]	[ ]	[ ]
17.4	if so, has the client been shown this written record?	[ ]	[ ]	[ ]
17.5	if the client was shown such a written record, does the lawyer ascertain:	[ ]	[ ]	[ ]
17.5.1	whether the client agreed the contents	[ ]	[ ]	[ ]
17.5.2	whether the client signed the written record	[ ]	[ ]	[ ]
17.6	if there has been a home search what evidence (if any) the police gained as a result?[17]	[ ]	[ ]	[ ]

Co-accuseds

		Yes	No	N/a

Questions 18 and 19 apply only where it appears from the file that there are co-accuseds.

18. Does the file show details of any co-accused, i.e.: **N/A** [ ]

    18.1   the co-accuseds' names?   [ ] [ ] [ ]

    18.2   some understanding if known by the client, of the client's view of the part played by the co- accuseds in the offence?   [ ] [ ] [ ]

    18.3   whether the co-accuseds have instructed other lawyers and, if so, their identity?   [ ] [ ] [ ]

    18.4   if known by the client, the co- accuseds' previous convictions?   [ ] [ ] [ ]

    18.5   some understanding of the co- accuseds' version of events?   [ ] [ ] [ ]

19. Where the lawyer is asked to act for any co- accused, is it apparent from the file whether the lawyer considered whether there is a conflict of interest (and whether it is appropriate to act)?   [ ] [ ] [ ]

Clients with Medical Problems

20. If it is apparent that the client is suffering from some medical condition that could be relevant to the alleged offence,[18] does the file show some understanding of: **N/A** [ ]

    20.1   its relevance to the allegation?[19]   [ ] [ ] [ ]

    20.2   the nature of the medical condition and its effects on the client?   [ ] [ ] [ ]

    20.3   if the condition is immediately relevant to the client's fitness for interview, did the lawyer seek to have a note made on the custody record?   [ ] [ ] [ ]

    20.4   the names and addresses of the client's G.P. and any other doctors or hospitals involved in the treatment of the client?   [ ] [ ] [ ]

    20.5   whether there were grounds to call the forensic medical examiner?   [ ] [ ] [ ]

Clients with Injuries

21. Where the client has suffered an injury during or after their detention, does the file show some understanding of: **N/A** [ ]

    21.1   a description of the injury?   [ ] [ ] [ ]

    21.2   the client's description of pain and discomfort?   [ ] [ ] [ ]

    21.3   the client's description of cause?   [ ] [ ] [ ]

    21.4   whether or not the injury affects the client's fitness for interview?   [ ] [ ] [ ]

    21.5   if so, did the lawyer seek to have a note made on the custody record?   [ ] [ ] [ ]

    21.6   whether a request was made for the forensic medical examiner to attend?   [ ] [ ] [ ]

		Yes	No	N/a

21.7   whether a request was made for photographs of the injuries to be taken?   [ ]   [ ]   [ ]

B. STRATEGIC DECISION MAKING

22.   If the client is due to be interrogated by the police, is it apparent from the file: N/A   [ ]

22.1   whether the lawyer considered the client's ability either to remain silent or cope with questioning (as advised)?[20]   [ ]   [ ]   [ ]

22.2   if it is clear to the lawyer that the client is unable to withstand questioning, has the lawyer sought to have this noted on the custody record?[21]   [ ]   [ ]   [ ]

22.3   where the lawyer did not attend the client during the interrogation, was a reason given on the file for not remaining?   [ ]   [ ]   [ ]

C. CLIENT COUNSELLING AND ADVICE

Prior to an Interrogation

23.   If the lawyer attended the client prior to an interrogation: N/A   [ ]

23.1   did the lawyer have a private interview with the client prior to that interrogation?[22]   [ ]   [ ]   [ ]

23.2   was the client advised as to whether they should answer questions or remain silent?   [ ]   [ ]   [ ]

23.3   if there is an alibi, was the client advised on whether any information on the alibi should be disclosed to the police?   [ ]   [ ]   [ ]

24. Presence During an Interrogation

    N/A   [ ]

Questions 25 to 27 only apply where the lawyer or their representative is present during a police interrogation of the client.

25.   Has the lawyer made a note of the interview including any relevant admissions and significant parts of the prosecution evidence disclosed by the police questioning and the replies of the client?[23]   [ ]   [ ]   [ ]

26.   Has the lawyer made a note of whether or not they intervened during the interview?   [ ]   [ ]   [ ]

27.   If the lawyer did intervene, has the nature of these interventions been recorded?[24]   [ ]   [ ]   [ ]

	Yes	No	N/a

28. Identification Procedures[25]

N/A [ ]

Questions 29 to 32 only apply where an identification procedure involving the client takes place.

		Yes	No	N/a
29.	If the client was the subject of an identification procedure where the lawyer decided not to attend the identity procedure, was a reason for non- attendance recorded?	[ ]	[ ]	[ ]
30.	If an identification procedure was to take place, is it evident from the file that the client was advised as to his/her rights and how to conduct him/herself?[26]	[ ]	[ ]	[ ]
31.	If the client was subject to an identification procedure and the lawyer attended, has the lawyer noted:	N/A		[ ]
31.1	the method of identification?	[ ]	[ ]	[ ]
31.2	the witness's original description of the subject to the police?	[ ]	[ ]	[ ]
31.3	a description of what occurred during the procedure?	[ ]	[ ]	[ ]
31.4	the time of the procedure?	[ ]	[ ]	[ ]
32.	If the identification procedure was not a parade:	N/A		[ ]
32.1	has the lawyer noted the reasons for using an alternative method?	[ ]	[ ]	[ ]
32.2	has the lawyer noted the representations made against the alternative methods?[27]	[ ]	[ ]	[ ]

Having left the Police Station

		Yes	No	N/a
33.	Has the lawyer agreed an immediate plan of action[28] with the client?	[ ]	[ ]	[ ]
34.	If the person giving advice at the police station was a junior member of staff,[29] was the advice checked subsequently by a supervisor?	[ ]	[ ]	[ ]
35.	Has the lawyer kept records of the following:[30]			
35.1	where relevant, time and details of any taking (or refusing) of samples?	[ ]	[ ]	[ ]
35.2	where relevant, that any medical examination has been entered on the custody record?	[ ]	[ ]	[ ]
35.3	where relevant, time and details of any unusual already mentioned features e.g. intimate search, disputes over property?	[ ]	[ ]	[ ]
35.4	where relevant, that any unusual features have been entered on the custody record?	[ ]	[ ]	[ ]
36.	Has the lawyer recorded the outcome of the client's detention, ie:	[ ]	[ ]	[ ]
36.1	details of charge and date of court hearing, or if the police do not charge the client, confirmation of that fact?	[ ]	[ ]	[ ]
36.2	police bail date and time if bail is granted, or if bail is refused, reasons for refusal?	[ ]	[ ]	[ ]

If police bail is refused the lawyer will need to consider taking instructions for a bail application at court the following morning. This will be audited under section III below.

If there is an evident complaint against the police then the lawyer will need to consider question 112 below.

II Taking Instructions Outside The Police Station

These criteria apply to cases where the client obtains initial advice at the solicitor's office, at court or at any other location outside the police station. The criteria do not apply to cases where initial instructions are taken at the police station.

A. GETTING INFORMATION

General Information

		Yes	No	N/a
37.	Does the file show the following:			
	37.1 the client's name?	[ ]	[ ]	[ ]
	37.2 the client's address?	[ ]	[ ]	[ ]
	37.3 the client's daytime or contact telephone number, if any?	[ ]	[ ]	[ ]
	37.4 the client's night- time or contact telephone number, if different from the daytime number?[31]	[ ]	[ ]	[ ]
	37.5 date of birth/age?	[ ]	[ ]	[ ]
	37.6 marital status?	[ ]	[ ]	[ ]
	37.7 age and relationship to the client of any dependants?	[ ]	[ ]	[ ]
	37.8 an understanding of the client's recent employment/unemployment history?	[ ]	[ ]	[ ]
38.	if the client is a juvenile or mentally handicapped, the name and address of an appropriate adult?	[ ]	[ ]	[ ]

The Offence

		Yes	No	N/a
39.	Does the file show some understanding of:			
	39.1 the substance of the allegation?	[ ]	[ ]	[ ]
	39.2 the client's version of events in relation to the allegation?[32]	[ ]	[ ]	[ ]
	39.3 the length of time (if any) the client spent in custody?	[ ]	[ ]	[ ]
	39.4 whether or not the client has been charged?	[ ]	[ ]	[ ]
	39.5 if the client has been charged:		N/A	[ ]
	39.5.1 the date of the next hearing?	[ ]	[ ]	[ ]
	39.5.2 the venue and time of the next hearing?	[ ]	[ ]	[ ]

		Yes	No	N/a

			Yes	No	N/a
39.6	if the client has not been charged, what stage has been reached in the investigation?		[ ]	[ ]	[ ]
39.7	whether the client is in breach of any court orders or is the subject of other criminal proceedings?[33]		[ ]	[ ]	[ ]
39.8	the identity of any Probation Officer or Social Worker, where one is involved with the client?		[ ]	[ ]	[ ]
39.9	where relevant, the names and (if possible) addresses of witnesses to the alleged offence or the alibi?[34]		[ ]	[ ]	[ ]

40. Does the file show:

			Yes	No	N/a
40.1	whether the client has already appeared in court in relation to this offence?		[ ]	[ ]	[ ]
40.2	if the client has already appeared in court for this offence, does the lawyer know whether any bail conditions were attached?		[ ]	[ ]	[ ]

41. Has the lawyer noted whether or not the client made any statement or confession to the police or other witnesses and if so, what was said?[35]   [ ] [ ] [ ]

Co-Accuseds

Questions 42 to 43 apply only where it appears from the file that there are co-accuseds.

				N/A	[ ]
42.	Does the file show details of any co-accused, i.e:-			**N/A**	[ ]
42.1	the co-accuseds' names	[ ]	[ ]	[ ]	
42.2	some understanding if known by the client, of the client's view of the part played by the co-accuseds' in the offence?	[ ]	[ ]	[ ]	
42.3	whether the co- accuseds have instructed other lawyers and, if so, their identity?	[ ]	[ ]	[ ]	

43. Where the lawyer is asked to act for any co-accused is it apparent from the file that the lawyer considered whether or not there is a conflict of interest (and whether or not it is appropriate to act)?   [ ] [ ] [ ]

Medical Condition

44. If it is apparent that the client is suffering from some medical condition that could be relevant to the offence,[36] does the file show some understanding of: **N/A** [ ]

			Yes	No	N/a
44.1	its relevance to the offence?		[ ]	[ ]	[ ]
44.2	the nature of the medical condition and its effects on the client		[ ]	[ ]	[ ]
44.3	the names and addresses of the client's G.P. and any other doctors or hospitals involved in the treatment of the client?		[ ]	[ ]	[ ]

B. STRATEGIC DECISION MAKING

45. Is it apparent from the file whether the lawyer has made some assessment of the client's version of events?   [ ] [ ] [ ]

C. CLIENT COUNSELLING AND ADVICE	Yes	No	N/a

C. CLIENT COUNSELLING AND ADVICE Yes   No   N/a

46. Has the lawyer explained the likely outcome on a potential guilty verdict and/or plea?[37]   [ ]   [ ]   [ ]

47. Has the lawyer agreed an immediate plan of action with the client?   [ ]   [ ]   [ ]

III   Initial Applications (Legal Aid and Bail)

The following questions apply to first applications for legal aid and bail.

Legal Aid

A. STRATEGIC DECISION MAKING

48. Where the Application for Legal Aid has not been successful: **N/A**   [ ]

    48.1   has the lawyer recorded the basis of any legal aid application made?[38]   [ ]   [ ]   [ ]

    48.2   has the lawyer related the client's application to the client's particular circumstances?   [ ]   [ ]   [ ]

B. THE HANDLING OF PROCEDURAL STEPS AND PREPARATION

49. Has the lawyer considered obtaining documentary evidence of earnings or benefits for the full Legal Aid application form?   [ ]   [ ]   [ ]

50. If legal aid has previously been refused, has the lawyer considered if there are grounds for re- applying to the court or applying to the Legal Aid Area Committee?[39]   [ ]   [ ]   [ ]

C. CLIENT COUNSELLING AND ADVICE

51. If instructed before an application for Legal Aid has been made and prior to attendance at court, has the lawyer advised the client of the likelihood of criminal legal aid being granted?   [ ]   [ ]   [ ]

52. Where legal aid is granted;   **N/A**   [ ]

    52.1   has the lawyer checked that the client has received a contribution notice from the court (if a contribution is payable).   [ ]   [ ]   [ ]

    52.2   if revocation occurs, was the client advised of the effect of revocation of the legal aid order?   [ ]   [ ]   [ ]

    51.3   has the lawyer advised the client of the duty to report changes of circumstances and address?   [ ]   [ ]   [ ]

    52.4   where a conflict of interest has become apparent after Legal Aid being granted, has the lawyer advised that seperate representation must be obtained and that it is for the new adviser to give advice regarding legal aid and to seek a transfer of any existing legal aid order.   [ ]   [ ]   [ ]

53. If Legal Aid is refused;   **N/A**   [ ]

		Yes	No	N/a

		Yes	No	N/a
53.1	has the lawyer informed the client of any right to appeal?[40]	[ ]	[ ]	[ ]
53.2	has the lawyer advised the client of the likely success or failure of an appeal?	[ ]	[ ]	[ ]
53.3	has the lawyer told the client that a new application can be made if any circumstances change?	[ ]	[ ]	[ ]

54. Bail

N/A [ ]

Questions 55 to 67 only apply where a lawyer has to make a bail application for their client.[41]

A. GETTING INFORMATION FROM THE CLIENT

55.	Has the lawyer obtained details of the objections to bail and considered how these may be countered?[42]	[ ]	[ ]	[ ]
56.	Does the file show some understanding of the following in preparing a bail application:			

56.1	details of the client's current address or proposed bail address if the client does not have an appropriate long- term address?	[ ]	[ ]	[ ]
56.2	who owns the property?	[ ]	[ ]	[ ]
56.3	in what capacity the client resides there?	[ ]	[ ]	[ ]
56.4	how long the client has lived there?	[ ]	[ ]	[ ]
56.5	if a surety is proposed, details of that person?[43]	[ ]	[ ]	[ ]
56.6	details of the client's community ties including:			

56.6.1	the client's date of birth	[ ]	[ ]	[ ]
56.6.2	where the client was born and brought up?	[ ]	[ ]	[ ]
56.6.3	whether the client is married or co- habiting?	[ ]	[ ]	[ ]
56.6.4	whether there are any children?	[ ]	[ ]	[ ]
56.6.5	where parent/partner/friends/relatives live?[44]	[ ]	[ ]	[ ]
56.6.6	whether the client has a job?	[ ]	[ ]	[ ]
56.6.7	if so, the client's length of employment	[ ]	[ ]	[ ]
56.6.8	if not, how long the client has been unemployed?	[ ]	[ ]	[ ]
56.6.9	what job prospects there are, if any?	[ ]	[ ]	[ ]

57.	Does the file show some understanding of the following:			
57.1	the client's previous criminal convictions, if any?	[ ]	[ ]	[ ]
57.2	the client's record of offending whilst on bail (if any)[45]	[ ]	[ ]	[ ]

		Yes	No	N/a

57.3   the client's previous record of answering bail[45] [ ] [ ] [ ]

58.   Has the lawyer considered what conditions of bail (if any) would be appropriate?[46] [ ] [ ] [ ]

59.   Has the lawyer considered the strength or otherwise of the evidence against the client? [ ] [ ] [ ]

60.   If it is clearly apparent that the client may wish to leave the jurisdiction, has the lawyer considered with the client whether a security could be given? [ ] [ ] [ ]

61.   If it is apparent that the court/C.P.S. may object to the client's current address or the client is of no fixed abode, has the lawyer considered with the client alternative addresses or bail hostels acceptable to the court. [ ] [ ] [ ]

B.   THE HANDLING OF PROCEDURAL STEPS AND PREPARATION

62.   Where there is an opportunity to do so,[47] did the lawyer attempt to contact the CPS and agree bail (with or without conditions)? [ ] [ ] [ ]

C.   CLIENT COUNSELLING AND ADVICE

63.   Has the lawyer advised the client on the likelihood of a successful bail application being made? [ ] [ ] [ ]

64.   If the lawyer has advised the client that bail is likely to be granted conditionally, has the lawyer considered with the client what bail conditions would be acceptable to both the client and the court?[48] [ ] [ ] [ ]

65.   If the client is granted bail has the lawyer advised the client in writing of the importance of answering to bail? [ ] [ ] [ ]

66.   If conditional bail is granted; **N/A** [ ]

66.1   has the lawyer noted the conditions imposed? [ ] [ ] [ ]

66.2   has the lawyer explained what the conditions involve? [ ] [ ] [ ]

66.3   has the lawyer advised on the consequences of breaching the bail conditions? [ ] [ ] [ ]

67.   If bail is withheld; **N/A** [ ]

67.1   has the lawyer noted the reasons for refusal? [ ] [ ] [ ]

67.2   has the lawyer noted the address at which the client will be held?[49] [ ] [ ] [ ]

67.3   has the lawyer explained the situation to the client including giving information on when and how future bail applications and appeals may be made including the Crown Court and the High Court? [ ] [ ] [ ]

67.4   has the lawyer contacted the client informing them of when it will be possible to visit in order to prepare the defence? [ ] [ ] [ ]

IV   Preparatory Work

68.   This section applies to all cases where criminal proceedings are instituted against the client. It covers the preparation of the client's case: taking full instructions; preparing details of the prosecution case; and preparing the defence (obtaining witness statements etc) **N/A** [ ]

A. The Handling Of Procedural Steps And Preparation

		Yes	No	N/a
69.	Has the lawyer met with the client and taken a full account of events (proof of evidence)?	[ ]	[ ]	[ ]
70.	Has the lawyer obtained the client's signature on the full account of events (proof of evidence)?	[ ]	[ ]	[ ]
71.	Has the lawyer received (or requested) from the Crown Prosecution Service (C.P.S.) or the Police (or any previous solicitor/Duty Solicitor acting for the client) the following:	[ ]	[ ]	[ ]
	71.1 details of charges?	[ ]	[ ]	[ ]
	71.2 copies of tape recorded interview(s)?[50]	[ ]	[ ]	[ ]
	71.3 advance disclosure/summary of evidence?	[ ]	[ ]	[ ]
	71.4 copies of previous convictions?	[ ]	[ ]	[ ]
	71.5 witness statements?	[ ]	[ ]	[ ]
	71.6 if the client gave a statement under caution, has the lawyer obtained a copy.	[ ]	[ ]	[ ]
72.	Has the lawyer obtained the names and addresses of witnesses to the alleged offence (or alibi) if any?[34]	[ ]	[ ]	[ ]
73.	Has the lawyer taken a proof of evidence from all relevant witnesses?[34]	[ ]	[ ]	[ ]
74.	Unless the case is an unequivocal guilty plea, has the lawyer requested or received a copy of the custody record from the police?	[ ]	[ ]	[ ]
75.	Has the lawyer considered whether expert or forensic evidence is relevant to the preparation of the Defence?[51]	[ ]	[ ]	[ ]
76.	If the lawyer is to seek the clients medical records, has the lawyer obtained a signed authority from the client to get relevant medical records.[52]	[ ]	[ ]	[ ]
77.	In minor cases has the lawyer considered the possibility of requesting the CPS to consider discontinuance, a caution or a binding over?[53]	[ ]	[ ]	[ ]

B. Client Counselling And Advice

		Yes	No	N/a
78.	Has the lawyer advised the client as to which court could/will deal with the offence?	[ ]	[ ]	[ ]
79.	Is it apparent from the file:			
	79.1 whether the lawyer explained what the prosecution will have to prove before the offence is made out and discussed the evidence?	[ ]	[ ]	[ ]
	79.2 whether the lawyer explained an outline of court procedure with the client?	[ ]	[ ]	[ ]
	79.3 whether the lawyer advised the client on how they should consider pleading?	[ ]	[ ]	[ ]
	79.4 whether the lawyer noted down the reaction of the client to the decided plan of action? (As a minimum this should include the client's consent to the proposed course of action going forward)[54]	[ ]	[ ]	[ ]

			Yes	No	N/a

79.5   whether the lawyer communicated to the client the steps that are to be taken in the client's defence?   [ ]   [ ]   [ ]

79.6   unless the case is an unequivocal guilty plea, whether the lawyer has advised the client about contacting witnesses of fact or gathering other relevant evidence as appropriate?   [ ]   [ ]   [ ]

79.7   whether the lawyer informed the client of when and in what form the next contact with the lawyer will take place?   [ ]   [ ]   [ ]

79.8   were any apparent queries from the client dealt with fully, promptly and politely?   [ ]   [ ]   [ ]

79.9   whether the client has been advised of how long they can expect to wait for the case to be concluded?[55]   [ ]   [ ]   [ ]

80.   Was the client given an opportunity to comment on documents/disclosures made by the prosecution (if any)?[56]   [ ]   [ ]   [ ]

V   Mode Of Trial Procedure/Committal

81.   This section applies to all cases triable 'either way' i.e. either summarily in the Magistrates Court or on indictment in the Crown Court.[57] It applies whether or not the client pleads guilty. The committal section applies to cases triable 'either way' or on indictment only.   **N/A**   [ ]

A.   Client Counselling and Advice

82.   If the offence is triable either way, has the lawyer explained mode of trial procedure to the client?   [ ]   [ ]   [ ]

83.   Has the lawyer advised on Mode of Trial?   [ ]   [ ]   [ ]

84.   Were the reasons for the advice as to mode of trial given?   [ ]   [ ]   [ ]

85.   Has the lawyer considered the circumstances of the client's case and the prosecution's view in giving such advice?   [ ]   [ ]   [ ]

86.   Have the client's express wishes on mode of trial been recorded and followed?[58]   [ ]   [ ]   [ ]

87.   **Committal**   **N/A**   [ ]

Questions 87 and 89 only apply where the court has directed or the client has elected for trial on indictment in the Crown Court.

88.   Has the lawyer advised the client on which style of committal the client should have and given reasons for the advice given?   [ ]   [ ]   [ ]

89.   Have the client's express wishes on committal been recorded and followed?[59]   [ ]   [ ]   [ ]

VI   Brief to Counsel

90.   This stage applies where there is a brief to Counsel.   **N/A**   [ ]

91.   Where there is a brief to Counsel, did the lawyer's summary: [ ]   [ ]   [ ]

		Yes	No	N/a
91.1	consider the evidence in the case?	[ ]	[ ]	[ ]
91.2	consider which witnesses (prosecution and defence) should attend at court?	[ ]	[ ]	[ ]
91.3	consider any law relevant to the hearing?[60]	[ ]	[ ]	[ ]
91.4	consider whether a conference is necessary?	[ ]	[ ]	[ ]
91.5	if a conference is necessary, discuss the issues to be considered at the conference?	[ ]	[ ]	[ ]
92.	Did the brief include all available witness statements?	[ ]	[ ]	[ ]

VII Magistrates' Court / Crown Court Trial

93. This stage deals with cases where a plea of not guilty is taken to trial. 'Cracked trials' (cases where the client changes the plea to guilty on the day of the trial) are also covered by this section. This section is not audited where the client initially indicates an intention to plead not guilty but subsequently in court pleads guilty, i.e. where a not guilty plea is never entered.   **N/A**   [ ]

A. THE HANDLING OF PROCEDURAL STEPS AND PREPARATION

No.	Question	Yes	No	N/a
94.	If the details of a location where an alleged incident occurred are relevant to the case, has a site inspection been made?[61]	[ ]	[ ]	[ ]
95.	Where relevant has consideration been given to photographs being taken or a plan drawn?[62]	[ ]	[ ]	[ ]
96.	Has the lawyer checked prosecution witness statements for points of weakness, dispute and any inadmissible evidence?[63]	[ ]	[ ]	[ ]
97.	Has the lawyer sought the client's comments on prosecution witness statements?	[ ]	[ ]	[ ]
98.	In the Crown Court, if counsel was instructed, was there a conference with counsel before trial?[64]	[ ]	[ ]	[ ]
99.	If the case has been placed on a warned list[65] has the lawyer written to all parties concerned:		**N/A**	[ ]
99.1	alerting them to the warned period?	[ ]	[ ]	[ ]
99.2	(in the case of non- expert witnesses/lay witnesses) explaining what the 'warned period' means?	[ ]	[ ]	[ ]
99.3	asking for objections if it is inconvenient for anyone?[66]	[ ]	[ ]	[ ]
100.	If the lawyer and client have decided to refuse to accept any written statements,[67] (notified to them on a 'Notice To Defendant-Proof By Written Statement') have the prosecution been notified and told that if the prosecution intend to rely on them, the defence will require those witnesses to give oral evidence?	[ ]	[ ]	[ ]

	Yes	No	N/a

101. Has the lawyer:

    101.1   where applicable, considered whether scientific or medical evidence is required?[68]   [ ] [ ] [ ]

    101.2   where expert evidence is to be used, served it on the CPS?   [ ] [ ] [ ]

    101.3   ensured/requested the prosecution to disclose any unused material?   [ ] [ ] [ ]

    101.4   considered whether any prosecution evidence can be agreed so that the witness is not required to attend court?   [ ] [ ] [ ]

    101.5   Where any police interrogation is to be questioned at the trial: **N/A** [ ]

        101.5.1 considered whether it was necessary to listen to the tape recording of the interview?   [ ] [ ] [ ]

        101.5.2 considered whether a full transcript of a taped interview was required?   [ ] [ ] [ ]

102. Has the lawyer contacted defence witnesses who are to appear, checking that they have been:[69]   **N/A** [ ]

    102.1   proofed adequately?[70]   [ ] [ ] [ ]

    102.2   warned of hearing date/time/place?[71]   [ ] [ ] [ ]

    102.3   reminded of evidence if appropriate?   [ ] [ ] [ ]

    102.4   advised of court procedures, dress and behaviour?   [ ] [ ] [ ]

103. If it was clear (to the defence) that the defence was unable to proceed on the date given by the court, was advance notice given to the court of this inability to proceed on that date?   [ ] [ ] [ ]

B. CLIENT COUNSELLING AND ADVICE

104. Has the lawyer contacted the client stating where and when the trial will be held?   [ ] [ ] [ ]

105. If it is the client's first trial, has the lawyer explained to the client what will happen at the trial, i.e. court procedure during and prior to the court appearance?[72]   [ ] [ ] [ ]

106. If the client is to give evidence, has the lawyer tried to meet with the client in order to discuss this?   [ ] [ ] [ ]

VIII Sentencing

107. This section applies to all cases where the client is sentenced by the courts on guilty or not guilty pleas.   **N/A** [ ]

Offence Specific Factors

108. If the offence is one contained in the sentencing guidelines of the Magistrates' Association, does the file show some understanding of all the information necessary to consider the seriousness indicators relevant to the particular offence(s) the client has committed as set out in these guidelines?[73]   [ ] [ ] [ ]

General Factors

		Yes	No	N/a
109.	Does the file show some understanding of information which may be used for a plea in mitigation:[74]	[ ]	[ ]	[ ]

			Yes	No	N/a
109.1	where the client has any drink, drugs, psychiatric or gambling problems, information on:			**N/A**	[ ]
	109.1.1	the extent/nature of this problem?	[ ]	[ ]	[ ]
	109.1.2	steps the client has taken, is taking or will take to deal with the problems (e.g. medical help, counselling, etc.)?	[ ]	[ ]	[ ]
109.2	if others were also involved in the offence, the extent of the client's role in the commission of the offence?		[ ]	[ ]	[ ]
109.3	if others were also involved in the offence, the influence of others in the client's commission of the offence?		[ ]	[ ]	[ ]
109.4	in cases of violence/assault, any provocation the client may have been subjected to?		[ ]	[ ]	[ ]
109.5	(guilty pleas only) any subsequent distress and remorse the client has shown at the commission of the offence?		[ ]	[ ]	[ ]
109.6	when a plea of guilt (if any) was made?		[ ]	[ ]	[ ]
109.7	the length of time the client has waited to be sentenced (if any)?		[ ]	[ ]	[ ]
109.8	the length of time the client has spent in custody or on remand (if any)?		[ ]	[ ]	[ ]
	109.8.1	whether this was the client's first conviction or not?	[ ]	[ ]	[ ]
109.9	any loss of employment the client may have incurred as a result of offending?		[ ]	[ ]	[ ]
109.10	in cases of theft/burglary, whether the client has given any assistance to the police in tracking down stolen property?[75]		[ ]	[ ]	[ ]
109.11	whether there has been any change in the client's circumstances since the commission of the offence?		[ ]	[ ]	[ ]
109.12	the availability of any character witnesses?		[ ]	[ ]	[ ]
109.13	the client's means and in particular any welfare benefits that the client receives?		[ ]	[ ]	[ ]

Aggravating Factors

			Yes	No	N/a
110.	Has the lawyer considered any 'aggravating' factors which might work against the client when it comes to sentencing, such as:		[ ]	[ ]	[ ]
	110.1	if the client's actions were premeditated, the extent/nature of such premeditation?	[ ]	[ ]	[ ]
	110.2	if the client's offence involved the use of weapons or threatened use of weapons, the nature of the weapon and the alleged use?	[ ]	[ ]	[ ]

		Yes	No	N/a

110.3   whether the offence was perpetrated against a vulnerable victim?[76]   [ ]   [ ]   [ ]

110.4   whether the commission of the offence involved a breach of personal trust?[77]   [ ]   [ ]   [ ]

Pre-Sentence Reports[78]

111.   Where a pre-sentence report was also written on the client for this offence, did the lawyer contact the Probation Service prior to the writing of a pre-sentence report with a view to discussing the client's case?   [ ]   [ ]   [ ]

IX   Transfer of Files and Complaints

Complaints about the Police

112.   If it is apparent that the client may have a complaint against the police, has the laywer recorded details of this complaint, including, in particular: [ ]   [ ]   [ ]

112.1   the nature of the complaint?   [ ]   [ ]   [ ]

112.2   a detailed statement of what happened?   [ ]   [ ]   [ ]

112.3   any information the client has that can help identify the officers involved (e.g. names, numbers and ranks)?   [ ]   [ ]   [ ]

112.4   whether or not the client wishes to make an official complaint?   [ ]   [ ]   [ ]

112.5   the advice given on whether or not a complaint should be made?   [ ]   [ ]   [ ]

Transfer of Files

113.   If the file is to be transferred to another office of the same organisation, department or fee earner:[79]   [ ]   [ ]   [ ]

113.1   is there evidence (letter/attendance note) of explanation to the client of the transfer?[80]   [ ]   [ ]   [ ]

113.2   was the client given the name of the person taking over the case?   [ ]   [ ]   [ ]

113.3   was the client asked for acknowledgement/approval of the transfer?   [ ]   [ ]   [ ]

Complaints against the laywer

114   Where the client makes a complaint regarding the lawyer or the lawyer's work, did the lawyer: [ ]   [ ]   [ ]

114.1   respond to it immediately?   [ ]   [ ]   [ ]

114.2   advise the client who else they can contact in the firm to consider the complaint?   [ ]   [ ]   [ ]

		Yes	No	N/a
114.3	if the problem was solved to the client's satisfaction, confirm the solution in writing?	[ ]	[ ]	[ ]
114.4	if the problem was not solved to the client's satisfaction, refer the client to the Solicitors' Complaints Bureau?	[ ]	[ ]	[ ]

Criminal—Notes to the Criteria

1. As published in *Transaction Criteria* by Sherr, Moorhead, Paterson (HMSO 1992). It was recognised at the time of drafting that this overlap with work beyond green form was a problem. This was unavoidable as such a wide variety of cases were being addressed in one "transaction" heading on the green form criteria. Comments about this overlap have been the most common specific comments received from practitioners on consultation and they have been dealt with in the restructured criteria here.

2. See, *Advising a suspect in the police station* (Law Society, 1991), p.11.

3. The information below may be on a DSPS 1 claim for costs.

4. The client may be reluctant to give this information. An alternative where such reluctance is shown, would be for the lawyer to record the custody number.

5. There should be a telephone number or an indication that there is no number and whether the number is for night and day or a different number for each.

6. This criterion will be 'not applicable' where it is apparent from the file that the client does not want anyone contacted.

7. e.g. A relative, guardian, or social worker.

8. This will usually be evidenced from completion of Form 'Advice At Police Stations Report'

9. e.g. Anything that has happened to the client/that the client has done or requested.

10. Not applicable if the suspect attended the Police Station as a volunteer. However, a volunteer may subsequently be arrested, and if this has occurred the criteria apply.

11. This may be evidenced from the custody record.

12. The police should be pressed for maximum information prior to the lawyer advising the client, p.22, *Advising a Suspect in the Police Station* (Law Society, 1991).

13. See *Advising a Suspect in the Police Station* (Law Society, 1991), p.12. Information as to the representative's status should be given at the initial attendance. If the suspect was not told of the representative's status until after the initial attendance, an omission will be recorded.

14. If this information was not given at the time, an omission should be recorded.

15. Details here includes name, address, etc.

16. If it was apparent from the file that the client does not wish to give any instructions then this would be 'not applicable'.

17. This question will be answered n/a if the file is silent as to whether or not there has been a home search.

18. e.g. Diabetes, drug addiction, alcoholism or kidney problems. Low intelligence could also be a factor.

19. It may provide a defence or be a reason for suggesting a caution or no further action.

20. If the client is medically unfit for interview then a doctor should be called to advise the client of that fact. See also, para 4.4.2: *Advising a Suspect in the Police Station*, (Law Society 1991).

21. This would apply where the client is medically unfit to have an interview or where the client is otherwise under a disability. It would not apply where, for example, the client is simply unwilling to follow the lawyer's advice.

22. This question will be "not applicable" if the police have refused to allow the lawyer to have a private interview with the client. Note, it cannot be assumed that all interviews with the client are private.

23. See, para 6.1.4, p.27: *Advising a Suspect in the Police Station*, (Law Society 1991).

24. See, para 6.1.4, p.27: *Advising a Suspect in the Police Station*, (Law Society 1991).

25. The four methods of identification are as follows: parade, group identification, video film, confrontation. These criteria are based on Chapter 8 of *Advising a Suspect in the Police Station*.

26. e.g. Advising the client not to give an oral response to any identification that might take place.

27. See para 8.2.2, *Advising a Suspect in the Police Station*, p.38. This would not apply where there was no need to make such representations, e.g. because the client wanted an alternative form of identification.

28. e.g. What client will do, what lawyer will do, next contact between them etc. If it is apparent that the matter has been concluded by the client's release without charge, an indication to the client that no further action is required will suffice.

29. Here junior member of staff includes all trainee solicitors, trainee legal executives and any person of less than two years experience of defence work in police stations. N.B. There is a new accreditation scheme being introduced by the Law Society.

30. The Law Society recommends that these records are kept. *Advising a suspect in the police station*, p.16.

31. There should be a telephone number or an indication that there is no number and whether the number is a night or day or a different number for each.

32. If it was apparent from the file that the client is unwilling to discuss the events then this would be 'not applicable'.

33. This will only apply where the client is the subject of bail or a probation order, etc.

34. This question relates to defence and prosecution witnesses.

35. The word 'confession' should be taken to include formal confessions and also admissions.

36. e.g. Diabetes, drug addiction, alcoholism or kidney problems. Low intelligence may also be a factor.

37. The extent and detail of such advice is a matter for the lawyer's discretion. A broad indication of likely outcome will satisfy a file audit.

38. A copy of the application form will satisfy this criterion.

39. Such grounds include the provision of further information as to why legal aid is required in the interests of justice. Under s.21 of the Legal Aid Act 1988 application may be made to the Legal Aid Area Committee by a person who has been refused legal aid in the case of an indictable or an either way offence where the refusal was not made on the grounds of means alone.

40. 'Regulation 14, Legal Aid in Criminal and Care Proceedings (General) Regulations, 1989, makes clear that an applicant whose application has been refused may renew his or her application either orally to the court or to the justices' clerk. This regulation should plainly be operated in the event of any new material becoming available. Under regulation 15, an application can be made for review to the appropriate area committee of the Legal Aid Board. However, this only lies after the first refusal of Legal Aid. The procedure is not available for summary only offences or where refusal was for financial reasons. The application should be made on form crim. 9 and must be lodged within 14 days of notification of the refusal but the time limit may for good reason be waived or extended by the area committee (reg. 16)' A. Edwards, Gazette 90/3 20 January 1993.

41. i.e. where the offence is one for which the court may remand in custody and the lawyer considers that a bail application is necessary whether or not it is opposed, bearing in mind that the decision regarding

bail remains with the CPS and the court. Where applications are made summarily and successfully i.e.instructions are taken at court and the matter is dealt with there and then, items 55–64 will not apply. Summary applications do not include cases where instructions are taken overnight for this purpose.

42. A lawyer should be in a position to answer the Prosecution's objections to bail as well as putting forward positive reasons for granting bail. It would usually be appropriate to discuss objections with the police (who may invite the CPS to object to bail) and the CPS.

43. See Magistrates' Court: A Guide To Good Practice, p.21. Details should cover: the surety's name; address, employment; criminal convictions; length of time the surety has known the defendant; the nature of their association; frequency and means of regular contact between surety and client; the surety's knowledge of current charge and clients antecedents; the surety's financial position and the nature of monies being offered in support of the suretyship.

44. Some evidence that the lawyer has considered who lives near the defendant will satisfy this criterion.

45. This information should appear on the record of previous convictions.

46. This will not apply where bail conditions are unlikely to be relevant (e.g. where bail is likely to be granted without conditions).

47. This question will not be audited on overnight bail applications as it is likely to be done at court and not noted.

48. For example: (Magistrates' Court: A Guide To Good Practice)

    A. A curfew, if the offence was allegedly committed at night/in the evening;

    B. A condition not to go to the area where the offence was allegedly committed or where offences of a similar nature often occur.

    C. If the offence is drink related, not to enter an off-licence or public house.

    D. Not to approach particular witnesses directly or through others or go within a specified distance of the witness's home address.

49. It may not be possible for this to be done immediately.

50. This would be satisfied by either a copy of the tape itself or the police record of the tape recorded interview. Practitioners should however be wary of relying heavily on a police summary (see, *Royal Commission on Criminal Justice 1993*, pp.41–42).

51. An omission should only be recorded here where no consideration is given although expert or forensic evidence is clearly in issue. Expert/Forensic evidence may be an issue in the following cases, among others:

    ■ in a murder case, an independent Pathologist's Report is usually obtained

    ■ where the client is suffering from a medical or psychiatric condition which may affect the question of guilt or provide mitigation.

    ■ where there is disputed handwriting

    ■ where the Prosecution has Forensic/Expert evidence which is not agreed, e.g. linking the defendant to the scene
       — fibres from clothing
       — particles of glass in clothing
       — blood stains
       — fingerprints

    The above examples are not exhaustive.

52. Authority to obtain the fee from the Legal Aid Board may also be necessary.

53. Auditors will assume that a case is not minor unless there is clear evidence to the contrary.

    The following are only some examples of minor cases:

    - Petty shoplifting
    - Small value criminal damage
    - Common Assault
    - Drunk and Disorderly

54. A note by the lawyer outlining a discussion between the lawyer and client will comprise evidence of agreement unless there is evidence to the contrary.

55. This should be based on a broad outline of the timescale that may be expected rather than a precise prediction of length of case.

56. It is for the lawyer to decide the most appropriate means for allowing comment. The client may not always need to see full copies of prosecution documents.

57. A list of offences classified as summary only, either way or indictable is contained in Appendix 6 of *The Magistrates Court: A Guide to Good Practice* (Law Society, 1992).

58. It will not be possible to follow the client's wishes if the court is not prepared to offer a summary trial, although this is what the client wishes. This is not audited as an omission. This question will be answered n/a where the client has been charged with a summary or indictable only offence; it is only applicable to either way offences.

59. It will not be possible to follow the client's wishes if the court declines a paper committal (s.6 (2)), although that is what the client wishes. This is not audited as an omission. The purpose of this question is to ascertain whether the lawyer has advised the client as to whether there should be an "old style" committal with witnesses being called (Section 6 (1) Magistrates' Courts Act 1980) or whether there should be a "paper" committal (Section 6 (2) Magistrates' Courts Act 1980).

60. The extent to which the lawyer's summary needs to consider the relevant law will depend on the complexity of the case. In a straight forward guilty plea, an indication of the common law or statutory provisions under which the client is charged will suffice, together with any relevant areas of sentencing law.

61. The Law Society: Magistrates' Courts: A Guide To Good Practice, p.64; "Consider the need for photographs and a plan of the scene of an incident or accident. You may need to visit the locus yourself to assess their value and so as to give instructions for their preparation". Inspection may be made by the lawyer, enquiry agent or expert witness. The location may be relevant where, e.g. the layout of the scene may have contributed to an accident or incident, where there is a dispute as to visibility or whether an incident could have been witnessed from a particular point.

62. Blake, p.297: "In some cases it will be worth going to the site of the alleged incident to try and check how things happened and make plans and take photographs (which will attract the interest of the jury to your case)." The Law Society, 'Magistrates' Courts: A Guide To Good Practice', p.64; "...obtain photographs of a client's relevant injuries urgently..."

63. This should be evident from the file. These may appear as handwritten comments on typed statements, questions to the client in correspondence, preparatory notes for trial etc.

64. This would be satisfied by a conference on the day.

65. The procedure by which a case enters the warned list has some local variations. Usually a preliminary warned list is sent out in advance indicating that a certain case will begin to come into the list in a number of weeks time.

66. The Law Society; 'Magistrates' Court: A Guide To Good Practice In The Preparation Of Cases', p.71

67. Section 9, C.J.A. 1967: Section 102, M.C.A. 1980: Rule 70, M.C. Rules 1981. A 'Notice To Defendant-Proof By Written Statement' is used to notify the defendant of an intention that written statements are to be used by witnesses.

68. This will only apply where there appear to be issues of a forensic/scientific or medical nature involved in the case.

69. The Law Society; 'Magistrates' Court: A Guide To Good Practice', p.71

70. This should consist of a full proof of evidence, signed by the witness if possible.

71. e.g. By refreshing their memories from their statements outside Court.

72. Unless it is clear from the file that the client had had a previous trial, there should be some discussion of court procedure. Previous convictions may not by themselves indicate previous trials as they may have resulted from guilty pleas.

73. Auditors will be issued with an up to date version of these guidelines and will refer to the guidelines for each specific offence in assessing this clause.

74. These were based on the Magistrates Court Guide to Good Practice.

75. This would only apply in cases where it was possible that the client could have made such help available.

76. For the purposes of audit, vulnerable victims includes: females, those over retiring age, or below 16, the mentally ill and the disabled.

77. e.g. Theft from an employer.

78. The nature of pre-sentence reports has changed significantly from the old Social Enquiry Reports. Ostensibly a more 'balanced' view of the offender, the probation service are asked to provide an indication of the seriousness of the offence and the suitability of particular punishments. This is based primarily on prosecution information (advance disclosure) provided to the probation service and an interview of the client. It seems vital that the defence solicitor has some input into the process if possible.

79. i.e. transferred from one main file handler to another. Firms working in teams would be expected to explain the approach to their clients at the outset of the case.

80. The Guide to the Professional Conduct of Solicitors (1993, Law Society), Ch 13, p.278, 13.02, 2.

Chapter Four:
Housing

This chapter sets out transaction criteria for three types of housing case:

1   Advising Clients with a Property in Disrepair (where the client rents a dwelling which is in disrepair);

2   Defending Possession Proceedings (where the client rents a dwelling and the landlord is threatening possession proceedings against the client);

3   Mortgage Repossession (where the client is an owner-occupier and the mortgage company is threatening possession proceedings against the client).

The criteria are based upon empirical work on legal aid files as well as relevant literature on housing law[1,2].

Each transaction is divided into 3 sections:

I.   Getting Information From The Client

II. Advising On That Information

III. Further Investigation, Research, and Action

1. Advising Clients with a Property in Disrepair

I Getting Information from the Client

			Yes	No	N/a
1.		Does the lawyer know:			
	1.1	the client's full name?	[ ]	[ ]	[ ]
	1.2	the client's address and telephone number?	[ ]	[ ]	[ ]
	1.3	the client's date of birth?	[ ]	[ ]	[ ]
	1.4	who lives with the client?	[ ]	[ ]	[ ]
	1.5	the age of any children living with the client?	[ ]	[ ]	[ ]
2.		Does the lawyer have an understanding of the property which is in disrepair? In particular:			
	2.1	how long the client has lived there;	[ ]	[ ]	[ ]
	2.2	the name and address of the landlord (unless the client doesn't know this);	[ ]	[ ]	[ ]
	2.3	when the landlord is not the local authority, whether or not there is a written agreement between the client and the landlord in relation to the house;	[ ]	[ ]	[ ]
	2.4	whether the client shares the property or any part of it with people other than their own family (e.g. is it a house or a flat?) and, if so, what action, if any, those people are or would be prepared to take:	[ ]	[ ]	[ ]
	2.5	if the rent has been paid up to date by the client;	[ ]	[ ]	[ ]
	2.6	the size of the property.	[ ]	[ ]	[ ]
3.		Does the lawyer have an understanding of each problem with the property? In particular:			
	3.1	any damage/defect in the property (or to goods within the property);	[ ]	[ ]	[ ]
	3.2	whereabouts in the property such damage is;	[ ]	[ ]	[ ]
	3.3	the apparent cause of such damage;	[ ]	[ ]	[ ]
	3.4	when the damage occurred and (if different) when the client first noticed a problem;	[ ]	[ ]	[ ]
	3.5	(if different from the damage itself) when the *cause of the* damage occurred and when the client first noticed this cause;	[ ]	[ ]	[ ]
	3.6	any repairs/cleaning up done by client because of the defect(s)/damage.	[ ]	[ ]	[ ]
4.		Does the lawyer have an understanding of the inconvenience and distress caused to the client and their family?	[ ]	[ ]	[ ]
5.		Does the lawyer know if the client and/or their family are suffering any health problems as a result of the disrepair?	[ ]	[ ]	[ ]

	Yes	No	N/a

6.   If so, does the lawyer know the names and addresses (if the client knows these) of any doctors, hospitals that have treated these health problems?   [ ]   [ ]   [ ]

7.   If it is apparent that the housing may be in a dangerous state, does the lawyer have an understanding of the nature of any danger?[3]   [ ]   [ ]   [ ]

8.   Does the lawyer have an understanding of:

      8.1   whether any complaints were made to the landlord?   [ ]   [ ]   [ ]

      8.2   when such complaints were made, and by whom?   [ ]   [ ]   [ ]

      8.3   if the complaints were made in writing, whether there are copies?   [ ]   [ ]   [ ]

      8.4   how the landlord responded to any complaints?   [ ]   [ ]   [ ]

9.   Does the lawyer have an understanding of repairs that will be necessary and whether or not the client would have to vacate the property for those repairs?   [ ]   [ ]   [ ]

10.   If there has been any building and/or repair work done on the property, does the lawyer have an understanding of: **N/A**   [ ]

      10.1   the nature of the work;   [ ]   [ ]   [ ]

      10.2   when the work was carried out;   [ ]   [ ]   [ ]

      10.3   on behalf of whom the work was carried out (i.e. the landlord or the client);   [ ]   [ ]   [ ]

      10.4   if the client had work carried out, who the work was carried out by, and (if contractors were used) the names and addresses of any builders used;   [ ]   [ ]   [ ]

11.   Does the lawyer know whether there have been any previous proceedings taken by the client or landlord which may be relevant?   [ ]   [ ]   [ ]

12.   For local authority housing, does the lawyer know whether any local authority action has previously been taken, and (if so) what action was taken?   [ ]   [ ]   [ ]

II   Advising on this Information

13.   Has the client been advised on the possibility of taking proceedings to ensure the landlord repairs the property?   [ ]   [ ]   [ ]

14.   Has the client been advised on the possibility of the lawyer negotiating with the Environmental Health Department or the landlord to ensure repairs are carried out?   [ ]   [ ]   [ ]

15.   Has the client been advised as to whether they should continue to make rent payments to the landlord?   [ ]   [ ]   [ ]

16.   Is the client advised on what to do if and when they are contacted by the landlord?   [ ]   [ ]   [ ]

17.   Is the client advised of the possibility of claiming damages for any damage to their property, personal injury, distress/inconvenience caused, and any other losses arising out of the defects?   [ ]   [ ]   [ ]

		Yes	No	N/a

18. If the client will have to vacate their housing whilst any repairs are carried out are they advised on claiming the costs of alternative accommodation?[4] **N/A** [ ]

    18.1 Was the limitation period for the action noted in a prominent place upon the file and was this correct?[5] [ ] [ ] [ ]

    18.2 Is there an indication that the client was advised of the limitation period? [ ] [ ] [ ]

Costs and funding of the case

19. Is there an indication of advice given to the client regarding costs and funding of the case? In particular: **N/A** [ ]

    19.1 the availability of green form advice and civil legal aid; [ ] [ ] [ ]

    19.2 the limits and extent of green form funding; [ ] [ ] [ ]

    19.3 whether or not the client will have to make a contribution to the case; [ ] [ ] [ ]

    19.4 the effects of the solicitor's and statutory charge on any damages received; [ ] [ ] [ ]

    19.5 the costs to the client should the case be lost; [ ] [ ] [ ]

    19.6 the nature and consequences of revocation and discharge of certificates (if one is granted); [ ] [ ] [ ]

    19.7 the duty to report changes of circumstance and address. [ ] [ ] [ ]

Progress of the case

20. Was the client advised how long they can expect to wait for the claim to be concluded? [ ] [ ] [ ]

21. Is there a firm indication of the steps a lawyer agrees to take in furtherance of the client's claim? [ ] [ ] [ ]

22. Is there an indication of the steps (if any) the lawyer has asked the client to take? [ ] [ ] [ ]

23. Is the client told when and in what form the next contact will take place? [ ] [ ] [ ]

24. Has the lawyer advised the client as to more than one possible course of action from which the client could choose?[6] [ ] [ ] [ ]

25 Did the lawyer indicate the likely outcome of the case? [ ] [ ] [ ]

26 Is there an indication that the client made an active choice on the lawyers suggested mode of action? [ ] [ ] [ ]

27. Has the lawyer noted down the reaction of the client to the decided resulting plan of action (as a minimum, this should include the client's consent to the action going forward)? [ ] [ ] [ ]

		Yes	No	N/a

28. If the lawyer is not going to represent the client at any hearing, is there an indication that alternative sources of representation or assistance were explained to the client? [ ] [ ] [ ]

29. Were any apparent queries from the client dealt with fully, promptly and politely ? [ ] [ ] [ ]

30. Did the lawyer deal with any evident emotional concerns of the client? [ ] [ ] [ ]

31. Any contact with the other side should be explained. In particular, did the lawyer explain when the other side will be contacted and why? [ ] [ ] [ ]

32. Did the lawyer advise the client as to what to do if contacted by the other side? [ ] [ ] [ ]

III Further Investigation, Research and Action

33. Where the landlord has not been contacted in writing to give notice that the client's property is in a state of disrepair, did either the lawyer or the client write to the landlord outlining the defects in need of repair? [ ] [ ] [ ]

34. If proceedings are being considered against a private landlord or a housing association was the local authority's Environmental Health Officer[7] requested to visit and inspect the property? [ ] [ ] [ ]

35. Where proceedings are being considered, was a report from a housing consultant sought (e.g. an environmental health and housing consultant)? [ ] [ ] [ ]

36. When instructing such a consultant, were the proposed grounds for any proceedings outlined? [ ] [ ] [ ]

37. Where proceedings are being considered on the basis that the housing defect has had and/or is having an effect on the client's physical or mental health, were any doctors involved in the treatment contacted for medical evidence? [ ] [ ] [ ]

38. When seeking medical evidence, were the proposed grounds for any proceedings outlined? [ ] [ ] [ ]

39. Were photographs of any damage to the dwelling and to the client's property sought? [ ] [ ] [ ]

40. Was it evident that all of the clients losses were being listed and quantified with receipts and invoices being collected for any replacements?[8] [ ] [ ] [ ]

41. If any of the damage stems from particular incidents, were any witnesses to these incidents contacted? [ ] [ ] [ ]

42. If the client does not know these at the first interview, is the name and address of the landlord sought? [ ] [ ] [ ]

43. Where the dispute involves a clause in a written tenancy, does the lawyer obtain a copy of the agreement? [ ] [ ] [ ]

44. If the client is advised to have repairs done and deduct the cost of this from rent payments, is the landlord warned of this intention and sent an estimate of the repair costs before they are carried out? [ ] [ ] [ ]

2. Defending Possession Proceedings

I Getting Information from the Client[9]

		Yes	No	N/a
45.	Does the lawyer know the following details?			
45.1	the client's full name;	[ ]	[ ]	[ ]
45.2	the address of the property;	[ ]	[ ]	[ ]
45.3	the client's telephone number;	[ ]	[ ]	[ ]
45.4	the client's date of birth;	[ ]	[ ]	[ ]
45.5	the nature of the property (i.e.- room/flat/house, shared accommodation);	[ ]	[ ]	[ ]
45.6	details of any other occupiers;	[ ]	[ ]	[ ]
45.7	in whose name(s) the tenancy is vested;	[ ]	[ ]	[ ]
45.8	if the client is in receipt of Housing Benefit, when it was claimed;	[ ]	[ ]	[ ]
46.	Does the lawyer know the following?			
46.1	the landlord's name, and (if possible) address and telephone number;	[ ]	[ ]	[ ]
46.2	the name, and (if possible) address and telephone number of any agent or solicitor;	[ ]	[ ]	[ ]
46.3	the rent (or licence fee);	[ ]	[ ]	[ ]
46.4	whether the rent includes anything which is not strictly 'rent' e.g. an element of service charge, amenity payment, or overpaid Housing Benefit;	[ ]	[ ]	[ ]
46.5	whether there are any arrears, and if so how much;	[ ]	[ ]	[ ]
46.6	whether any payment is being made to the landlord by the DSS in respect of rent arrears;	[ ]	[ ]	[ ]
46.7	the date of commencement of tenancy;	[ ]	[ ]	[ ]
46.8	the date of commencement of occupancy (if different);	[ ]	[ ]	[ ]
46.9	whether or not the client has received a notice to quit or notice of intention to seek possession, and (if so) when;	[ ]	[ ]	[ ]
46.10	details of any Court Proceedings (previous and/or current proceedings, hearing date, date of receipt of summons, etc.);	[ ]	[ ]	[ ]
46.11	details of any verbal communications with landlord/agent;	[ ]	[ ]	[ ]
46.12	details of any previous arrangements to remedy default (i.e. arrangements for paying off arrears, etc.);	[ ]	[ ]	[ ]
46.13	if it is apparent from the advice to the client that they are in imminent danger of losing possession, does the lawyer have an understanding of their rehousing entitlement[10] (i.e. does the client and/or any member of his/her family living with him/her, have a priority need? e.g. dependent children, old age, medical condition, pregnancy etc.)	[ ]	[ ]	[ ]

46.14   if the client succeeded to the tenancy on the death of a previous tenant, does the lawyer have an understanding of the circumstances leading to that succession, and details of the preceding tenancy agreement (if any)?   [ ] [ ] [ ]

46.15   if the client was assigned the tenancy, does the lawyer know the circumstances of that assignment?   [ ] [ ] [ ]

46.16   does the lawyer know if the tenant occupies the property as their only or principal home?   [ ] [ ] [ ]

47.   Has the lawyer taken a client statement on the matters contained in the landlord's alleged ground for possession?   [ ] [ ] [ ]

48.   If possession is sought on the basis of rent arrears, or persistent delay in paying rent, does the lawyer have an understanding of: **N/A** [ ]

48.1   whether or not the client agrees with the landlord's view of arrears or persistent delays?   [ ] [ ] [ ]

48.2   whether the landlord has and/or is refusing to accept rent?   [ ] [ ] [ ]

48.3   whether the landlord has tried or considered other collection methods (i.e. apart from court proceedings)?   [ ] [ ] [ ]

48.4   if the arrears, or any part of them, represent money that has been used by the tenant to pay repairs as a result of the landlord's default, whether there is a report or other evidence available on the pre-repair condition of the property and steps taken by the client to get the landlord to effect repairs?   [ ] [ ] [ ]

48.5   if the client is claiming Housing Benefit, does the lawyer know if the landlord has paid the correct amount of H.B. into the client's rent account and whether or not the benefit authority has sought to recoup any overpayment of H.B. by adjusting the client's rent account?[11]   [ ] [ ] [ ]

48.6   the client's regular financial commitments (e.g. maintenance payments, payments under court order, credit/HP payments)?   [ ] [ ] [ ]

48.7   details of the client's welfare benefits, income and savings?   [ ] [ ] [ ]

48.8   details of what the client might be able to afford by way of paying off arrears/paying into court?   [ ] [ ] [ ]

48.9   (private sector tenants only) whether there is a registered fair rent, and if so, what?   [ ] [ ] [ ]

48.10   if there is an alleged breach of covenant/tenancy obligation, whether the landlord has accepted rent knowing of the breach?   [ ] [ ] [ ]

49.   Where the Landlord will have to show that suitable alternative accommodation[12] is available: **N/A** [ ]

49.1   where the landlord is not the local authority, does the lawyer know whether the local housing authority has issued a Certificate that it will provide suitable alternative accommodation?   [ ] [ ] [ ]

49.2   where the landlord is the housing authority, or there is no Certificate, is the lawyer aware of the distance the tenant and any members of his/her family would commonly have to travel to get to and from their new home?   [ ]   [ ]   [ ]

49.3   does the lawyer know the nature of the proposed alternative accommodation and any objections the client has to these premises?   [ ]   [ ]   [ ]

49.4   does the lawyer know whether the tenant has received other offers of alternative accommodation?   [ ]   [ ]   [ ]

50.   Where it is apparent that the dwelling may have been let in relation to the client's employment, does the lawyer have an understanding of: **N/A**   [ ]

50.1   whether the tenant was in the employment of the landlord or a former landlord at the time when the premises were let?   [ ]   [ ]   [ ]

50.2   whether the tenancy was granted strictly in consequence of an employee/employer relationship?   [ ]   [ ]   [ ]

50.3   if the tenant is still employed by the same employer?   [ ]   [ ]   [ ]

51.   Where the action is for forfeiture (this applies only to fixed term tenancies created before 15/1/1989 or leases):   **N/A**   [ ]

51.1   has the lawyer asked the client whether the landlord has expressly or impliedly waived the relevant breach of covenant e.g. by the landlord demanding, or the client paying rent which accrues after the cause of forfeiture?   [ ]   [ ]   [ ]

51.2   where there is an alleged arrears of service charges: does the lawyer have an understanding of the basis of any objections to the payment of such service charges?   [ ]   [ ]   [ ]

52.   If possession is claimed on the ground that the premises are required for occupation by a landlord or landlord's family, does the lawyer have details of the hardship that will be caused by the grant of a possession order to all people who may be affected by such grant?   [ ]   [ ]   [ ]

53.   If possession is claimed on the ground that there is a returning owner-occupier, does the lawyer have an understanding of: **N/A**   [ ]

53.1   whether or not the landlord occupied the same premises at any time before the grant of the tenancy?   [ ]   [ ]   [ ]

53.2   whether the tenant received written notice before the grant of the tenancy, that the owner occupier could return and reclaim possession?   [ ]   [ ]   [ ]

54.   Where possession is sought on the basis that the tenancy was an out of season holiday let, does the lawyer have an understanding of the following: **N/A**   [ ]

54.1   whether or not the intention of the parties was to create an out of season holiday let?   [ ]   [ ]   [ ]

54.2   whether or not the tenant received written notice before the grant of the tenancy that possession could be reclaimed on the basis that the dwelling was an off-season holiday let?   [ ]   [ ]   [ ]

			Yes	No	N/a

55. Where possession is sought because the premises were let in connection with an educational establishment, agricultural employment, a religious ministry, as a redundant farmhouse, as a retirement home, or as a letting to servicemen, does the lawyer know if the tenant received written notice before the commencement of the tenancy that possession could be sought on this ground?   [ ]   [ ]   [ ]

56. If the tenancy is a protected shorthold tenancy created before 15/1/89, does the lawyer know if and when the client received written notice of the landlord's ability to recover possession under the statutory grounds applying to protected shorthold tenancies?   [ ]   [ ]   [ ]

57. If it is claimed by the landlord that the tenancy was created after 15/1/89, but the client had been living in the dwelling before that date, does the lawyer have an understanding of the nature of the agreement between the two parties prior to that date?   [ ]   [ ]   [ ]

58. Where the landlord claims that the client has an Assured Shorthold Tenancy, does the lawyer have an understanding of: **N/A**   [ ]

    58.1 whether notice in the prescribed form had been served before the commencement of the tenancy, stating that the tenancy would be an assured shorthold one?   [ ]   [ ]   [ ]

    58.2 whether the tenant was previously an assured tenant of the same landlord?   [ ]   [ ]   [ ]

59. If the tenancy was created before 15/1/1989 and where the original contractual Rent Act protected tenancy has been validly determined by e.g. Notice to Quit, forfeiture, or the expiry of a fixed term tenancy, has the lawyer asked the client: **N/A**   [ ]

    59.1 whether the tenant was residing in the premises when the contractual tenancy was terminated?   [ ]   [ ]   [ ]

    59.2 if the tenant has not subsequently remained in residential occupation of the premises,[13] does the lawyer know: **N/A**   [ ]

        59.2.1 if the tenant has sublet the whole of the premises?   [ ]   [ ]   [ ]

        59.2.2 how long the period(s) of absence have been?   [ ]   [ ]   [ ]

        59.2.3 the reason for the absence?   [ ]   [ ]   [ ]

        59.2.4 whether or not the client has a definite intention to return?   [ ]   [ ]   [ ]

        59.2.5 whether the tenant has left personal belongings and furniture on the premises?   [ ]   [ ]   [ ]

        59.2.6 whether there are any other people in occupation of the premises, and if so, their relationship to the tenant, and the dates of their occupation?   [ ]   [ ]   [ ]

II Advising on that Information

			Yes	No	N/a

60. If the client is in rent arrears, has the lawyer discussed methods of maximising their income, including receipt of welfare benefits?   [ ]   [ ]   [ ]

61. Has the client been advised of the status of their tenancy?   [ ]   [ ]   [ ]

	Yes	No	N/a
62. Where it is apparent that proceedings are likely, has the lawyer advised the client as to how the court is likely to exercise its powers?	[ ]	[ ]	[ ]
63. If it is apparent that the client is likely to lose possession, has the lawyer explained what will happen should the landlord be successful in seeking a possession order?[10]	[ ]	[ ]	[ ]
64. If it is apparent that the client is likely to lose possession, has the lawyer explained the extent of the local authority's obligation to rehouse the client?	[ ]	[ ]	[ ]

Costs and funding of the case

	Yes	No	N/a
65. Is there an indication of advice given to the client regarding the costs and funding of the case? In particular;	[ ]	[ ]	[ ]
65.1 the availability of green form advice and civil legal aid:	[ ]	[ ]	[ ]
64.2 the limits and extent of green form funding.	[ ]	[ ]	[ ]
65.3 whether or not the client will have to make a contribution to the case;	[ ]	[ ]	[ ]
65.4 the effects of the solicitor's and statutory charge on any damages received;	[ ]	[ ]	[ ]
65.5 the costs to the client should the case be lost;	[ ]	[ ]	[ ]
65.6 the nature and consequences of discharge and revocation of certificates (if one is granted);	[ ]	[ ]	[ ]
65.7 the duty to report changes of circumstance and address;	[ ]	[ ]	[ ]
65.8 where there is more than one defendant to the possession proceedings, the possibility that the Legal Aid Board may call for contributions from non- legally aided persons;	[ ]	[ ]	[ ]

Progress of the case

	Yes	No	N/a
66. Did the lawyer advise the client how long the case is likely to take?	[ ]	[ ]	[ ]
67. Is there a firm indication of the steps the lawyer has agreed to take, and have these been communicated to the client?	[ ]	[ ]	[ ]
68. Is there a firm indication of the things the lawyer has asked the client to do and the time limits within which they ought to be completed?	[ ]	[ ]	[ ]
69. Has the client been told when and in what form the next contact will take place?	[ ]	[ ]	[ ]
70. Has the lawyer advised the client as to more than one possible course of action?	[ ]	[ ]	[ ]
71. Did the lawyer indicate the likely outcome of the case?	[ ]	[ ]	[ ]

		Yes	No	N/a
72.	Is there an indication that the client made an active choice on the lawyers suggested mode of action?	[ ]	[ ]	[ ]
73.	Has the lawyer noted down the reaction of the client to the decided plan of action (as a minimum, this should include the client's consent to the action going forward)?	[ ]	[ ]	[ ]
74.	If the lawyer is not going to represent the client at any hearing, is there an indication that alternative sources of representation or assistance were explained to the client?	[ ]	[ ]	[ ]
75.	Were any apparent queries from the client dealt with fully, promptly and politely ?	[ ]	[ ]	[ ]
76.	Did the lawyer deal with any evident emotional concerns of the client?	[ ]	[ ]	[ ]
77.	Any contact with the other side should be explained. In particular, did the lawyer explain when the other side will be contacted and why?	[ ]	[ ]	[ ]
78.	Did the lawyer advise the client as to what to do if contacted by the other side?	[ ]	[ ]	[ ]

III Further Investigation, Research and Action

		Yes	No	N/a
79.	Has the lawyer attempted to obtain copies of any relevant correspondence between the client and the landlord?	[ ]	[ ]	[ ]
80.	If the rent has been increased recently, has the lawyer sought documentary evidence of an intention to seek an increase of rent?	[ ]	[ ]	[ ]
81.	Has the lawyer sought a copy of any Notice to Quit/Notice of Intention to Seek Possession?	[ ]	[ ]	[ ]
82.	Has the lawyer sought a copy of written Tenancy Agreement, and/or rent book/rent receipts?	[ ]	[ ]	[ ]
83.	Did the lawyer write to the client confirming in a comprehensible manner;	[ ]	[ ]	[ ]

		Yes	No	N/a

83.1   the basis on which the action for possession may be resisted and/or the basis of any defence/counter-claim?   [ ]   [ ]   [ ]

83.2   an outline of the advice given, including, in particular, areas of uncertainty/difficulty?   [ ]   [ ]   [ ]

84.   Was the client kept informed of significant developments with the other side?   [ ]   [ ]   [ ]

3. Mortgage Repossession

I Getting Information from the Client

		Yes	No	N/a
85.	Has the lawyer recorded the following information:			
85.1	the client's address and telephone number of the property;	[ ]	[ ]	[ ]
85.2	the client's and any other occupiers full names, dates of birth, occupations, relationships between occupiers;	[ ]	[ ]	[ ]
85.3	the income and savings of the client and the client's family;	[ ]	[ ]	[ ]
85.4	the legal owner(s) name, address, relationship to occupier(s) (if different from above);	[ ]	[ ]	[ ]
85.5	the legal title (i.e. freehold/leasehold, registered/ unregistered);	[ ]	[ ]	[ ]
85.6	date of commencement of occupancy?	[ ]	[ ]	[ ]
86.	Does the solicitor know:			
86.1	the Mortgagee's name, address and telephone number;	[ ]	[ ]	[ ]
86.2	the mortgage reference number;	[ ]	[ ]	[ ]
86.3	the priority of the mortgagee (i.e. whether 1st or 2nd mortgage etc);	[ ]	[ ]	[ ]
86.4	details of the mortgagee's solicitors;	[ ]	[ ]	[ ]
86.5	the type of mortgage (e.g. endowment, repayment/annuity or pension)	[ ]	[ ]	[ ]
86.6	the date of mortgage;	[ ]	[ ]	[ ]
86.7	the payments i.e. amount of monthly instalments (and life insurance premium if relevant) and the amount of arrears;	[ ]	[ ]	[ ]
86.8	the approximate amount required to redeem the mortgage;	[ ]	[ ]	[ ]
86.9	the estimated value of the property with vacant possession;	[ ]	[ ]	[ ]
86.10	the regular financial commitments (e.g. maintenance payments, payments under court order, credit/HP payments etc) of the client?	[ ]	[ ]	[ ]
87.	Where there are other adults in occupation with the client,[14] does the lawyer have an understanding of, in particular:		N/A	[ ]
87.1	details of contributions made by occupying non-legal owner(s) towards:	[ ]	[ ]	[ ]
87.1.1	purchase price;	[ ]	[ ]	[ ]
87.1.2	deposit;	[ ]	[ ]	[ ]
87.1.3	mortgage (any regular and substantial direct financial contributions);	[ ]	[ ]	[ ]

		Yes	No	N/a

87.2   if apparent, any details of other contributions[15]   [ ]   [ ]   [ ]

87.3   whether any person in occupation at the date of execution of a
mortgage and making such contributions, knew of the creation of
the lender's interest?   [ ]   [ ]   [ ]

88.   Does the lawyer know details of any previous or current court proceedings
(i.e. hearing dates, date of receipt of summons)?   [ ]   [ ]   [ ]

89.   Does the lawyer know if there have been any previous arrangements between
the client and the lender to remedy default?   [ ]   [ ]   [ ]

90.   Does the lawyer have an understanding of the client (and their family's)
rehousing entitlement (does client have a 'priority' need? e.g. dependent
children, pregnancy, old age, medical condition etc.)?   [ ]   [ ]   [ ]

91.   Where the borrower is unemployed or sick, are they protected by a mortgage
protection plan?   [ ]   [ ]   [ ]

92.   Whether there are any problems with the property which could give rise to a
counter claim (e.g. for negligence or breach of warranty arising out of a
survey report on the condition of the mortgaged property)?   [ ]   [ ]   [ ]

II Advising on that Information

		Yes	No	N/a

93.   Has the lawyer discussed methods of maximising the client's income, including receipt of welfare benefits?   [ ]   [ ]   [ ]

94.   Has the lawyer discussed methods of reducing mortgage costs?[16]   [ ]   [ ]   [ ]

95.   Has the lawyer advised the client of the court's powers to prevent the lender
obtaining possession, and the likely basis on which the mortgagee's claim
would be postponed?[17]   [ ]   [ ]   [ ]

96.   Has the lawyer explained what will happen should the mortgagee be
successful in seeking a possession order or the terms of any suspended order
be broken, and the legal options available to the client at that late stage? [ ]   [ ]   [ ]

97.   If a possession order seems likely, has the lawyer advised the client that they
will be entitled to any surplus funds left over once the mortgage has been
redeemed, and have arrangements been made for the payment of such sums to
the client?   [ ]   [ ]   [ ]

98.   Has the lawyer advised the client that s/he may, in principle, be sued by the
mortgagee on the personal covenant in the mortgage deed for any shortfall,
where sale proceeds are less than the outstanding mortgage?   [ ]   [ ]   [ ]

99.   Where a possession order seems likely, has the lawyer advised the client
regarding the possibility of rehousing by the local authority?   [ ]   [ ]   [ ]

Costs and funding of the case

100.   Is there an indication of advice given to the client regarding the costs and
funding of the case given?
In particular;   [ ]   [ ]   [ ]

100.1   the availability of green form advice and civil legal aid;   [ ]   [ ]   [ ]

100.2   the limits and extent of green form funding;   [ ]   [ ]   [ ]

		Yes	No	N/a
100.3	whether or not the client will have to make a contribution to the case;	[ ]	[ ]	[ ]
100.4	the effect of the statutory charge on any damages received;	[ ]	[ ]	[ ]
100.5	the costs to the client should the case be lost;	[ ]	[ ]	[ ]
100.6	the nature of discharge and revocation of certificates (if one is awarded);	[ ]	[ ]	[ ]
100.7	the duty to report changes of circumstance and address;	[ ]	[ ]	[ ]
100.8	where there is more than one defendant to the possession proceedings, the possibility that the Legal Aid Board may call for contributions from non-legally aided persons;	[ ]	[ ]	[ ]

Progress of the case

101.	Did the lawyer advise the client as to what to do if contacted by the other side?	[ ]	[ ]	[ ]
102.	Is there an indication of the steps the lawyer has agreed to take, and have these been communicated to the client?	[ ]	[ ]	[ ]
103.	Is there an indication of the things the lawyer has asked the client to do and the time limits within which they ought to be completed?	[ ]	[ ]	[ ]
104.	Has the client been told when and in what form the next contact will take place?	[ ]	[ ]	[ ]
105.	Has the lawyer advised the client as to more than one possible course of action?[18]	[ ]	[ ]	[ ]
106.	Did the lawyer indicate the likely outcome of the case?	[ ]	[ ]	[ ]
107.	Is there an indication that the client made an active choice on the lawyers suggested mode of action?	[ ]	[ ]	[ ]
108.	Has the lawyer noted down the reaction of the client to the decided plan of action (as a minimum, this should include the client's consent to the action going forward)?	[ ]	[ ]	[ ]
109.	If the lawyer is not going to represent the client at any hearings, is there an indication that alternative sources of representation of assistance were explained to the client?	[ ]	[ ]	[ ]
110.	Were any apparent queries from the client dealt with fully, promptly and politely?	[ ]	[ ]	[ ]
111.	Did the lawyer deal with any evident emotional concerns of the client?	[ ]	[ ]	[ ]
112.	Any contact with the other side should be explained. In particular, did the lawyer explain when the other side will be contacted and why?	[ ]	[ ]	[ ]

III Further Investigation, Research and Action

		Yes	No	N/a
113.	Was evidence of the client's current and (if different) future financial circumstances being collected?[19]	[ ]	[ ]	[ ]

		Yes	No	N/a

114. Did the lawyer collect the mortgage deed and copies of relevant correspondence between the client and the mortgagee? [ ] [ ] [ ]

115. Did the lawyer write to the client confirming in a comprehensible manner;

    115.1 the available financial options; [ ] [ ] [ ]

    115.2 the basis on which the action for possession may be resisted and/or (if applicable) the basis of any defence/counter-claim; [ ] [ ] [ ]

    115.3 an outline of the advice given, including, in particular, areas of uncertainty/difficulty? [ ] [ ] [ ]

116. Was the client kept informed of significant developments with the other side? [ ] [ ] [ ]

Housing—Notes to the Criteria

1. In particular, 'Repairs: Tenants' Rights' (LAG 1986) by Jan Luba; 'Landlord and Tenant' by Lewis and Holland (Casdec 1988, 4th Ed.); and 'Manual of Housing Law' by Andrew Arden (Sweet and Maxwell 1986, 3rd Ed.).

2. See, in particular: Defending Possession Proceedings (2nd Ed. LAG 1989) by Jan Luba, Nic Madge, and Derek O'Connell.

3. This will be "not applicable" if there is no reference to the housing being dangerous in either the client's statement, attendance notes or correspondence.

4. This will be "not applicable" if there is no reference to the client having to vacate the housing in either the client's statement, attendance notes or correspondence.

5. This is generally three years from any personal injury, or six years from the date that a landlord is given notice of disrepair. Sometimes the limitation period runs from the date that the defect arose even if the defect was not apparent when it first arose). See Luba, op.cit., p.42.

6. i.e. on the different options for resolving the matter.

7. Many solicitors prefer to instruct their own expert rather than use the local authority's Environmental Health Officer.

8. These should include any damage to the fabric of the house, furniture, carpets, clothing, cleaning costs, extra heating costs to dry out damp items, etc.

9. A number of crieria in this section apply only to certain grounds for possession. Furthermore, the applicability of certain questions will depend on the date the tenancy came into being and the type of tenancy. This will be apparent from the questions themselves.

10. This will be "not applicable" if there is no reference to the client being in imminent danger of losing possession in either the client's statement, attendance notes or correspondence.

11. This will be "not applicable" unless the landlord is a Local Authority.

12. Suitable Alternative Accommodation is an individual ground for Rent Act Protected Tenancies (s 98 Rent Act 1977) and for Assured Tenancies under the Housing Act 1988 (Part III, Schedule 2). There are a number of grounds for seeking possession for Secure Tenancies where the landlord must show that there is suitable alternative accommodation in addition to making out the primary charitable landlords, tied accommodation, disabled accommodation, special accommodation provided by Housing Associations/Trusts, etc, special needs accommodation, under accommodation (Housing Act 1985; Part II, Sch. 2).

13. If this is the case, it could raise questions as to the reasonableness of continuing work under the green form.

14. i.e. other adults in occupation with the client who are not legal owners of the property and are party to the mortgage.

15. e.g. helping with the construction of the property pooling of resources or other assistance, relieving the legal owners from expenditure on the property.

16. e.g. requesting the lender accept interest-only payments, so that the capital repayments of annuity mortgages (e.g. straight repayment mortgages) can be deferred in the short term: or (annuity mortgages only) requesting lender extend the term of the loan (and possibly the capitalization of existing arrears) in order to reduce monthly capital repayments; or (endowments mortgages only) switching to an annuity mortgage, if reduced monthly repayments would result; or (especially where mortgage is with a fringe,

high interest mortgage company) requesting local authority/building society remortgage the lender, or sale and lease back i.e. persuading local authority or a housing association to purchase and to allow the borrower to remain in occupation as a public sector tenant.

17. e.g. the High Court's inherent discretion to grant a short adjournment of for example 28 days, to allow any default to be remedied or for the loan to be redeemed, or an adjournment on the basis of specified monthly payments, with a suspended order for possession, also the Court's power to grant relief under the Consumer Credit Act 1974 (i.e. time order, suspended possession order).

18. i.e. on the different options for resolving the matter e.g. defend, give up possession, agree to the sale of the house.

19. e.g. letter of confirmation from DSS concerning payment of mortgage interest, evidence of future regular employment from a new employer, evidence of a forthcoming loan from friends/relatives, evidence of remortgage facilities, estate agents' valuation of the property statements of income and expenditure.

Chapter Five:
Debt

The transaction criteria set out in this chapter are based on a review of files as well as on a survey of literature on debt problems and general legal practice, and relevant literature on housing and debt law[1].

There are two transactions.

- Fuel debts, rent arrears and consumer debts

- Mortgage repossession

The first of these is a general debt transaction covering fuel debts, rent arrears and consumer debts. The second covers mortgage possession cases and applies to cases where the client is an owner-occupier and the mortgage company is threatening or taking possession proceedings against the client.

Each transaction is divided into 3 sections:

I.   Getting Information from the Client

II. Advising On That Information

III. Further Investigation, Research and Action.

1. Rent Arrears, Fuel Debts and Consumer Debts[2]

I Getting Information from the Client

		Yes	No	N/a
1.	Does the lawyer know the client's:			
1.1	name?	[ ]	[ ]	[ ]
1.2	address and telephone number?	[ ]	[ ]	[ ]
1.3	date of birth?	[ ]	[ ]	[ ]
1.4	marital status?[3]	[ ]	[ ]	[ ]
1.5	dependants' ages, relationship to client?	[ ]	[ ]	[ ]
1.6	details of non-dependants in household (if applicable)?	[ ]	[ ]	[ ]
1.7	details of relevant medical condition (if any) of client, and members of household?	[ ]	[ ]	[ ]
1.8	the employment details of the client and the client's partner (i.e. employed, self-employed, in part time work, or unemployed and the name and address of any employer)?	[ ]	[ ]	[ ]
2.	Has the lawyer compiled a financial statement[4] containing details of all the client's income? Including, in particular:		N/A	[ ]
2.1	if the client is employed, wages of client;	[ ]	[ ]	[ ]
2.2	if the client's partner is employed, wages of partner;	[ ]	[ ]	[ ]
2.3	a breakdown of all the welfare benefits the client (and their partner) receives;	[ ]	[ ]	[ ]
2.4	maintenance and other payments from any third parties?	[ ]	[ ]	[ ]
3.	Does the financial statement[4] contain details of all the client's essential[5] expenditure? In particular:		N/A	[ ]
3.1	rent/mortgage (including any arrears);	[ ]	[ ]	[ ]
3.2	community charge;	[ ]	[ ]	[ ]
3.3	water rates;	[ ]	[ ]	[ ]
3.4	life assurance;	[ ]	[ ]	[ ]
3.5	house insurance;	[ ]	[ ]	[ ]
3.6	telephone;	[ ]	[ ]	[ ]
3.7	gas and electricity;	[ ]	[ ]	[ ]
3.8	housekeeping;	[ ]	[ ]	[ ]
3.9	payments under court order;	[ ]	[ ]	[ ]
3.10	credit/HP/catalogue payments;	[ ]	[ ]	[ ]

			Yes	No	N/a
	3.11	bank/finance house loans including second and subsequent charges;	[ ]	[ ]	[ ]
	3.12	maintenance payments (if any);	[ ]	[ ]	[ ]
	3.13	travelling expenses[6] (and why these are essential);	[ ]	[ ]	[ ]
	3.14	clothing;	[ ]	[ ]	[ ]
	3.15	child care expenses;	[ ]	[ ]	[ ]
	3.16	prescription charges;	[ ]	[ ]	[ ]
	3.17	other essential expenditure;	[ ]	[ ]	[ ]

4. Does the financial statement[4] contain details of all the client's non-essential expenditure? In particular:

			Yes	No	N/a
	4.1	TV and video rental;	[ ]	[ ]	[ ]
	4.2	car running costs;	[ ]	[ ]	[ ]
	4.3	cigarettes;[7]	[ ]	[ ]	[ ]
	4.4	alcohol;	[ ]	[ ]	[ ]
	4.5	newspapers/magazines;	[ ]	[ ]	[ ]
	4.6	entertainment (pub/restaurant/cinema etc);	[ ]	[ ]	[ ]
	4.7	pocket money for children;	[ ]	[ ]	[ ]

5. Does the lawyer have details of the client's savings and assets?   [ ]   [ ]   [ ]

6. Does the lawyer have details of each of the client's creditors?
In particular: **N/A**   [ ]

			Yes	No	N/a
	6.1	name and address;	[ ]	[ ]	[ ]
	6.2	reference/account number;	[ ]	[ ]	[ ]
	6.3	outstanding amount;	[ ]	[ ]	[ ]
	6.4	arrears;	[ ]	[ ]	[ ]
	6.5	details of any assets on which loan/credit is secured;	[ ]	[ ]	[ ]

7. If the client has unpaid fines or unpaid maintenance/affiliation orders, does the lawyer have details of these?   [ ]   [ ]   [ ]

8. Does the lawyer have an understanding of any communication between the client and the creditors?   [ ]   [ ]   [ ]

9. Does the lawyer have an understanding of any previous arrangements to remedy default?   [ ]   [ ]   [ ]

10. Does the lawyer have an understanding of any current or previous Court Proceedings?   [ ]   [ ]   [ ]

139

	Yes	No	N/a

11. Does the lawyer have an understanding of the reasons for the client's debt problem?[8]   [ ] [ ] [ ]

12. Where the debt is a fuel debt, does the lawyer know: **N/A** [ ]

    12.1 whether the client has received notice of disconnection, and if so, when?   [ ] [ ] [ ]

    12.2 whether there is a bona fide dispute over the level of charges, and if so, has this been communicated to the supplier?   [ ] [ ] [ ]

    12.3 whether the debt (or any part of it) is in the name of a previous occupier?   [ ] [ ] [ ]

    12.4 whether the client can supply credit references/guarantors?   [ ] [ ] [ ]

    12.5 where the debt is in a landlord's name—has the landlord been paid by the client/tenant?   [ ] [ ] [ ]

13. Where the debt is a consumer debt,[9] has the lawyer: **N/A** [ ]

    13.1 identified the particular type(s) of agreement(s) in respect of which a debt problem arises?[10]   [ ] [ ] [ ]

    13.2 where it is a contract for goods/services has the lawyer asked the client whether s/he feels s/he has any grounds for grievance against the seller/supplier in relation to the credit financed contract? (e.g. poor quality goods etc)?   [ ] [ ] [ ]

    13.3 if the client is or has been self-employed, does the lawyer know whether the credit was provided to an individual/partnership, or a company?   [ ] [ ] [ ]

    13.4 If the agreement is a regulated Consumer Credit Agreement, does the lawyer have an understanding of whether the agreement was properly executed? i.e. there should be an understanding of: **N/A** [ ]

        13.4.1 when the contract was entered into?   [ ] [ ] [ ]

        13.4.2 whether it was signed by debtor and creditor/agent?   [ ] [ ] [ ]

        13.4.3 whether it contains the name and address of debtor and creditor?   [ ] [ ] [ ]

        13.4.4 description and cash price of goods;   [ ] [ ] [ ]

        13.4.5 timing of repayments;   [ ] [ ] [ ]

        13.4.6 amounts of repayments;   [ ] [ ] [ ]

        13.4.7 Annual Percentage Rate;   [ ] [ ] [ ]

        13.4.8 where the debtor signed the agreement;   [ ] [ ] [ ]

        13.4.9 what was said by both parties before the signing of the agreement;   [ ] [ ] [ ]

		Yes	No	N/a

		Yes	No	N/a
13.4.10	whether (and when) the debtor received a notice setting out the rights of cancellation;	[ ]	[ ]	[ ]
13.4.11	whether the debtor received a copy of the agreement within 7 days of the signing of the contract;	[ ]	[ ]	[ ]
13.4.12	how much the client has paid off under the agreement;	[ ]	[ ]	[ ]
13.4.13	whether the client has received a default notice;	[ ]	[ ]	[ ]

14. Where the debt is for rent arrears, is there evidence that the lawyer has considered the following: **N/A** [ ]

		Yes	No	N/a
14.1	whether or not the client agrees with the landlord's view of arrears or persistent delays?	[ ]	[ ]	[ ]
14.2	whether the rent includes anything which is not strictly 'rent' e.g. an element of service charge, amenity payment, or overpaid housing benefit?	[ ]	[ ]	[ ]
14.3	if the arrears, or any part of them, represent money that has been used by the tenant to pay repairs as a result of the landlord's default, is there a report or other evidence available on the pre-repair condition of the property and steps taken by the client to get the landlord to effect repairs?	[ ]	[ ]	[ ]
14.4	if the client is claiming Housing Benefit, does the lawyer know if the landlord has paid the correct amount of H.B. into the client's rent account and whether or not the benefit authority has sought to recoup any overpayment of H.B. by adjusting the client's rent account?	[ ]	[ ]	[ ]
14.5	collection methods the landlord has tried or considered?	[ ]	[ ]	[ ]
14.6	whether the landlord has refused to accept rent?	[ ]	[ ]	[ ]
14.7	the circumstances surrounding any previous rent increase?	[ ]	[ ]	[ ]
14.8	Has the lawyer sought a copy of the tenancy agreement/rent book/ rent receipts?	[ ]	[ ]	[ ]

II Advising on that Information

		Yes	No	N/a
15.	Has the lawyer discussed methods of maximising the client's income?	[ ]	[ ]	[ ]
16.	Where the client has multiple debt problems, has the lawyer prioritised the client's debts?	[ ]	[ ]	[ ]
17.	Has the lawyer calculated levels of affordable repayments?	[ ]	[ ]	[ ]
18.	If a court order has been made against the client, or it appears likely that there will be such an order made, has the lawyer advised the client about the procedure for varying sums payable under a court order?	[ ]	[ ]	[ ]
19.	Has the lawyer advised the client about the remedies available to the relevant creditors, and the likely way in which the creditors will seek to recover the debts?	[ ]	[ ]	[ ]

		Yes	No	N/a

20. Has the lawyer advised the client about the consequences of breaching a likely court order e.g. for payment of arrears? [ ] [ ] [ ]

21. Has the lawyer warned the client of the effect a court judgment in favour of the creditor may have on the client's ability to obtain credit and mortgage facilities in the future? [ ] [ ] [ ]

22. If it is apparent that the debt is likely to be totally unmanageable, has the lawyer discussed the possibility of the client presenting a bankruptcy petition, or seeking an administration order or voluntary arrangement, and the respective consequences of these measures? [ ] [ ] [ ]

23. Where a debt is in the landlord's name (e.g. a fuel debt), and the landlord has been paid the money for that debt by the client, has the lawyer advised the client about contacting the local authority Environmental Health Department for assistance? [ ] [ ] [ ]

24. Where the debt is a consumer debt: **N/A** [ ]

   24.1 has the lawyer determined whether any lender to whom the client is indebted, holds the requisite licence[11] [ ] [ ] [ ]

   24.2 if the lender does not hold a licence, has the lawyer advised on the enforceability of the contract? [ ] [ ] [ ]

   24.3 where the creditor has not complied with the necessary contractual formalities, has the lawyer advised the client on the agreement's enforceability? [ ] [ ] [ ]

   24.4 if the agreement is a cancellable agreement, has the lawyer advised the client whether the agreement is still cancellable, and if it is cancellable, how the cancellation rights may be exercised? [ ] [ ] [ ]

   24.5 if the agreement is an H.P. or Conditional Sale Agreement which has been properly executed, and cancellation is not available, has the lawyer advised how the client may terminate the agreement? [ ] [ ] [ ]

   24.6 where goods have already been repossessed under an H.P. or Conditional Sale agreement or where repossession is inevitable, has the lawyer discussed the possibility of seeking the H.P. company's permission for the client to sell the goods privately? [ ] [ ] [ ]

   24.7 has the lawyer advised the client about his/her right for early discharge of his/her total indebtedness under the relevant agreement, by e.g. cheaper financing? [ ] [ ] [ ]

25. Where the APR is very high (e.g. more than 40%), or the agreement otherwise grossly contravenes the ordinary principles of fair dealing, has the lawyer explained the court's powers in relation to extortionate credit bargains? [ ] [ ] [ ]

26. Where credit has been extended to the client in respect of goods (between £100 and £30,000) by a party other than the supplier (e.g. by a credit card purchase), and the client has grounds for alleging misrepresentation/breach of contract, has the lawyer advised the client that s/he can also claim against the creditor? [ ] [ ] [ ]

		Yes	No	N/a

27. Where there is evidence of harassment by creditors, has the lawyer advised the client of the remedies available , (e.g. persuade police to prosecute, notify local Trading Standards or Consumer Protection Department)?   [ ]   [ ]   [ ]

Costs and Funding of the Case

28. Is there an indication of advice given to the client regarding the costs and funding of the case? In particular: **N/A**   [ ]

    28.1   the availability of green form advice and civil legal aid   [ ]   [ ]   [ ]

    28.2   the limits and extent of green form funding   [ ]   [ ]   [ ]

    28.3   whether or not the client will have to make a contribution to the case;   [ ]   [ ]   [ ]

    28.4   the effects of the solicitor's and statutory charge on any damages received (if these are being claimed);   [ ]   [ ]   [ ]

    28.5   the costs to the client should the case be lost;   [ ]   [ ]   [ ]

    28.6   the nature and consequences of revocation and discharge of certificates (if one is granted);   [ ]   [ ]   [ ]

    28.7   the duty to report changes of circumstance and address;   [ ]   [ ]   [ ]

Progress of the Case

    29.1   Did the lawyer advise the client of how long the case is likely to take?   [ ]   [ ]   [ ]

    29.2   Is there an indication of the steps the lawyer has agreed to take and have these been communicated to the client?   [ ]   [ ]   [ ]

    29.3   Is there an indication of the things the lawyer has asked the client to do and the time limits within which they ought to be completed?   [ ]   [ ]   [ ]

    29.4   Has the client been told when and in what form the next contact with the lawyer will take place?   [ ]   [ ]   [ ]

    29.5   Has the lawyer advised the client as to more than one possible course of action?   [ ]   [ ]   [ ]

    29.6   Did the lawyer indicate the likely outcome of the case?   [ ]   [ ]   [ ]

    29.7   Is there an indication that the client made an active choice on the lawyers suggested mode of action?   [ ]   [ ]   [ ]

    29.8   Has the lawyer noted down the reaction of the client to the decided plan of action (as a minimum, this should include the client's consent to the action going forward)?   [ ]   [ ]   [ ]

    29.9   If the lawyer is not going to represent the client at any hearings, is there an indication that alternative sources of representation or assistance were explained to the client?   [ ]   [ ]   [ ]

    29.10   Were any apparent queries from the client dealt with fully, promptly and politely?   [ ]   [ ]   [ ]

29.11   Did the lawyer deal with any evident emotional concerns of the client?   [ ] [ ] [ ]

29.12   Any contact with the other side should be explained. In particular did the lawyer explain when the other side will be contacted and why?   [ ] [ ] [ ]

29.13   Did the lawyer advise the client of what to do if contacted by the other side?   [ ] [ ] [ ]

III   Further Investigation, Research and Action

30.   Does the lawyer have or seek copies of all relevant documents, notices, and correspondence?   [ ] [ ] [ ]

31.   Did the lawyer write to the client confirming in a comprehensible manner an outline of the advice given, including in particular, any areas of difficulty/uncertainty?   [ ] [ ] [ ]

32.   Was the client kept informed of any significant developments?   [ ] [ ] [ ]

33.   Did the lawyer write to creditors covering the following matters: [ ] [ ] [ ]

33.1   if the debts are queried by the client, requesting proofs of debts?   [ ] [ ] [ ]

33.2   where the client wishes the creditor to continue to supply (e.g. fuel supplier), attempting to negotiate for supply to continue?   [ ] [ ] [ ]

33.3   negotiating affordable repayment schedule (uncontested debts only)?   [ ] [ ] [ ]

2. Mortgage Repossession

This transaction applies to cases where the client is an owner-occupier and the mortgage company is threatening or taking possession proceedings against the client.

I Getting Information from the Client

		Yes	No	N/a
34.	Has the lawyer recorded the following information?			
34.1	the address of the property;	[ ]	[ ]	[ ]
34.2	the occupier(s) full name(s), date(s) of birth, occupation(s), relationship(s) between occupier(s);	[ ]	[ ]	[ ]
34.3	the income and savings of the client and the client's family;	[ ]	[ ]	[ ]
34.4	the legal owner(s) name, address, relationship to occupier(s) (if different from above);	[ ]	[ ]	[ ]
34.5	the legal title (i.e. freehold/leasehold, registered/unregistered);	[ ]	[ ]	[ ]
34.6	date of commencement of occupancy.	[ ]	[ ]	[ ]
35.	Does the solicitor know the following details?			
35.1	the mortgagee's name, address and telephone number;	[ ]	[ ]	[ ]
35.2	the mortgage reference number;	[ ]	[ ]	[ ]
35.3	the priority of the mortgagee (i.e. whether 1st or 2nd mortgage, etc.);	[ ]	[ ]	[ ]
35.4	details of the mortgagee's solicitors;	[ ]	[ ]	[ ]
35.5	the type of mortgage (e.g. endowment, repayment/annuity or pension)	[ ]	[ ]	[ ]
35.6	date of the mortgage;	[ ]	[ ]	[ ]
35.7	the payments, i.e. amount of monthly instalments (and life insurance premium if relevant) and the amount of arrears;	[ ]	[ ]	[ ]
35.8	the amount required to redeem mortgage;	[ ]	[ ]	[ ]
35.9	the estimated value of the property with vacant possession;	[ ]	[ ]	[ ]
35.10	the regular financial commitments (e.g. maintenance payments, payments under court order, credit/HP payments, etc.) of the client;	[ ]	[ ]	[ ]
36.	Where there are other adults in occupation with the client, does the lawyer have an understanding of the following matters? In particular:		**N/A**	[ ]
36.1	details of contributions made by occupying non-legal owner(s) towards:			

		Yes	No	N/a

		Yes	No	N/a
(a) purchase price;		[ ]	[ ]	[ ]
(b) deposit;		[ ]	[ ]	[ ]
(c) mortgage (any regular and substantial direct financial contributions).		[ ]	[ ]	[ ]
36.2	if apparent, any details of other contributions;[12]	[ ]	[ ]	[ ]
36.3	whether any person in occupation at the date of execution of a mortgage and making such contributions, knew of the creation of the lender's interest.	[ ]	[ ]	[ ]
37.	Does the lawyer know details of any previous or current court proceedings (i.e. hearing dates, date of receipt of summons)?	[ ]	[ ]	[ ]
38.	Does the lawyer have an understanding of any previous arrangements between the client and the lender to remedy default.	[ ]	[ ]	[ ]
39.	Does the lawyer have an understanding of the client's (and their family's) rehousing entitlement (does the client have a priority need? e.g. dependent children, pregnancy, old age, medical condition etc.)	[ ]	[ ]	[ ]
40.	Where the borrower is unemployed or sick, whether they are protected by a mortgage protection plan?	[ ]	[ ]	[ ]
41.	Does the lawyer know whether there are any problems with the property which could give rise to a counterclaim (e.g. for negligence or breach of warranty arising out of a survey report on the condition of the mortgaged property).	[ ]	[ ]	[ ]

II Advising on that information

		Yes	No	N/a
42.	Has the lawyer discussed methods of maximising the client's income, including receipt of welfare benefits?	[ ]	[ ]	[ ]
43.	Has the lawyer discussed methods of reducing mortgage costs?[13]	[ ]	[ ]	[ ]
44.	Has the lawyer advised the client of the court's powers to prevent the lender obtaining possession, and the likely basis on which the mortgagee's claim would be postponed?[14]	[ ]	[ ]	[ ]
45.	Has the lawyer explained what would happen should the mortgagee be successful in seeking a possession order, or the term of any suspended order be broken, and the legal options available to the client at that late stage?	[ ]	[ ]	[ ]
46.	If a possession order seems likely, has the lawyer advised the client that they will be entitled to any surplus funds left over once the mortgage has been redeemed, and have arrangements been made for the payment of such sums to the client?	[ ]	[ ]	[ ]
47.	Has the lawyer advised the client that they may, in principle, be sued by the mortgagee on the personal covenant in the mortgage deed for any shortfall, where sale proceeds are less than the outstanding mortgage?	[ ]	[ ]	[ ]
48.	Where a possession order seems likely, has the lawyer advised the client regarding the possibility of re-housing by the local authority?	[ ]	[ ]	[ ]

Costs and Funding of the Case

		Yes	No	N/a
49.	Has advice to the client regarding the costs of the case been given? In particular;			
49.1	the availability of green form advice and civil legal aid;	[ ]	[ ]	[ ]
49.2	the limits and extent of green form funding;	[ ]	[ ]	[ ]
49.3	whether or not the client will have to make a contribution to the case;	[ ]	[ ]	[ ]
49.4	the costs to the client should the case be lost;	[ ]	[ ]	[ ]
49.5	the duty to report changes of circumstances and address;	[ ]	[ ]	[ ]
49.6	the nature and consequences of discharge and revocation of certificates (if granted);	[ ]	[ ]	[ ]
49.7	where there is more than one defendant to the possession proceedings, the possibility that the Legal Aid Board may call for contributions from non-legally aided persons.	[ ]	[ ]	[ ]

Progress of the Case

		Yes	No	N/a
50.1	Did the lawyer advise the client of how long the case is likely to take?	[ ]	[ ]	[ ]
50.2	Is there an indication of the steps the lawyer has agreed to take, and have these been communicated to the client?	[ ]	[ ]	[ ]
50.3	Is there an indication of the things that the lawyer has asked the client to do and the time limits within which they ought to be completed?	[ ]	[ ]	[ ]
50.4	Has the client been told when and in what form the next contact from the lawyer will take place?	[ ]	[ ]	[ ]
50.5	Has the lawyer advised the client as to more than one possible course of action?	[ ]	[ ]	[ ]
50.6	Did the lawyer indicate the likely outcome of the case?	[ ]	[ ]	[ ]
50.7	Is there an indication that the client made an active choice on the lawyer's suggested mode of action?	[ ]	[ ]	[ ]
50.8	Has the lawyer noted down the reaction of the client to the decided plan of action (as a minimum, this should include the client's consent to the action going forward)?	[ ]	[ ]	[ ]
50.9	If the lawyer is not going to represent the client at any hearings, is there an indication that alternative sources of representation or assistance were explained to the client?	[ ]	[ ]	[ ]
50.10	Were any apparent queries from the client dealt with fully, promptly and politely?	[ ]	[ ]	[ ]
50.11	Did the lawyer deal with any evident emotional concerns of the client?	[ ]	[ ]	[ ]

	Yes	No	N/a

51. Any contact with the other side should be explained. In particular;   **N/A**   [ ]

51.1 Did the lawyer explain when the other side would be contacted and why?   [ ]   [ ]   [ ]

51.2 Did the lawyer advise the client of what to do if contacted by the other side?   [ ]   [ ]   [ ]

III Further Action, Investigation and Research

52. Was evidence of the client's current and (if different) future financial circumstances being collected?[15]   [ ]   [ ]   [ ]

53. Did the lawyer collect the mortgage deed and copies of relevant correspondence between the client and the mortgagee?   [ ]   [ ]   [ ]

54. Did the lawyer write to the client confirming in a comprehensible manner;

54.1 the available financial options;   [ ]   [ ]   [ ]

54.2 the basis on which the action for possession may be resisted and/or (if applicable) the basis of any defence/counterclaim;   [ ]   [ ]   [ ]

54.3 an outline of the advice given, including, in particular, areas of uncertainty/difficulty?   [ ]   [ ]   [ ]

55. Was the client kept informed of significant developments with the other side?   [ ]   [ ]   [ ]

Debt—Notes to the Criteria

1. *Defending Possession Proceedings* (2nd ed. LAG 1989) by Jan Luba, Nic Madge, and Derek McConnell and the Money Advice Services *Debt Counselling Handbook* (1991).

2. A number of questions in this transaction apply only to specific categories of debt. The text of the question will indicate where this is the case.

3. Includes co-habitees.

4. The information may be contained in the CLA 4, statement, attendance notes or any resume completed by the client. It does not have to be contained in a single document in the file.

5. This should include details of the clients obligation and the payments they are making towards these items.

6. Only if they appear excessive.

7. 4.3–4.6 are often recorded as housekeeping expenses, so as not to antagonise creditors.

8. e.g. Sickness, lost overtime, short-time working, strike, marital breakdown, pregnancy, etc.

9. Consumer debts would include general debts other than fuel or rent, in particular pure loans in relation to goods or services (including credit card debts). Inland Revenue debts are not covered by consumer debts.

10. i.e. A contract for supply of goods/services with no credit provisions, hire-purchase (a bailment of goods with an option to purchase), conditional sale (a sale of goods with price payable by instalments and property not to pass to buyer until certain conditions are fulfilled), credit sale (similar to conditional sale, but property passes immediately), personal loan, credit card, charge card, budget account in shops, overdraft.

11. under Part III of the Consumer Credit Act 1974.

12. e.g. helping with the construction of the property pooling of resources or other assistance relieving the legal owner(s) from expenditure on the property.

13. e.g. requesting the lender accept interest-only payments, so that the capital repayments of annuity mortgages (e.g. straight repayment mortgages) can be deferred in the short term; or (annuity mortgages only) requesting lender extend the term of the loan (and possibly the capitalisation of existing arrears) in order to reduce monthly capital repayments; or (endowment mortgages only) switching to an annuity mortgage, if reduced monthly repayments would result; or (especially where mortgage is with a fringe, high interest mortgage company) requesting local authority/building society remortgage the lender; or sale and lease back i.e. persuading local authority or a housing association to purchase the property and to allow the borrower to remain in occupation as a public sector tenant.

14. e.g. the High Court's inherent discretion to grant a short adjournment of for example 28 days, to allow any default to be remedied or for the loan to be redeemed; or an adjournment on the basis of specified monthly payments, with a suspended order for possession; also the Court's power to grant relief under Consumer Credit Act 1974 (i.e. time order, suspended possession order).

15. e.g. letter of confirmation from DSS concerning payment of mortgage interest; evidence of future regular employment from a new employer; evidence of a forthcoming loan from friends/relatives; evidence of remortgage facilities; estate agent's valuation of the property, statements of income and expenditure.

Chapter Six:
Welfare Benefits

This chapter contains criteria covering three transactions:

- Overpayment of Income Support

- Invalidity Benefit Appeals (Draft)

- Good Cause for Backdating of Claims (Draft)

The first set of criteria were developed during the research project and are based upon a review of legal aid files and literature on welfare benefits work[1]. In addition to this transaction, the Board has drafted two further transactions in welfare benefits. These were drafted by Board staff with extensive experience in the category of work following the process established by the research project. These transactions are still in draft and at the time of writing are the subject of testing and consultation. We include them here for information. Any comments should be sent to the Legal Department, Legal Aid Head Office.

Each transaction is divided into 3 sections:

I.   Getting Information from the Client

II.   Advising On That Information

III. Further Investigation, Research and Action.

Recognising the Need for Welfare Benefits Advice

The Board has decided after testing the "Recognition Criteria" previously published (Transaction Criteria, HMSO 1992), many of which are now out of date, to substitute a management audit of the requirement to ensure that initially one person and then all caseworkers/advisers are able to recognise the need for Welfare Benefits advice and refer the client to an appropriate source of advice.

1. Overpayment of Income Support

This transaction covers situations where a client faces repayment of Income Support because of an allegation of misrepresentation or failure to disclose a material fact[2].

I GETTING INFORMATION

General Information

		Yes	No	N/a
1.	Does the file show:			
1.1	the client's full name?	[ ]	[ ]	[ ]
1.2	the client's address and telephone number?	[ ]	[ ]	[ ]
1.3	the client's date of birth?	[ ]	[ ]	[ ]

Information on the Alleged Overpayment

		Yes	No	N/a
2.	Does the file show some understanding of:			
2.1	the reason given by the Benefits Agency for the alleged overpayment?	[ ]	[ ]	[ ]
2.2	if misrepresentation or failure to disclose is alleged, whether the claimant is accused of fraud?	[ ]	[ ]	[ ]
3.	If misrepresentation is alleged, does the file show some understanding of:		**N/A**	[ ]
3.1	the facts the client is alleged to have misrepresented?	[ ]	[ ]	[ ]
3.2	what the client put on any forms in relation to those facts?	[ ]	[ ]	[ ]
3.3	whether the caseworker obtained from the client their version of events?	[ ]	[ ]	[ ]
3.4	the client's view on whether they misrepresented, and the basis for this view?	[ ]	[ ]	[ ]
3.5	what the client has said to Benefits Agency staff in relation to the allegedly misrepresented facts?	[ ]	[ ]	[ ]
4.	If failure to disclose is alleged, does the file show some understanding of:		**N/A**	[ ]
4.1	whether the client had knowledge of the fact(s) that they allegedly failed to disclose?	[ ]	[ ]	[ ]
4.2	whether the client informed the Benefits Agency of the fact(s) (either orally, in writing or on a form)?	[ ]	[ ]	[ ]
4.3	if the client informed an individual at the Benefits Agency:			
4.3.1	whether they can identify that person, and, if so, who that person is?	[ ]	[ ]	[ ]

		Yes	No	N/a

4.3.2   when?   [ ] [ ] [ ]

4.4   if the client knew the fact(s) but did not tell the Benefits Agency does the file show an understanding of why and whether it would be reasonable to expect the client to disclose the facts in these circumstances.   [ ] [ ] [ ]

5.   Does the file show how much the alleged overpayment is?   [ ] [ ] [ ]

6.   Does the file show the amount of any deductions which have been made from the client's benefit?   [ ] [ ] [ ]

7.   If the client's benefit was suspended, does the file show some understanding of the reason given for the suspension?   [ ] [ ] [ ]

8.   Has the caseworker considered whether the overpayment was due to a clerical error by the Benefits Agency?   [ ] [ ] [ ]

II   Advising on this Information

9.   Was the client advised as to whether they misrepresented or failed to disclose facts relevant to their Income Support claim?   [ ] [ ] [ ]

10.   Was the client advised whether any misrepresentation or failure to disclose actually led to an overpayment?   [ ] [ ] [ ]

11.   Was the client advised whether to appeal against the Benefits Agency decision?   [ ] [ ] [ ]

12.   If the client is advised to appeal, were they advised not to repay any money to the Benefits Agency for the alleged overpayment until after the appeal?   [ ] [ ] [ ]

13.   If the client faced, or seemed likely to face an allegation of fraud, were they advised what to do if contacted by the Benefits Agency?   [ ] [ ] [ ]

14.   If the client's benefit was suspended: N/A [ ]

14.1   were they advised whether the Benefits Agency was entitled to suspend their benefit?   [ ] [ ] [ ]

14.2   were they advised to make a further claim if they subsequently met the qualifying conditions for Income Support?   [ ] [ ] [ ]

15.   If deductions were made from the client's benefit, were they advised whether the rate of deduction was correct?   [ ] [ ] [ ]

Costs and Funding of the Case

16.   Did the file show that the client was advised in respect of the following matters:

16.1   the availability of green form advice and the extent and limits of green form funding?   [ ] [ ] [ ]

16.2   whether the client will have to make a contribution to the case?   [ ] [ ] [ ]

		Yes	No	N/a
16.3	the costs to the client of taking a case to an appeal tribunal?	[ ]	[ ]	[ ]
16.4	the effect of the solicitor's charge on any money received and the result of the case?	[ ]	[ ]	[ ]

Progress of the Case

		Yes	No	N/a
17.1	Was the client advised how long the case is likely to take?	[ ]	[ ]	[ ]
17.2	Is there an indication of the steps the caseworker has agreed to take and were these communicated to the client?	[ ]	[ ]	[ ]
17.3	Is there an indication of any steps the client has been asked to take, and the time within which these must be completed?	[ ]	[ ]	[ ]
17.4	Was the client told when and in what form the next contact would take place?	[ ]	[ ]	[ ]
17.5	Was the client advised as to the possible courses of action?	[ ]	[ ]	[ ]
17.6	Was the client advised of the likely outcome of the case?	[ ]	[ ]	[ ]
17.7	Is there an indication that the client made an active choice on the suggested mode of action?	[ ]	[ ]	[ ]
17.8	Does the file show the reaction of the client to the decided plan of action (as a minimum, this should include the client's consent to the action going forward)?	[ ]	[ ]	[ ]
17.9	If no representation is to be organised for the client at any hearings, is there an indication that alternative sources of representation or assistance were explained to the client?	[ ]	[ ]	[ ]
17.10	Were any apparent queries from the client dealt with fully, promptly and politely?	[ ]	[ ]	[ ]
17.11	Were any evident emotional concerns of the client dealt with?	[ ]	[ ]	[ ]
17.12	If it appears likely that the other side will contact the client direct, was the client advised as to what they should do in the event that the other side does contact them?	[ ]	[ ]	[ ]

III   Further Investigation, Research, and Action.

The following criteria apply where the case extends beyond initial advice.
18.   Was the Benefits Agency asked for:

		Yes	No	N/a
18.1	a written statement of the reasons for the Adjudication Officer's decision?	[ ]	[ ]	[ ]
18.2	a breakdown of how the overpayment was calculated?	[ ]	[ ]	[ ]
19.	Where both the following apply, was an appeal lodged within three months?	[ ]	[ ]	[ ]

		Yes	No	N/a

a)   the client has been advised to appeal

b)   they first consulted the caseworker within three months of being sent the Adjudication Officer's decision.

		Yes	No	N/a
20.	Where there is to be an appeal, was the Adjudication Officer invited to review the decision which is to be appealed?	[ ]	[ ]	[ ]
21.	Did the letter notifying the Benefits Agency of the appeal state the grounds for that appeal?	[ ]	[ ]	[ ]
22.	Was the client given an opportunity to read and comment on any written decisions which the caseworker received from the Benefits Agency or the Independent Tribunals Service?	[ ]	[ ]	[ ]
23.	Where the client was not to be represented by the caseworker at an appeal hearing, were written submissions prepared for the client?	[ ]	[ ]	[ ]
24.	Where the client was not to be represented by the caseworker at an appeal hearing, was a letter sent to the client advising him/her of the main points to pursue at the hearing?	[ ]	[ ]	[ ]
25.	Where an appeal is to be made to the Social Security Commissioner:		**N/A**	[ ]
25.1	was leave sought from the Chairman of the Social Security Appeal Tribunal (SSAT)?	[ ]	[ ]	[ ]
25.2	if the SSAT Chairman refused leave, was leave sought from the Commissioner within six weeks of being sent the refusal by the SSAT?	[ ]	[ ]	[ ]
25.3	if leave was granted by the SSAT Chairman, was notice of appeal sent to the Commissioner within six weeks of leave being granted?	[ ]	[ ]	[ ]

2. Invalidity Benefit Appeals

This transaction applies to a refusal of Invalidity Benefit to the client on the grounds that s/he is fit for work.

I. GETTING INFORMATION

General Information

		Yes	No	N/a
1.	Does the file show:			
1.1	the client's full name?	[ ]	[ ]	[ ]
1.2	the client's address and telephone number?	[ ]	[ ]	[ ]
1.3	the client's date of birth?	[ ]	[ ]	[ ]

Information on the Client's Medical Condition

		Yes	No	N/a
2.	Does the file show some understanding of:			
2.1	whether the client considers him/herself fit for work?	[ ]	[ ]	[ ]
2.2	if the client does not consider him/herself fit for work, what are the reasons for this?	[ ]	[ ]	[ ]
2.3	the name and address of the client's General Practitioner?	[ ]	[ ]	[ ]
2.4	whether the client was covered by a medical certificate when s/he first saw the caseworker?	[ ]	[ ]	[ ]
2.5	if the client is not covered by a medical certificate, has the caseworker discussed the possibility of approaching the client's General Practitioner for a further certificate?	[ ]	[ ]	[ ]
2.6	if applicable, the reason given by the client's General Practitioner for his/her incapacity for work?	[ ]	[ ]	[ ]
2.7	whether the client has consulted a medical specialist(s) in connection with his/her relevant illness or disability?	[ ]	[ ]	[ ]
2.8	if so, the name and address of any such person?	[ ]	[ ]	[ ]
2.9	whether the client is currently a patient of any such person?	[ ]	[ ]	[ ]
2.10	whether the client has been examined by a doctor on behalf of the Benefits Agency?	[ ]	[ ]	[ ]

Information on the Client's Employment

		Yes	No	N/a
3.	Does the file show some understanding of:			
3.1	what job(s) the client did in the past?	[ ]	[ ]	[ ]
3.2	what tasks those jobs involved?	[ ]	[ ]	[ ]

			Yes	No	N/a
3.3	when the client worked in any such jobs?		[ ]	[ ]	[ ]
3.4	the client's education and training?		[ ]	[ ]	[ ]
3.5	if the client has been working while receiving Invalidity Benefit:				
	3.5.1	for how many hours each week?	[ ]	[ ]	[ ]
	3.5.2	what tasks the client's job involves?	[ ]	[ ]	[ ]
	3.5.3	what are the client's reasons for working?	[ ]	[ ]	[ ]
	3.5.4	what is the attitude to this of the client's doctor?	[ ]	[ ]	[ ]
	3.5.5	how much (if anything) the client earns?	[ ]	[ ]	[ ]
	3.5.6	whether the Benefits Agency views any such earnings as therapeutic?	[ ]	[ ]	[ ]

Information on the History of the Client's Claim

4.	Does the file show some understanding of:				
4.1	the date when the client first claimed Invalidity Benefit?		[ ]	[ ]	[ ]
4.2	how the client's Invalidity Benefit was calculated?		[ ]	[ ]	[ ]
4.3	whether the client was receiving Invalidity Benefit when s/he first saw the caseworker?		[ ]	[ ]	[ ]
4.4	if the client's Invalidity Benefit has been suspended, has the caseworker advised the client to register as unemployed and claim Unemployment Benefit/Income Support? (The client will not have to register as unemployed if s/he cares for dependents, or is aged over 50 and has not worked for 10 years)		[ ]	[ ]	[ ]
	4.4.1	if the client has been advised to register as unemployed, has the caseworker explained to the client that this will not prejudice any appeal against the refusal of Invalidity Benefit?	[ ]	[ ]	[ ]
	4.4.2	if the client registered as unemployed, did the caseworker advise him/her to keep a note of all unsuccessful attempts to obtain a job?	[ ]	[ ]	[ ]
4.5	whether the caseworker considered the client's entitlement to any other benefits?		[ ]	[ ]	[ ]

II Advising on this Information

		Yes	No	N/a
5.	has the caseworker advised the client whether s/he has grounds for appealing against the decision to refuse Invalidity Benefit?	[ ]	[ ]	[ ]
6.	if the client has already appealed, has the caseworker advised the client whether the appeal is likely to succeed?	[ ]	[ ]	[ ]

Costs and Funding of the Case

			Yes	No	N/a
7.	Did the caseworker advise the client in respect of the following matters:				
7.1	the availability of green form advice and the extent and limits of green form funding.		[ ]	[ ]	[ ]

	Yes	No	N/a

7.2   whether the client will have to make a contribution to the case.   [ ] [ ] [ ]

7.3   the costs to the client of taking the case to an appeal tribunal.   [ ] [ ] [ ]

Progress of the Case

8.1   Was the client advised of how long the case is likely to take?   [ ] [ ] [ ]

8.2   Is there an indication of the steps the caseworker has agreed to take and were these communicated to the client?   [ ] [ ] [ ]

8.3   Is there an indication of the steps the caseworker has asked the client to take (if any)?   [ ] [ ] [ ]

8.4   Was the client told when and in what form the next contact would take place?   [ ] [ ] [ ]

8.5   Was the client advised as to more than one possible course of action?   [ ] [ ] [ ]

8.6   Did the caseworker indicate the likely outcome of the case?   [ ] [ ] [ ]

8.7   Is there an indication that the client made an active choice on the caseworker's suggested mode of action?   [ ] [ ] [ ]

8.8   Has the caseworker noted down the reaction of the client to the decided plan of action (as a minimum, this should include the client's consent to the action going forward)?   [ ] [ ] [ ]

8.9   If the caseworker is not going to represent the client at any hearings, is there an indication that alternative sources of representation or assistance were explained to the client?   [ ] [ ] [ ]

8.10   Were any apparent queries from the client dealt with fully, promptly and politely?   [ ] [ ] [ ]

8.11   Did the caseworker deal with any evident emotional concerns of the client?   [ ] [ ] [ ]

8.12   If it appears likely that the other side will contact the client direct, was the client advised as to what s/he should do in the event that the other side does contact him/her?   [ ] [ ] [ ]

III   Further Investigation, Research, and Action

The following criteria apply where the case extends beyond initial advice.

9.   Where all the following apply, was an appeal lodged within three months?   [ ] [ ] [ ]

a)   the Adjudication Officer has made a decision that the client is not entitled to Invalidity Benefit.

b)   the client has been advised to appeal;

c)   s/he first consulted the caseworker within three months of being sent the Adjudication Officer's decision.

		Yes	No	N/a

10. Did the letter notifying the Benefits Agency of the appeal state the grounds for the appeal? [ ] [ ] [ ]

11. If an appeal is made, has the caseworker obtained a medical report from: **N/A** [ ]

    11.1 the client's General Practitioner? [ ] [ ] [ ]

    11.2 the client's specialist? [ ] [ ] [ ]

12. Upon receipt of any medical report, did the caseworker: **N/A** [ ]

    12.1 allow the client to comment upon it or a summary of its conclusions? [ ] [ ] [ ]

    12.2 if the report was unfavourable, consider the possibility of seeking a further report? [ ] [ ] [ ]

13. Was the client given an opportunity to read and comment on any written decisions and/or submissions which the caseworker may have received from the Benefits Agency or the Independent Tribunals Service? [ ] [ ] [ ]

14. The Adjudication Officer will have provided job descriptions for a range of jobs which s/he thinks the client can do. Has the caseworker considered whether it is reasonable to expect the client to do these jobs? [ ] [ ] [ ]

15. Where the client was not to be represented by the caseworker at an appeal hearing, were written submissions prepared for the client? [ ] [ ] [ ]

16. Where the client was not to be represented by the caseworker at an appeal hearing, was a letter sent to the client advising him/her of the main points to pursue at the hearing? [ ] [ ] [ ]

17. Where an appeal is to be made to the Social Security Commissioner: **N/A** [ ]

    17.1 was leave to appeal sought from the Chairman of the Social Security Appeal Tribunal (SSAT)? [ ] [ ] [ ]

    17.2 if the SSAT Chairman refused leave, was leave sought from the Commissioner within six weeks of being sent the refusal by the SSAT? [ ] [ ] [ ]

    17.3 if leave was granted by the SSAT Chairman, was notice of appeal sent to the Commissioner within six weeks of leave being granted? [ ] [ ] [ ]

3. 'Good Cause' for Backdating of Claims

This transaction applies to the following benefits: Income Support, Housing Benefit, Family Credit, Council Tax Benefit, Disability Working Allowance, Unemployment Benefit, Sickness Benefit, Invalidity Benefit, Severe Disablement Allowance, Industrial Injuries Benefits. The transaction covers situations where the client is applying for a benefit to be paid in respect of a period before the date when s/he first claimed it and has good reasons for not having claimed earlier.

I. GETTING INFORMATION

General Information

		Yes	No	N/a
1.	Does the file show:			
1.1	the client's full name?	[ ]	[ ]	[ ]
1.2	the client's address and telephone number?	[ ]	[ ]	[ ]
1.3	the client's date of birth?	[ ]	[ ]	[ ]

Information on Good Cause for a Late Claim

		Yes	No	N/a
2.	Does the file show some understanding of:			
2.1	the date when the client first satisfied the qualifying conditions for the benefit which is the subject of the claim for backdating?	[ ]	[ ]	[ ]
2.2	the date when the client claimed that benefit?	[ ]	[ ]	[ ]
2.3	the client's reasons for failing to claim the benefit before that date?	[ ]	[ ]	[ ]
2.4	the earliest date to which these reasons apply?	[ ]	[ ]	[ ]
2.5	whether the reasons have applied continuously to the client's failure to claim from that date to the date of claim.	[ ]	[ ]	[ ]
2.6	the client's background, including his or her:			
2.6.1	state of health (physical and/or mental)	[ ]	[ ]	[ ]
2.6.2	experience of the benefits system	[ ]	[ ]	[ ]
2.6.3	education and literacy	[ ]	[ ]	[ ]
2.6.4	ability to speak and understand English	[ ]	[ ]	[ ]
2.6.5	responsibility for any dependants	[ ]	[ ]	[ ]
2.7	whether the client has ever made any enquiries about his/her entitlement to benefits, and, if so:		N/A	[ ]
2.7.1	to whom the enquiry was made?	[ ]	[ ]	[ ]
2.7.2	when?	[ ]	[ ]	[ ]

160

			Yes	No	N/a
	2.7.3	what the client was told?	[ ]	[ ]	[ ]
2.8		whether someone else made such enquiries on behalf of the client, and, if so:		N/A	[ ]
	2.8.1	what was that person's relationship to the client?	[ ]	[ ]	[ ]
	2.8.2	whether the person was acting in a formal capacity as the client's representative? (this includes appointees, solicitors, advice workers etc.)	[ ]	[ ]	[ ]

II Advising on this Information

		Yes	No	N/a
3.	Was the client advised whether s/he had 'good cause' for making a late claim?	[ ]	[ ]	[ ]
4.	Was the client advised of the amount of backdated benefit s/he may be able to recover? (such advice may be given as a sum in pounds or by reference to a number of weeks' entitlement).	[ ]	[ ]	[ ]
5.	Except in the case of Industrial Injuries Benefits, was the client advised that benefit could be backdated no more than 12 months?	[ ]	[ ]	[ ]
6.	Where the client may be entitled to backdated benefit, was s/he advised to how to claim it?	[ ]	[ ]	[ ]
7.	If backdated benefit has been refused to the client, was s/he advised to appeal?	[ ]	[ ]	[ ]

Costs and Funding of the Case

			Yes	No	N/a
8.		Did the caseworker advise the client in respect of the following matters:			
	8.1	the availability of green form advice and the extent and limits of green form funding?	[ ]	[ ]	[ ]
	8.2	whether the client will have to make a contribution to the case?	[ ]	[ ]	[ ]
	8.3	the costs to the client of taking the case to an appeal tribunal?	[ ]	[ ]	[ ]

Progress of the Case

			Yes	No	N/a
9.1		Was the client advised of how long the case is likely to take?	[ ]	[ ]	[ ]
	9.2	Is there an indication of the steps the caseworker has agreed to take and were these communicated to the client?	[ ]	[ ]	[ ]
	9.3	Is there an indication of the steps the caseworker has asked the client to take (if any)?	[ ]	[ ]	[ ]
	9.4	Was the client told when and in what form the next contact would take place?	[ ]	[ ]	[ ]
	9.5	Was the client advised as to more than one possible course of action?	[ ]	[ ]	[ ]
	9.6	Did the caseworker indicate the likely outcome of the case?	[ ]	[ ]	[ ]

9.7   Is there an indication that the client made an active choice on the caseworker's suggested mode of action?   [ ]   [ ]   [ ]

9.8   Has the caseworker noted down the reaction of the client to the decided plan of action (as a minimum, this should include the client's consent to the action going forward)?   [ ]   [ ]   [ ]

9.9   If the caseworker is not going to represent the client at any hearings, is there an indication that alternative sources of representation or assistance were explained to the client?   [ ]   [ ]   [ ]

9.10   Were any apparent queries from the client dealt with fully, promptly and politely?   [ ]   [ ]   [ ]

9.11   Did the caseworker deal with any evident emotional concerns of the client?   [ ]   [ ]   [ ]

9.12   If it appears likely that the other side will contact the client direct, was the client advised as to what s/he should do in the event that the other side does contact him/her?   [ ]   [ ]   [ ]

III   Further Action, Investigation and Research

The following criteria apply where the case extends beyond initial advice.

10.   If the client may be entitled to backdated benefit and this has been refused, was the Benefits Agency (or, if applicable, the Local Authority) asked for a written statement of the reasons for that decision?   [ ]   [ ]   [ ]

11.   Where all the following apply, was a written request for a review made within six weeks?   [ ]   [ ]   [ ]

     a)   the claim is for Housing Benefit and/or Council Tax Benefit;

     b)   the client has been advised to appeal;

     c)   s/he first consulted the caseworker within six weeks of being sent the Housing Benefit Officer's decision.

12.   Where all the following apply, was a written request for a further review made within 28 days?   [ ]   [ ]   [ ]

     a)   the claim is for Housing Benefit and/or Council Tax Benefit;

     b)   the client has been advised to appeal;

     c)   the decision to refuse backdated benefit was reviewed but not revised.

13.   Where all the following apply, was an appeal lodged within three months?   [ ]   [ ]   [ ]

     a)   the claim is for any of the other benefits to which this set of transaction criteria applies;

     b)   the client has been advised to appeal;

     c)   s/he first consulted the caseworker within three months of being sent the Adjudication Officer's decision.

		Yes	No	N/a

14. Did the letter notifying the Benefits Agency (or, if applicable, the Local Authority) of the appeal state the grounds for the appeal? [ ] [ ] [ ]

15. Was the client given an opportunity to read and comment on any written decisions which the caseworker may have received from the Benefits Agency, the Local Authority or the Independent Tribunals Service? [ ] [ ] [ ]

16. Where the client was not to be represented by the caseworker at an appeal hearing, were written submissions prepared for the client? [ ] [ ] [ ]

17. Where the client was not to be represented by the caseworker at an appeal hearing, was a letter sent to the client advising him/her of the main points to pursue at the hearing? [ ] [ ] [ ]

18. Where an appeal is to be made to the Social Security Commissioner: **N/A** [ ]

    18.1 was leave to appeal sought from the Chairman of the Social Security Appeal Tribunal (SSAT)? [ ] [ ] [ ]

    18.2 if the SSAT Chairman refused leave, was leave sought from the Commissioner within six weeks of being sent the refusal by the SSAT? [ ] [ ] [ ]

    18.3 if leave was granted by the SSAT Chairman, was notice of appeal sent to the Commissioner within six weeks of leave being granted? [ ] [ ] [ ]

19. Where the claim is for Housing Benefit and/or Council Tax Benefit and the Housing Benefit Review Board has reviewed but has not revised the Local Authority's determination, has the caseworker considered the possibility of Judicial Review? [ ] [ ] [ ]

Welfare Benefits—Notes to the Criteria

1. In particular CPAG's *National Welfare Benefits Handbook* (24th ed. 1994/95); CPAG's *Rights Guide to Non-Means Tested Benefits* (17th ed. 1994/95); *Disability Rights Handbook*; and '*The Law of Social Security*' by AI Ogus and EM Barendt (Butterworths, London 1988).

2. The transaction does not apply to situations where the apparent overpayment is due to the late payment of another benefit (other than income support) which reduces the level of the client's income support entitlement. Overpayments in such circumstances have to be repaid, regardless of whether or not the late payment was the fault of the client. See, *National Welfare Benefits Handbook*; 24th ed. (1994/95).

Chapter Seven:
Employment

This chapter contains three transactions which apply if the client is advised that they may have a case under that heading:

- Wrongful Dismissal;

- Unfair Dismissal;

- Redundancy.

The transactions are split into three main categories:

I.   Getting Information from the Client.

II. Advising On This Information.

III. Further Investigation, Research and Action.

The transactions are **preceded** by a general section of information to be collected in all dismissal/ redundancy cases.

The transaction criteria set out are based around a review of relevant files in the research project, as well as a survey of literature on employment law and general legal practice[1].

1. Dismissal/Redundancy—General Information

I Getting Information from the Client

Background Information

		Yes	No	N/a
1.	Does the lawyer know the client's:			
1.1	name	[ ]	[ ]	[ ]
1.2	date of birth;	[ ]	[ ]	[ ]
1.3	address and telephone number;	[ ]	[ ]	[ ]
1.4	relevant employment history?	[ ]	[ ]	[ ]
2.	Does the lawyer know:			
2.1	the name and address of the employer;	[ ]	[ ]	[ ]
2.2	the nature of the business;	[ ]	[ ]	[ ]
2.3	the size of the firm?	[ ]	[ ]	[ ]
3.	If it is unclear whether or not the client worked under a contract of employment or a contract for services, does the lawyer know:		N/A	[ ]
3.1	who bears responsibility for tax/N.I.;	[ ]	[ ]	[ ]
3.2	the extent of any benefits provided by the 'employer';	[ ]	[ ]	[ ]
3.3	whether there was a prohibition on working for other companies or individuals;	[ ]	[ ]	[ ]
3.4	whether the client was subject to control by the employer's disciplinary code;	[ ]	[ ]	[ ]
3.5	whether or not the client provides his own equipment, hires his own helpers, takes a degree of financial risk, or does anything else which would suggest s/he is an independent contractor?	[ ]	[ ]	[ ]
3.6	Does the lawyer appear to know whether there is any possibility of the contract being rendered illegal and unenforceable?	[ ]	[ ]	[ ]
3.7	Does the lawyer have, or has the lawyer asked for details of the client's terms of employment, including (where available) a copy of the client's contract/ written statement of terms and any variations (if applicable)?	[ ]	[ ]	[ ]
4.	Does the file demonstrate that the lawyer had an understanding of all the following:[2]			
4.1	date employment began;	[ ]	[ ]	[ ]
4.2	the date the last period of employment began;[3]	[ ]	[ ]	[ ]
4.3	if the client was previously employed on the same premises by different employers over a period of time, did the lawyer know the date of this previous employment?	[ ]	[ ]	[ ]

		Yes	No	N/a
4.4	scale or rate of remuneration and intervals of pay;	[ ]	[ ]	[ ]
4.5	hours of work/overtime;	[ ]	[ ]	[ ]
4.6	the period of notice required to determine the contract;	[ ]	[ ]	[ ]
4.7	job title and/or representation of the hierarchy within which the employee's job is located;	[ ]	[ ]	[ ]
4.8	disciplinary rules and grievance procedures;	[ ]	[ ]	[ ]
4.9	if contract is for a fixed term, the date when the contract expires;	[ ]	[ ]	[ ]
4.10	terms relating to holidays; holiday pay; sickness (including sickness pay); and pension schemes?	[ ]	[ ]	[ ]
4.11	Has the lawyer asked whether the client is a member of a union?	[ ]	[ ]	[ ]

2. Wrongful Dismissal   N/A   [   ]

I Getting Information From the Client

		Yes	No	N/a
5.	Does the file demonstrate that the lawyer has an understanding of the following:			
5.1	how and when the contract was terminated;	[ ]	[ ]	[ ]
5.2	a description of the incidents leading up to dismissal and the dismissal itself (including the names and addresses of any witnesses, and verbal reasons given for the dismissal);	[ ]	[ ]	[ ]
5.3	whether the client has tried to return to work;	[ ]	[ ]	[ ]
5.4	the minimum statutory notice period that the client is entitled to;[4]	[ ]	[ ]	[ ]
5.5	what (if anything) the client has done to mitigate his/her loss;	[ ]	[ ]	[ ]
5.6	whether the client is or was receiving any welfare benefits post-dismissal;	[ ]	[ ]	[ ]
5.7	whether wages/salary was paid in lieu of notice?[5]	[ ]	[ ]	[ ]
5.8	If it is likely that the client has been involved in a serious breach of the conditions of their employment (e.g. gross misconduct) has the possibility of the client's repudiatory breach been raised?	[ ]	[ ]	[ ]

II Advising on that Information

		Yes	No	N/a
6.	Has the client been advised on what they can claim for, including, in particular:			
6.1	the period of time over which wages can be claimed;	[ ]	[ ]	[ ]
6.2	other fringe benefits[6] (where relevant);	[ ]	[ ]	[ ]
6.3	accrued holiday pay;	[ ]	[ ]	[ ]
6.4	where notice if given would mean the client would have been continuously employed for more than 2 years, was there an approximate evaluation of the loss to the client of the chance of bringing a claim for unfair dismissal?	[ ]	[ ]	[ ]
6.5	the prospects of such a claim?	[ ]	[ ]	[ ]
7.	Has the client been advised of what would be deducted from such a claim? In particular:			
7.1	earnings from a subsequent job (if any);	[ ]	[ ]	[ ]
7.2	unemployment benefit/income support (if any);	[ ]	[ ]	[ ]
7.3	Has the lawyer explained the relative advantage of a negotiated settlement because of common law deductions?	[ ]	[ ]	[ ]

		Yes	No	N/a

| 7.4 | Has the client been advised of the role of ACAS? | [ ] | [ ] | [ ] |

| 7.5 | If it is apparent that the client has share option rights in the former employer company, has the lawyer considered with the client any advantage that might be secured if the client elects to treat the contract as continuing, and presents himself for work? | [ ] | [ ] | [ ] |

| 7.6 | Has the lawyer considered with the client the choice of venue (small claims court/county court/high court)? | [ ] | [ ] | [ ] |

| 7.7 | Has the lawyer advised the client that if, after dismissal, something comes to the employer's attention which would have justified the dismissal, that reason may then be relied on by the employer? | [ ] | [ ] | [ ] |

Costs and Funding of the Case

8. Is there an indication of advice given to the client regarding the costs of the case? In particular:

8.1	the availability of green form advice and civil legal aid:	[ ]	[ ]	[ ]
8.2	the limits and extent of green form funding.	[ ]	[ ]	[ ]
8.3	the effects of the solicitor's and statutory charge on any damages received;	[ ]	[ ]	[ ]
8.4	the costs to the client should the case be lost;	[ ]	[ ]	[ ]
8.5	if a certificate is granted, the nature and consequence of revocation and discharge of certificates;	[ ]	[ ]	[ ]
8.6	the duty to report changes of circumstance and address;	[ ]	[ ]	[ ]
8.7	whether or not the client will have to make a contribution to the case;	[ ]	[ ]	[ ]

Progress of the Case

9.1	Did the lawyer tell the client how long the claim might take to be concluded?	[ ]	[ ]	[ ]
9.2	Is there an indication of the steps the lawyer has agreed to take, and have these been communicated to the client?	[ ]	[ ]	[ ]
9.3	Is there an indication of the things the lawyer has asked the client to do and the time within which these steps must be completed?	[ ]	[ ]	[ ]
9.4	Has the client been told when and in what form the next contact with the lawyer will take place?	[ ]	[ ]	[ ]
9.5	Has the lawyer advised the client as to the possible courses of action?[7]	[ ]	[ ]	[ ]
9.6	Did the lawyer indicate the likely outcome of the case?	[ ]	[ ]	[ ]
9.7	Was the client given more than one choice of action from which they could choose?	[ ]	[ ]	[ ]

9.8 Has the lawyer noted down the reaction of the client to the decided plan of action (as a minimum, this should include the client's consent to the action going forward)?   [ ] [ ] [ ]

9.9 If the lawyer is not going to represent the client at any hearing, is there an indication that alternative sources of representation or assistance were explained to the client?   [ ] [ ] [ ]

9.10 Were any apparent queries from the client dealt with fully, promptly and politely?   [ ] [ ] [ ]

9.11 Did the lawyer deal with any evident emotional concerns of the client?   [ ] [ ] [ ]

9.12 Any contact with the other side should be explained. In particular, did the lawyer explain when the other side will be contacted and why?   [ ] [ ] [ ]

9.13 Did the lawyer advise the client as to what they should do in the event that the other side contacted them?   [ ] [ ] [ ]

9.14 Did the lawyer note the limitation period for the action in a prominent place on the file?   [ ] [ ] [ ]

10. Did the lawyer consider the client's entitlement to welfare benefits, in particular: **N/A** [ ]

10.1 if the client (and any partner of the client) is working less than 16 hours a week, has the lawyer advised the client as to the possibility of claiming income support?   [ ] [ ] [ ]

10.2 if the client (and any partner of the client) is working less than 16 hours, and it seems possible, from the above advice, that income support will be available, has the lawyer advised the client as to help they might receive with housing costs. In particular: **N/A** [ ]

  10.2.1 if they live in rented accommodation, how much of their rent should they be able to claim for;   [ ] [.] [ ]

  10.2.2 if they live in owner occupied accommodation, that they will only be able to claim for the interest on any mortgage payments;   [ ] [ ] [ ]

  10.2.3 if they live in owner occupied accommodation, claims for mortgage interest payments for the first sixteen weeks of an income support claim may be reduced;   [ ] [ ] [ ]

10.3 if the client (or their partner) is in paid work for more than 16 hours per week, and has at least one child under the age of 16 (or under 19 and in full time education) was the client advised of the possibility of claiming Family Credit?   [ ] [ ] [ ]

10.4 if the client is currently unemployed, did the lawyer advise them of the possibility of claiming Unemployment Benefit?[8]   [ ] [ ] [ ]

10.5 where the client is pregnant, and has ceased to work because of her pregnancy, has the lawyer advised her of the possibility of claiming statutory maternity pay or statutory maternity allowance?   [ ] [ ] [ ]

III Further Investigation, Research and Action

			Yes	No	N/a

11. Did the lawyer write to the client confirming in a comprehensible manner:

    11.1   the basis of the client's claim;   [ ] [ ] [ ]

    11.2   an outline of the advice given, including (where appropriate) areas of uncertainty/difficulty;   [ ] [ ] [ ]

    11.3   Was the client kept informed of significant developments with the other side?   [ ] [ ] [ ]

    11.4   Were any witnesses contacted and interviewed if possible?   [ ] [ ] [ ]

    11.5   Was the client given an opportunity to read any witness statements and reports, and to comment upon these?   [ ] [ ] [ ]

    11.6   Were letters to the client comprehensible?   [ ] [ ] [ ]

    11.7   If the client does not have a written statement of reasons, did the lawyer seek a written statement of reasons from the employer?   [ ] [ ] [ ]

    11.8   Did the lawyer contact the employer informing them of the basis of the client's claim, and outlining what damages and/or remedies are sought?   [ ] [ ] [ ]

3. Unfair Dismissal

I Getting Information from the Client

			Yes	No	N/a
12.	Does the file demonstrate that the lawyer has dealt with the following:				
	Whether the client satisfies eligibility requirements; i.e.:				
	12.1	is an employee;	[ ]	[ ]	[ ]
	12.2	is below the normal retiring age for employees in the particular undertaking;	[ ]	[ ]	[ ]
	12.3	has been in 2 years continuous employment;	[ ]	[ ]	[ ]
	12.4	has been dismissed;[9]	[ ]	[ ]	[ ]
	12.5	does not ordinarily work outside Great Britain;	[ ]	[ ]	[ ]
	12.6	is not a member of an excluded class of employee?[10]	[ ]	[ ]	[ ]
	12.7	how and when the contract was terminated?	[ ]	[ ]	[ ]
	12.8	the Effective Date of Termination "EDT"?	[ ]	[ ]	[ ]
13.	Has the lawyer raised the following matters:				
	13.1	the possibility of the continuous employment term being previously broken?	[ ]	[ ]	[ ]
	13.2	whether the client has at any stage been absent because of strikes/lockouts, and if so for how long?	[ ]	[ ]	[ ]
	13.3	the possibility the client has effectively contracted out of his/her rights?[11]	[ ]	[ ]	[ ]
	13.4	if it is likely that the client has been involved in a serious breach of the conditions of their employment (e.g. gross misconduct) has the possibility of the client's repudiatory breach been raised?	[ ]	[ ]	[ ]
	13.5	whether there is any possibility of the contract of employment being rendered illegal or unenforceable.	[ ]	[ ]	[ ]
14.	Has the lawyer asked the client:				
	14.1	for the employers written statement of reasons for dismissal?	[ ]	[ ]	[ ]
	14.2	what was the verbal reason given (if any) at the time of dismissal and whether there were any witnesses to the dismissal or any incidents connected with the dismissal?	[ ]	[ ]	[ ]
15.	If the client is a member of a trades union, does the lawyer have an understanding of:		N/A	[ ]
	15.1	whether there is any evidence to suggest the dismissal may be union-related?	[ ]	[ ]	[ ]

		Yes	No	N/A

15.2   if the dismissal appears to be the result of industrial action, whether all employees taking part in the dispute were dismissed, and if any have been given offers of re-engagement?   [ ]   [ ]   [ ]

16.   If dismissed for misconduct, does the lawyer have an understanding of: **N/A**   [ ]

  16.1   the nature of the misconduct?   [ ]   [ ]   [ ]

  16.2   whether this was an isolated incident?   [ ]   [ ]   [ ]

  16.3   the history of previous disciplinary measures taken against the client[12]   [ ]   [ ]   [ ]

17.   If dismissed because of 'redundancy', does the lawyer have an understanding of: **N/A**   [ ]

  17.1   whether the selection was in contravention of any customary arrangements or agreed procedures?   [ ]   [ ]   [ ]

  17.2   whether the selection criteria were applied objectively?   [ ]   [ ]   [ ]

  17.3   whether reasonable warning was given of impending redundancies?   [ ]   [ ]   [ ]

  17.4   whether any volunteers were asked for?   [ ]   [ ]   [ ]

  17.5   whether the union,(or if none, the workforce) was consulted regarding selection criteria for redundancy?   [ ]   [ ]   [ ]

  17.6   whether alternative employment within the firm was considered?   [ ]   [ ]   [ ]

  17.7   whether the employer has offered to renew the contract or to re-engage the employee?   [ ]   [ ]   [ ]

18.   If dismissed because of pregnancy, does the lawyer have an understanding of: **N/A**   [ ]

  18.1   whether the client was incapable of adequately doing the work she was employed to do because of pregnancy, or would have become so by the EDT?   [ ]   [ ]   [ ]

  18.2   whether continued employment in the particular position would have involved the contravention of a duty or restriction imposed by or under any enactment?   [ ]   [ ]   [ ]

  18.3   whether there was a suitable available vacancy, and if so was it offered to her?   [ ]   [ ]   [ ]

19.   If dismissed because of lack of capability, does the lawyer have an understanding of: **N/A**   [ ]

  19.1   the nature of the 'incapability'?   [ ]   [ ]   [ ]

  19.2   the nature of the dismissal procedure?   [ ]   [ ]   [ ]

20.   If dismissed because of a reason connected with a transfer of the employer's undertaking (and where the EDT falls after the date of transfer), does the lawyer have an understanding of: **N/A**   [ ]

  20.1   name and address of transferee?   [ ]   [ ]   [ ]

		Yes	No	N/A

20.2   whether the recognised trades union (or the workforce, if no trades union) was consulted?   [ ]   [ ]   [ ]

20.3   whether transferee has changed the client's terms of employment?   [ ]   [ ]   [ ]

20.4   any alleged economic, technical or organisational reason that it is maintained will entail a change in the workforce?   [ ]   [ ]   [ ]

II   Advising on that Information

21.   Has the client been advised of how the basic award will be calculated in unfair dismissal claims?   [ ]   [ ]   [ ]

22.   Has the client been advised of the role of ACAS?   [ ]   [ ]   [ ]

23.   Has the client been advised of how a further compensatory award will be calculated in unfair dismissal claims? In particular: **N/A** [ ]

23.1   immediate loss of earnings from date of dismissal to date of hearing   [ ]   [ ]   [ ]

23.2   future loss of earnings;   [ ]   [ ]   [ ]

23.3   any other fringe benefits;   [ ]   [ ]   [ ]

23.4   loss of statutory protection;   [ ]   [ ]   [ ]

23.5   expenses involved in looking for work.   [ ]   [ ]   [ ]

24.   Has the client been advised of the possibility of deductions being made from their award for, in particular: **N/A** [ ]

24.1   contributory fault (if any);   [ ]   [ ]   [ ]

24.2   payments made at the time of dismissal (if any);   [ ]   [ ]   [ ]

24.3   unreasonable refusal of reinstatement (if any);   [ ]   [ ]   [ ]

24.4   deduction where the EDT falls after client's 64th birthday;   [ ]   [ ]   [ ]

24.5   failure to mitigate (if any)?   [ ]   [ ]   [ ]

25.   Has the client been advised of the likely impact of an award or settlement on receipt of benefits?   [ ]   [ ]   [ ]

26.   Where the client has already received some payments from their former employer (e.g. salary in lieu of notice/ex gratia payments) has the lawyer explained the benefits of a negotiated settlement because of, for example, recoupment regulations?   [ ]   [ ]   [ ]

27.   Has the tribunal procedure been explained to the client, including the range of possible orders an Industrial Tribunal may make?[13]   [ ]   [ ]   [ ]

28.   Has the relevant time limit for complaint to the Industrial Tribunal been noted in a prominent place on the file?   [ ]   [ ]   [ ]

29.   Has the relevant time limit for complaint to the Industrial Tribunal been explained to the client?[14]   [ ]   [ ]   [ ]

Costs and Funding of the Case

		Yes	No	N/A

30. Is there an indication of advice given to the client regarding the costs and funding of the case. In particular:

		Yes	No	N/A
30.1	the availability of green form advice and the limits and extent of green form funding;	[ ]	[ ]	[ ]
30.2	whether or not the client will have to make a contribution to the case;	[ ]	[ ]	[ ]
30.3	the effects of the solicitor's charge on any damages received;	[ ]	[ ]	[ ]
30.4	the costs to the client of taking a case to the Industrial Tribunal	[ ]	[ ]	[ ]

Progress of the Case

		Yes	No	N/A
31.1	Did the lawyer tell the client how long the claim might take to be concluded?	[ ]	[ ]	[ ]
31.2	Is there a firm indication of the steps the lawyer has agreed to take, and have these been communicated to the client?	[ ]	[ ]	[ ]
31.3	Is there a firm indication of the things the lawyer has asked the client to do and of the time within which these steps must be completed?	[ ]	[ ]	[ ]
31.4	Has the client been told when and in what form the next contact will take place?	[ ]	[ ]	[ ]
31.5	Was the client given more than one choice of action from which they could choose?[7]	[ ]	[ ]	[ ]
31.6	Did the lawyer indicate to the client the prospects of success for their claim?	[ ]	[ ]	[ ]
31.7	Is there an indication that the client made an active choice on the lawyer's suggested mode of action?	[ ]	[ ]	[ ]
31.8	Has the lawyer noted down the reaction of the client to the decided plan of action (as a minimum, this should include the client's consent to the action going forward)?	[ ]	[ ]	[ ]
31.9	If the lawyer is not going to represent the client at any hearing, is there an indication that alternative sources of representation or assistance were explained to the client?	[ ]	[ ]	[ ]
31.10	Were any apparent queries from the client dealt with fully, promptly and politely?	[ ]	[ ]	[ ]
31.11	Did the lawyer deal with any evident emotional concerns of the client?			
31.12	Any contact with the other side should be explained. In particular, did the lawyer explain when the other side will be contacted and why?	[ ]	[ ]	[ ]
31.13	Did the lawyer advise the client as to what they should do in the event that the other side contacted them?	[ ]	[ ]	[ ]

32. Did the lawyer consider the client's entitlement to welfare benefits? In particular:

32.1   if the client (and any partner of the client) is working less than 16 hours a week, has the lawyer advised the client as to the possibility of claiming income support?   [ ]   [ ]   [ ]

32.2   if the client (and any partner of the client) is working less than 16 hours, and it seems possible, from the above advice, that income support will be available, has the lawyer advised the client as to help they might receive with housing costs. In particular: **N/A**   [ ]

32.2.1   if they live in rented accommodation, how much of their rent they should be able to claim for;   [ ]   [ ]   [ ]

32.2.2   if they live in owner occupied accommodation, that they will only be able to claim for the interest on any mortgage payments;   [ ]   [ ]   [ ]

32.2.3   if they live in owner occupied accommodation that claims for mortgage interest payments for the first sixteen weeks of an income support claim may be reduced;   [ ]   [ ]   [ ]

32.3   if the client (or their partner) is in paid work for more than 16 hours per week, and has at least one child under the age of 16 (or under 19 and in full time education) was the client advised of the possibility of claiming Family Credit?   [ ]   [ ]   [ ]

32.4   if the client is currently unemployed, did the lawyer advise them of the possibility of claiming Unemployment Benefit?[8]   [ ]   [ ]   [ ]

32.5   where the client is pregnant, and has ceased to work because of her pregnancy, has the lawyer advised her of the possibility of claiming statutory maternity pay or statutory maternity allowance?   [ ]   [ ]   [ ]

III Further Investigation, Research and Action

33. Did the lawyer write to the client confirming in a comprehensible manner:

33.1   the basis of the client's claim?   [ ]   [ ]   [ ]

33.2   an outline of the advice given, including (where appropriate) areas of uncertainty/difficulty?   [ ]   [ ]   [ ]

33.3   Was the client kept informed of significant developments with the other side?   [ ]   [ ]   [ ]

33.4   Were any witnesses contacted and interviewed if possible?   [ ]   [ ]   [ ]

33.5   Was the client given an opportunity to read any witness statements and reports, and to comment upon these?   [ ]   [ ]   [ ]

33.6   Were letters to the client comprehensible?   [ ]   [ ]   [ ]

33.7   If the client does not have these, did the lawyer seek a written statement of reasons from the employer?   [ ]   [ ]   [ ]

		Yes	No	N/a

33.8   Did the lawyer contact the employer explaining the basis of the client's claim, and outlining what damages and/or remedies are sought?   [ ]   [ ]   [ ]

33.9   Where the client will not be represented by the lawyer, are written submissions prepared for the client?   [ ]   [ ]   [ ]

33.10   Where the client will not be represented by the lawyer, was a letter sent to the client advising them of the main points to pursue at an appeal hearing?   [ ]   [ ]   [ ]

4 REDUNDANCY

I Getting Information from the Client

34. Does the file demonstrate that the lawyer has dealt with whether the client satisfies eligibility requirements? In particular:

34.1 the client is an employee; [ ] [ ] [ ]

34.2 the client is below the normal retiring age for employees in the particular undertaking; [ ] [ ] [ ]

34.3 the client has been in 2 years continuous employment with the last employer; [ ] [ ] [ ]

34.4 the client does not ordinarily work outside Great Britain; [ ] [ ] [ ]

34.5 the client is not a member of an excluded class of employees;[15] [ ] [ ] [ ]

34.6 that the client has been dismissed by reason of redundancy;[16] [ ] [ ] [ ]

34.7 what the 'effective date of termination' was (EDT). [ ] [ ] [ ]

35. Has the lawyer raised the following matters:

35.1 whether the client has at any stage been absent because of strikes/lockouts, and if so for how long? [ ] [ ] [ ]

35.2 the possibility of continuity of employment being preserved on previous change of employer (if relevant); [ ] [ ] [ ]

35.3 the possibility the client has effectively contracted out of his/her rights?[17] [ ] [ ] [ ]

35.4 if it is likely that the client has been involved in a serious breach of the conditions of their employment (e.g. gross misconduct) has the possibility of the client's repudiatory breach been raised? [ ] [ ] [ ]

36. Has the lawyer asked the client:

36.1 for the employer's written statement of reasons for dismissal? [ ] [ ] [ ]

36.2 what was the verbal reason given (if any) at the time of dismissal and were there any witnesses? [ ] [ ] [ ]

36.3 if the client is a member of a trades union, does the lawyer have an understanding of: N/A [ ]

36.4 whether there is any evidence to suggest the redundancy may be union related? [ ] [ ] [ ]

36.5 if the redundancy appears to be the result of industrial action, whether all employees taking part in the dispute were dismissed, and if any have been given offers of re-engagement? [ ] [ ] [ ]

37.   Does the lawyer have an understanding of:

    37.1   whether the client's selection was in contravention of a customary arrangement or agreed procedure;   [   ]   [   ]   [   ]

    37.2   were the selection criteria applied objectively;   [   ]   [   ]   [   ]

    37.3   whether reasonable warning was given of impending redundancies;   [   ]   [   ]   [   ]

    37.4   whether the union, (or if none, the workforce) was consulted regarding selection criteria;   [   ]   [   ]   [   ]

    37.5   whether alternative employment within the firm was considered;   [   ]   [   ]   [   ]

    37.6   whether the employer has offered to renew the contract or to re-engage the employee;   [   ]   [   ]   [   ]

    37.7   the terms of any proposed re-engagement, and whether they will involve any additional burdens for the employee (e.g. commuting distance, costs, etc);   [   ]   [   ]   [   ]

    37.8   the financial position of the employer;   [   ]   [   ]   [   ]

    37.9   whether the client has been allowed reasonable time off work to look for alternative employment?   [   ]   [   ]   [   ]

II   Advising on that Information

    38.1   Was the client advised as to how any redundancy payment they can claim will be calculated?   [   ]   [   ]   [   ]

    38.2   Where the employer has failed to comply with the union consultation requirements has the possibility of a Protective Award been raised?   [   ]   [   ]   [   ]

    38.3   In Union related cases, has the possibility of a Special Award/Interim Relief been raised?   [   ]   [   ]   [   ]

Costs and Funding of the Case

39.   Is there an indication of advice given to the client regarding the costs and funding of the case. In particular:

    39.1   the availability of green form advice and the limits and extent of green form funding;   [   ]   [   ]   [   ]

    39.2   whether or not the client will have to make a contribution to the case;   [   ]   [   ]   [   ]

    39.3   the effects of the solicitor's charge on any damages received;   [   ]   [   ]   [   ]

    39.4   the costs to the client of taking the case to an Industrial Tribunal;   [   ]   [   ]   [   ]

Progress of the Case

    40.1   Did the lawyer tell the client how long the claim might take to be concluded?   [   ]   [   ]   [   ]

    40.2   Is there a firm indication of the steps the lawyer has agreed to take, and have these been communicated to the client?   [   ]   [   ]   [   ]

		Yes	No	N/A

40.3 Is there a firm indication of the things the lawyer has asked the client to do and the time within which these steps must be completed? [ ] [ ] [ ]

40.4 Has the client been told when and in what form the next contact will take place? [ ] [ ] [ ]

40.5 Has the lawyer advised the client as to more than one possible course of action?[7] [ ] [ ] [ ]

40.6 Did the lawyer indicate the likely outcome of the case? [ ] [ ] [ ]

40.7 Is there an indication that the client made an active choice on the lawyers suggested mode of action? [ ] [ ] [ ]

40.8 Has the lawyer noted down the reaction of the client to the decided plan of action (as a minimum, this should include the client's consent to the action going forward)? [ ] [ ] [ ]

40.9 If the lawyer is not going to represent the client at any hearing, is there an indication that alternative sources of representation or assistance were explained to the client? [ ] [ ] [ ]

40.10 Were any apparent queries from the client dealt with fully, promptly and politely? [ ] [ ] [ ]

40.11 Did the lawyer deal with any evident emotional concerns of the client? [ ] [ ] [ ]

40.12 Any contact with the other side should be explained. In particular, did the lawyer explain when the other side will be contacted and why? [ ] [ ] [ ]

40.13 Did the lawyer advise the client as to what they should do in the event that the other side contacts them? [ ] [ ] [ ]

41. Did the lawyer consider the client's entitlement to welfare benefits, in particular:

41.1 if the client is working less than 16 hours a week, has the lawyer advised the client as to the possibility of claiming income support? [ ] [ ] [ ]

41.2 if the client is working less than 16 hours, and it seems possible, from the above advice, that income support will be available, has the lawyer advised the client as to help they might receive with housing costs. In particular: N/A [ ]

    41.2.1 if they live in rented accommodation, how much of their rent they should be able to claim for; [ ] [ ] [ ]

    41.2.2 if they live in owner occupied accommodation, that they will only be able to claim for the interest on any mortgage payments; [ ] [ ] [ ]

    41.2.3 if they live in owner occupied accommodation that claims for mortgage interest payments for the first sixteen weeks of an income support claim may be reduced; [ ] [ ] [ ]

41.3 if the client is in paid work for more than 16 hours per week, and has at least one child under the age of 16 (or under 19 and in full time education) was the client advised of the possibility of claiming Family Credit? [ ] [ ] [ ]

		Yes	No	N/A

41.4   if the client is currently unemployed, did the lawyer advise them of the possibility of claiming Unemployment Benefit?[8]   [ ]   [ ]   [ ]

41.5   where the client is pregnant, and has ceased to work because of her pregnancy, has the lawyer advised her of the possibility of claiming statutory maternity pay or statutory maternity allowance?   [ ]   [ ]   [ ]

III Further Action, Investigation and Research

42.   Did the lawyer write to the client confirming in a comprehensible manner:

42.1   the basis of the client's claim;   [ ]   [ ]   [ ]

42.2   an outline of the advice given, including (where appropriate) areas of uncertainty/difficulty?   [ ]   [ ]   [ ]

42.3   Was the client kept informed of significant developments with the other side?   [ ]   [ ]   [ ]

42.4   Were any witnesses contacted and interviewed if possible?   [ ]   [ ]   [ ]

42.5   Was the client given an opportunity to read any witness statements and reports, and to comment upon these?   [ ]   [ ]   [ ]

42.6   Were letters to the client comprehensible?   [ ]   [ ]   [ ]

42.7   Has the time limit for complaint to the Tribunal (6 months from the client's EDT) been noted in a prominent position on the file and explained to the client?[18]   [ ]   [ ]   [ ]

42.8   If the client does not have these, did the lawyer seek a written statement of reasons from the employer?   [ ]   [ ]   [ ]

42.9   Did the lawyer contact the employer explaining the basis of the client's claim, and outlining what damages and/or remedies are sought?   [ ]   [ ]   [ ]

42.10   Where the client will not be represented by the lawyer, are written submissions prepared for the client?   [ ]   [ ]   [ ]

42.11   Where the client will not be represented by the lawyer, was a letter sent to the client advising them of the main points to pursue at an appeal hearing?   [ ]   [ ]   [ ]

Employment—Notes to the Criteria

1. In particular, Tolley's Employment Handbook (5th Edition, 1988).

2. This should extend beyond any written terms describing the terms and dates of a client's employment to what actually occurred in practice.

3. This question is intended to cover situations where there has been a break in the client's employment with the employer against who the claim is being made.

4. If the client has been continuously employed for less than 2 years but more than one month then they are entitled to one week's notice. If the client has been employed for 2 years or more then the client is entitled to one weeks notice for each year worked up to a maximum of 12 weeks.

5. i.e. Any payments made by the employer either during or after the dismissal, with the employer representing that the client would have earned the money had s/he worked out the proper notice period.

6. These could include: company car, luncheon vouchers, private health insurance, pension scheme, discount on goods, life cover, death in service benefits and accommodation.

7. i.e. on the different options for resolving the matter.

8. This is "not applicable" if the client is unemployed and already in receipt of unemployment benefit.

9. i.e. Contract terminated by employer with or without notice, or fixed term contract and not renewed under that contract, or contract terminated by client with or without notice by way of constructive dismissal.

10. In unfair dismissal cases the following are excluded:

    a. members of the armed forces

    b. police service

    c. share fisherman.

11. This can occur where the client has worked under contract for a fixed term of a year or more, and the dismissal consists only of the expiry of the fixed term. Furthermore the client had to agree in writing, before that expiry date, to exclude the right to claim for unfair dismissal.

12. e.g. Warnings, suspensions etc.

13. The relief available is reinstatement, re-engagement, compensation orders and interim relief.

14. i.e. 3 months from the clients EDT.

15. In redundancy cases the following are excluded:

    a. crown employees

    b. certain domestic servants.

    c. share fisherman

16. i.e. The employer has ceased, or intends to cease to carry on the business for the purposes for which the client was so employed, or has ceased, or intends to cease to carry on the business in the place where the client was so employed; or the requirement for the client to carry out work of a particular kind, or to do so in the place where he was so employed, has ceased or diminished or is expected to cease or diminish.

17. This may occur where the client has worked under a contract for a fixed term of 2 years or more, and the dismissal consists only of the expiry of that term. Furthermore the client must have agreed in writing to exclude the right to a redundancy payment before the expiry date.

18. The time limit must be noted on the file in a position which is easily visible. Reference to the time limit in an attendance note/letter is not sufficient.

Chapter Eight:
Immigration/Nationality

The criteria in this chapter cover two transactions:

- Advising clients seeking political asylum;
- Advising clients with a partner seeking leave to enter and remain in the U.K.

The transactions are divided into three sections:

I.   Getting Information from the Client

II.   Advising on that Information

III. Further Investigation, Research and Action

The transaction criteria are based upon a review of legal aid files as well as relevant literature on immigration law and practice[1,2].

1. Advising Clients Seeking Political Asylum

These criteria apply to cases where the client seeks political asylum from their country of origin because of fear of persecution. They have been based in particular on the ILPA guide to best practice[2].

I. Getting Information from the Client

Questions relating to the client and the client's social background

1. Does the file show some understanding of the following in relation to the client:

		Yes	No	N/a
1.1	full name (plus any aliases, if applicable)?	[ ]	[ ]	[ ]
1.2	address, telephone number and any other permanent contact number/address?	[ ]	[ ]	[ ]
1.3	nationality?	[ ]	[ ]	[ ]
1.4	place and date of birth?	[ ]	[ ]	[ ]
1.5	history of residences to date?	[ ]	[ ]	[ ]
1.6	ownership of property?	[ ]	[ ]	[ ]
1.7	education and work history to date?	[ ]	[ ]	[ ]
1.8	religion, ethnic group and language?	[ ]	[ ]	[ ]
1.9	details of the client's family[3]?	[ ]	[ ]	[ ]

Questions relating to processing of claims to date

2. Does the file show some understanding of reasons for having made or wanting to make a claim or asylum in the UK, particularly:

		Yes	No	N/a
2.1	whether there has been a claim for political asylum since arrival?	[ ]	[ ]	[ ]
2.2	if so, is there an understanding of:			
2.2.1	when and how such a claim was made?	[ ]	[ ]	[ ]
2.2.2	what was said (or copies of what was written)?	[ ]	[ ]	[ ]
2.3	whether a Political Asylum Questionnaire (PAQ) has been completed?	[ ]	[ ]	[ ]
2.4	if a PAQ was completed, is it known whether it was completed with an adviser?	[ ]	[ ]	[ ]
2.5	the client's current immigration status[4] and any appeal rights?	[ ]	[ ]	[ ]
2.6	whether the client currently has to report because of temporary admission or release conditions	[ ]	[ ]	[ ]
2.7	whether the client has been refused the opportunity to claim political asylum in the UK in the past?	[ ]	[ ]	[ ]

			Yes	No	N/a
2.8		whether the client has an interview date in relation to his or her claim for political asylum and, if so, the date?	[ ]	[ ]	[ ]

Questions relating to the client's arrival in the UK

3. Does the file show an understanding of:

			Yes	No	N/a
3.1		the client's date of arrival in UK?	[ ]	[ ]	[ ]
3.2		how the client obtained their travel documents, i.e.:			
	3.2.1	any exit visa?	[ ]	[ ]	[ ]
	3.2.2	any passport and in whose name the passport is/was?	[ ]	[ ]	[ ]
3.3		if entry required a visa:		N/A	[ ]
	3.3.1	how the client obtained a visa for the UK	[ ]	[ ]	[ ]
	3.3.2	what type of visa was obtained?	[ ]	[ ]	[ ]
	3.3.3	if there were any problems obtaining the visa, what was said to obtain the visa and why?	[ ]	[ ]	[ ]
3.4		If the client had any difficulties leaving his or her country, what they were (e.g. having to use bribes etc.)?	[ ]	[ ]	[ ]
3.5		mode of transport to the UK?	[ ]	[ ]	[ ]
3.6		how and where the ticket(s) were purchased?	[ ]	[ ]	[ ]
3.7		all countries travelled through coming to the UK and why no claim for asylum was made in each?	[ ]	[ ]	[ ]
3.8		time of arrival in the UK?	[ ]	[ ]	[ ]
3.9		the client's mental and physical state on entering the country[5]	[ ]	[ ]	[ ]

Clients Questioned on Entry

			Yes	No	N/a
4.		If the client was questioned on entry, does the file show some understanding of:		N/A	[ ]
	4.1	who was the client questioned by and for how long?	[ ]	[ ]	[ ]
	4.2	whether the client was also searched?	[ ]	[ ]	[ ]
	4.3	whether any documents were taken?	[ ]	[ ]	[ ]
	4.4	whether anything about the process was explained to the client at the time?	[ ]	[ ]	[ ]
	4.5	if needed, whether there was an adequate interpreter present?	[ ]	[ ]	[ ]
	4.6	the client's view of the immigration officer's behaviour?	[ ]	[ ]	[ ]

		Yes	No	N/a

4.7 whether the client's relatives or friends came to meet the client at the airport, and whether the client was told of their presence [ ] [ ] [ ]

4.8 what the client said on arrival and why? [ ] [ ] [ ]

4.9 whether the client was pressured to speak by fear/threats of detention? [ ] [ ] [ ]

4.10 whether the client claimed asylum, and, if not, why? [ ] [ ] [ ]

4.11 whether the client was happy that what the client said was accurately recorded and, if not, why? [ ] [ ] [ ]

4.12 whether the client had a representative present? [ ] [ ] [ ]

4.13 whether what the client said was read back to the client for checking? [ ] [ ] [ ]

4.14 whether the client signed a statement? [ ] [ ] [ ]

Questions relating to Fear of Persecution

5. Does the file show an understanding of:

5.1 what the client is afraid of? [ ] [ ] [ ]

5.2 when this fear arose? [ ] [ ] [ ]

Political opinion

6. Where the client fears persecution on the basis of political opinion, does the file show some understanding of the client's political beliefs/involvement, including[6]; **N/A** [ ]

6.1 the nature of the political beliefs and the reason for holding them? [ ] [ ] [ ]

6.2 the circumstances in which the client acquired those beliefs? [ ] [ ] [ ]

6.3 whether the client is a member or sympathiser of specific political parties/associations[7] or has refused membership of a ruling party? [ ] [ ] [ ]

6.4 if the client is willing to provide the information, the structure of the party or association of which client is a member and full names of those with whom client worked? [ ] [ ] [ ]

6.5 if the client is a member of any such organisations; political posts held, functions performed and political activities engaged in by the client? [ ] [ ] [ ]

6.6 any incidents with the authorities, including (where applicable) demonstrations [ ] [ ] [ ]

Religion

7. Where the client fears persecution on the basis of religion, does the file show some understanding of the client's religious beliefs/involvement, including: **N/A** [ ]

7.1 the nature of the religious beliefs? [ ] [ ] [ ]

7.2 the circumstances in which the client acquired those beliefs? [ ] [ ] [ ]

		Yes	No	N/a

7.3   if the client is a member of any religious organisations; posts held, functions performed and activities engaged in by the client?   [ ]   [ ]   [ ]

7.4   any incidents with the authorities, including (where applicable) demonstrations?   [ ]   [ ]   [ ]

7.5   whether the client has continued to worship in the UK?   [ ]   [ ]   [ ]

Race and Nationality

8.   Where the client fears persecution on the basis of race and/or nationality, does the file show some understanding of the client's race/nationality, including: N/A   [ ]

8.1   a description of race/nationality, including (where appropriate) any tribe or sub-clan?   [ ]   [ ]   [ ]

8.2   any activities which associated the client with their nationality or racial group?   [ ]   [ ]   [ ]

8.3   any incidents with the authorities, including (where applicable) demonstrations?   [ ]   [ ]   [ ]

Social Group

9.   Where the client fears persecution on the basis of social group, does the file show some understanding of the client's social group, including: N/A   [ ]

9.1   the nature of the social group and the reason for the client being within that group?   [ ]   [ ]   [ ]

9.2   the circumstances surrounding the client's membership of that group?   [ ]   [ ]   [ ]

9.3   whether the client is a member or sympathiser of any organisation connected with that group?   [ ]   [ ]   [ ]

9.4   if the client is willing to provide the information, structure of the social group of which client is a member and full names of those with whom client worked   [ ]   [ ]   [ ]

9.5   if the client is a member of any organisations connected with that group, posts held, functions performed and activities engaged in by the client?   [ ]   [ ]   [ ]

9.6   any incidents with the authorities, including (where applicable) demonstrations   [ ]   [ ]   [ ]

The Effects of Persecution

10.   Does the file show some understanding of the effect of persecution/fear of persecution on the client, in particular:

10.1   where applicable, details of the following:

10.1.1   harassment?   [ ]   [ ]   [ ]

	Yes	No	N/a
10.1.2 restriction on activities	[ ]	[ ]	[ ]
10.1.3 searches?	[ ]	[ ]	[ ]
10.1.4 periods in hiding?	[ ]	[ ]	[ ]
10.1.5 discrimination?	[ ]	[ ]	[ ]
10.2 where the client has been detained or arrested, the names of prisons/ detention centres?	[ ]	[ ]	[ ]
10.3 where applicable, details of any torture or ill-treatment the client has suffered	[ ]	[ ]	[ ]
10.4 where the client has been tried, convicted and/or punished, an understanding of the basis for such persecution/punishment?	[ ]	[ ]	[ ]
10.5 where applicable, whether the client ever received medical treatment of any type as a result of his/her treatment by the authorities?	[ ]	[ ]	[ ]
10.6 the effect on education and/or job?	[ ]	[ ]	[ ]
10.7 the effect of political activity on property and extended family?	[ ]	[ ]	[ ]
11. Does the file show some understanding of whether there is any political involvement of the client's extended family, and (if so) have any been recognised as refugees in this country or elsewhere?	[ ]	[ ]	[ ]
12. Does the file show some understanding of			
12.1 why it was not reasonable to escape from persecution in country of origin?	[ ]	[ ]	[ ]
12.2 if client has been out of country of origin since start of persecution, whether the client made a claim for political asylum or sought protection?	[ ]	[ ]	[ ]
12.2.1 if so, details of claim and why the client left?	[ ]	[ ]	[ ]
12.2.2 if not, why no claim was made in that country?	[ ]	[ ]	[ ]
12.3 what the client believes would happen if the client were returned?	[ ]	[ ]	[ ]

Questions relating to supporting documentation

	Yes	No	N/a
13. Does the file show that the lawyer has asked for and/or received any documents that the client has relating to the flight and political activities[8]	[ ]	[ ]	[ ]

II. Advising on this Information

Advice given to the client, and recorded on the file (either in attendance notes or in confirmatory letters to the client), should cover the following. Questions 14–23 apply only to clients who are to make an application for asylum. Question 24 considers refusals and appeals.

	Yes	No	N/a
14. Was the client advised of whether the claim is likely to be successful[9]	[ ]	[ ]	[ ]

		Yes	No	N/a

15. Was the client advised of their status during processing of the claim, in particular:

    15.1   that the client can not be returned to the country of origin during the currency of the claim for asylum?   [ ]   [ ]   [ ]

    15.2   that there is no entitlement to family reunion whilst the claim is processed[10]?   [ ]   [ ]   [ ]

16. Was the client advised of the consequences of a successful claim[11]   [ ]   [ ]   [ ]

17. Was the client advised of the consequences of an unsuccessful claim[12]   [ ]   [ ]   [ ]

18. If the client either does not have leave to enter the country, is being treated as an illegal entrant, and/or has been served with a notice of intention to deport: **N/A**   [ ]

    18.1   was the client advised that they are liable to be detained?   [ ]   [ ]   [ ]

    18.2   were the possibilities of being released if detained explained?   [ ]   [ ]   [ ]

19. Has the client been advised of the possibility that they may be granted exceptional leave to remain rather than refugee status?   [ ]   [ ]   [ ]

20. Has the client been advised of the effect on their status should they be granted refugee status or exceptional leave to remain (e.g. in relation to their ability to work, gain housing, education, and claim social security)?   [ ]   [ ]   [ ]

21. Has the client been advised of the likely possibility of being able to settle permanently in this country and how long it will be before they could settle?   [ ]   [ ]   [ ]

22. Was the client advised of the client's entitlement to income support, housing benefit, and (after six months) to work?   [ ]   [ ]   [ ]

23. Has the client been advised of the possibility of claiming urgent payment under income support?   [ ]   [ ]   [ ]

Refusals and Appeals

24. If the client's application for refugee status has been refused (here a refusal includes circumstances where the client has only been granted exceptional leave to remain):   **N/A**   [ ]

    24.1   has the lawyer advised the client on whether or not to appeal?   [ ]   [ ]   [ ]

    24.2   has the lawyer advised the client of what will happen to the client should they not appeal?   [ ]   [ ]   [ ]

    24.3   has the client been advised of the time limits for such an appeal?   [ ]   [ ]   [ ]

    24.4   unless the client clearly does not wish to appeal, has the limitation period for an appeal been noted in a prominent place upon the file?   [ ]   [ ]   [ ]

Costs and Funding of the Case

25. Is there an indication of the advice given to the client regarding the costs and funding of the case?   [ ]   [ ]   [ ]

    In particular:

    25.1   the availability of green form advice and the limits and extent of green form funding?   [ ]   [ ]   [ ]

		Yes	No	N/a

25.2   whether or not the client will have to make a contribution to the case?   [ ]   [ ]   [ ]

Progress of the Case

26. Was the client advised how long they can expect to wait for their application to be decided?   [ ]   [ ]   [ ]

27. Is there an indication of the steps the lawyer agrees to take in furtherance of the client's claim?   [ ]   [ ]   [ ]

28. Is there an indication of the steps the lawyer has asked the client to take (if any)?   [ ]   [ ]   [ ]

29. Was the client advised when and in what form the next contact between lawyer and client will take place?   [ ]   [ ]   [ ]

30. Was the client advised as to more than one possible course of action?   [ ]   [ ]   [ ]

31. Did the lawyer indicate the likely outcome of the case?   [ ]   [ ]   [ ]

32. Is there an indication that the client made an active choice on the lawyer's suggested mode of action?   [ ]   [ ]   [ ]

33. Has the lawyer noted down the reaction of the client to the decided resulting plan of action (as a minimum, this should include the client's consent to the action going forward)?   [ ]   [ ]   [ ]

34. If the lawyer is not going to represent the client at any hearing, is there an indication that alternative sources of representation or assistance were explained to the client?   [ ]   [ ]   [ ]

35. Were any apparent queries from the client dealt with fully, promptly and politely?   [ ]   [ ]   [ ]

36. Did the lawyer deal with any evident emotional concerns of the client?   [ ]   [ ]   [ ]

37. Did the lawyer explain any contact with the other side?   [ ]   [ ]   [ ]

   37.1   In particular, when they will be contacted and why?   [ ]   [ ]   [ ]

38. If it apppears likely that the other side will contact the client directly, was the client advised as to what they should do in the event that the other side does contact them?   [ ]   [ ]   [ ]

III.   Further Action, Investigation and Research

39. Did the lawyer seek the client's passport (or a copy)?   [ ]   [ ]   [ ]

40. If there has been no previous formal application for asylum: N/A   [ ]

   40.1   did the lawyer write to the Home Office to make a formal application   [ ]   [ ]   [ ]

   40.2   was a full application made within 3 months of the Home Office sending an application form?   [ ]   [ ]   [ ]

		Yes	No	N/a

40.3   did the application include a full statement of facts in support of the client's application (covering all points outlined above in "getting information")?   [ ]   [ ]   [ ]

41.   If the client has been interviewed by the immigration authorities, did the lawyer seek a copy of any interview transcripts?   [ ]   [ ]   [ ]

42.   If any evidence is in a language other than English, did the lawyer arrange for certified translations of the documents, and were copies of the documents (and translations) included in the asylum application?   [ ]   [ ]   [ ]

43.   Was the client kept informed of any significant developments?   [ ]   [ ]   [ ]

44.   If a Political Asylum Questionnaire (PAQ) has been completed has the lawyer sought a copy, together with copies of any correspondence to and from the Home Office?   [ ]   [ ]   [ ]

45.   If the client does not already have one, has the lawyer ensured that the client has been issued with a Standard Acknowledgement Letter (SAL)[13]   [ ]   [ ]   [ ]

46.   If the case involves torture or ill-treatment, has the lawyer considered obtaining a medical report and, if so, an authority from the client to do so?   [ ]   [ ]   [ ]

47.   Has the lawyer considered obtaining a letter from any other doctor or social worker who has been treating the client for any significant condition either in his/her country of origin or in the UK and, if so, an authority from the client to do so?   [ ]   [ ]   [ ]

48.   In cases involving fear on the basis of religion, has the lawyer considered seeking a letter in support of the client's claim from the relevant religious organisation?   [ ]   [ ]   [ ]

2. Advising Clients with Partners Seeking Leave to Enter and Remain

These transaction criteria apply to clients who have a spouse or fiancé(e) (hereafter referred to as the 'applicant') who wishes to enter and remain in the country.

I. Getting Information

			Yes	No	N/a
49.	Does the lawyer know:				
	49.1	the dates of birth of:			
		49.1.1 the client?	[ ]	[ ]	[ ]
		49.1.2 the applicant?	[ ]	[ ]	[ ]
	49.2	the full names of:			
		49.2.1 the client?	[ ]	[ ]	[ ]
		49.2.2 the applicant?	[ ]	[ ]	[ ]
	49.3	the addresses and telephone number(s) of:			
		49.3.1 the client?	[ ]	[ ]	[ ]
		49.3.2 the applicant?	[ ]	[ ]	[ ]
	49.4	details of employment of:			
		49.4.1 the client?	[ ]	[ ]	[ ]
		49.4.2 the applicant	[ ]	[ ]	[ ]
	49.5	age and relationship to the client and applicant of any dependants?	[ ]	[ ]	[ ]
	49.6	whether the applicant has ever visited the U.K. previously?	[ ]	[ ]	[ ]
	49.7	if the applicant has visited the U.K. previously, does the lawyer know:		N/A	[ ]
		49.7.1 the dates, places, and lengths of stay in this country?	[ ]	[ ]	[ ]
		49.7.2 who they stayed with, and for what purpose (e.g. social, studies, visit, etc.)?	[ ]	[ ]	[ ]
	49.8	whether the applicant has made other immigration applications?	[ ]	[ ]	[ ]
	49.9	client's citizenship (where the client was born, what the client's passport is, etc.)?	[ ]	[ ]	[ ]
	49.10	how the applicant, client or their family proposes to pay for the fare across to the U.K.?	[ ]	[ ]	[ ]
50.	If the client is unable to support the applicant financially, does the lawyer have an understanding of whether or not someone is prepared to sponsor the applicant (i.e. guarantee financial support for the applicant)?		[ ]	[ ]	[ ]

194

		Yes	No	N/a

51.   If there is a sponsor for the applicant does the lawyer have an understanding of the sponsor's financial position?   **N/A**   [ ]

In particular:

51.1   the sponsor's employment (their salary, the stability of that employment, years worked, etc.)?   [ ]   [ ]   [ ]

51.2   the sponsor's debts and savings (i.e. are there any, and if so details of these)?   [ ]   [ ]   [ ]

51.3   the sponsor's ownership of property (and mortgage payments outstanding)?   [ ]   [ ]   [ ]

51.4   regular financial commitments of the sponsor, (e.g. expenses in keeping their own immediate family)?   [ ]   [ ]   [ ]

52   Does the lawyer know:

52.1   where the client and applicant will live once reunited?   [ ]   [ ]   [ ]

52.2   whether it is the intention of the client and applicant to live together?   [ ]   [ ]   [ ]

52.3   whether or not the housing will be adequate?   [ ]   [ ]   [ ]

53.   Does the lawyer have an understanding of the nature of the relationship of client and applicant? In particular:

53.1   whether they are married?   [ ]   [ ]   [ ]

53.2   when and where they were married?   [ ]   [ ]   [ ]

53.3   if the marriage was arranged, how the marriage was arranged and by whom?   [ ]   [ ]   [ ]

53.4   whether there are any marriage certificates and, if so, how the lawyer or client could obtain these?   [ ]   [ ]   [ ]

53.5   if the client and applicant have lived together since their marriage, how long was this for, when was this and where?   [ ]   [ ]   [ ]

53.6   whether there are any children from the relationship?   [ ]   [ ]   [ ]

53.7   whether there has been any post-nuptial correspondence (or other contact) between client and applicant?   [ ]   [ ]   [ ]

53.8   if, when, and where the parties have met?   [ ]   [ ]   [ ]

53.9   how the relationship (if any) developed between the parties?   [ ]   [ ]   [ ]

53.10   whether there are photographs or other evidence of meetings between the client and applicant?   [ ]   [ ]   [ ]

53.11   why the client and applicant are not currently living together (in the applicant's country of origin)?   [ ]   [ ]   [ ]

53.12   the intention of client and applicant in entering into the marriage[14]   [ ]   [ ]   [ ]

		Yes	No	N/a

53.13   the religion and customs surrounding the marriage of the client and applicant in relation to, in particular, its arrangement (if applicable), and the customary arrangements for living together afterwards[15]   [ ]   [ ]   [ ]

54.   If there are medical reasons for allowing entry of the applicant does the lawyer have an understanding of these medical reasons, and are the names and addresses of relevant doctors/hospitals known?   [ ]   [ ]   [ ]

55.   If the marriage between the client and the applicant is (or would be) a polygamous one, does the lawyer have an understanding of whether any of the husband's other wives have entry clearance, a certificate of entitlement or have been to the UK other than as a visitor (temporarily or illegally)?   [ ]   [ ]   [ ]

56.   If the client or applicant has been accused of dishonesty (e.g. by attempting to mislead the immigration officer at interview) does the lawyer have an understanding of: **N/A**   [ ]

56.1   whether the client appeared to have been dishonest?   [ ]   [ ]   [ ]

56.2   the client's explanation of any inconsistencies?   [ ]   [ ]   [ ]

57.   If the client and applicant are not yet married, does the lawyer have an understanding of: **N/A**   [ ]

57.1   whether there are any reasons the couple are not yet married?[16]   [ ]   [ ]   [ ]

57.2   whether the applicant will be fully supported and accommodated up until the period of the marriage?   [ ]   [ ]   [ ]

57.3   the applicant's employment prospects post-marriage?   [ ]   [ ]   [ ]

57.4.   If the client has been refused leave, does the lawyer know: **N/A**   [ ]

57.4.1   the date when such a refusal was made,   [ ]   [ ]   [ ]

57.4.2   whether the client has a copy of the original application including any sponsorship declaration?   [ ]   [ ]   [ ]

II.   Advising on this Information

Advice given to the client, and recorded on the file (either in attendance notes or in confirmatory letters to the client), should cover the following.

58.   If an application is to be made, whether to request an oral hearing for the application?   [ ]   [ ]   [ ]

59.   If an appeal is considered, was the client advised on the time limits for appealing to the adjudicator[17]   [ ]   [ ]   [ ]

60.   If the adjudicator has refused the applicant's application, was the client advised on the time limits for appealing the adjudicator's decision[18]   [ ]   [ ]   [ ]

61.   If the applicant and client are not yet married are they advised:

61.1   that should the applicant be granted leave to enter this will usually be for up to six months in which time the couple should marry and then apply for an extension of stay?   [ ]   [ ]   [ ]

		Yes	No	N/a

61.2   the applicant will be unable to work until after the couple have married and the applicant has been granted leave to work?   [ ]   [ ]   [ ]

Costs and Funding of the Case

62. Is there an indication of the advice given to the client regarding the costs of the case?   [ ]   [ ]   [ ]

In particular:

62.1   the availability of green form advice and the limits and extent of green form funding?   [ ]   [ ]   [ ]

62.2   whether or not the client will have to make a contribution to the case?   [ ]   [ ]   [ ]

Progress of the Case

63. Was the client advised of how long they can expect to wait for their application to be concluded?   [ ]   [ ]   [ ]

64. Is there an indication of the steps the lawyer agrees to take in furtherance of the applicant's claim?   [ ]   [ ]   [ ]

65. Is there an indication of the steps the lawyer has asked the client to take (if any)?   [ ]   [ ]   [ ]

66. Is the client told when and in what form the next contact will take place?   [ ]   [ ]   [ ]

67. Has the lawyer advised the client as to more than one possible course of action?   [ ]   [ ]   [ ]

68. Did the lawyer indicate the likely outcome of the case?   [ ]   [ ]   [ ]

69. Is there an indication that the client made an active choice on the lawyer's suggested mode of action?   [ ]   [ ]   [ ]

70. If the lawyer is not going to represent the client at any hearing, is there an indication that alternative sources of representation or assistance were explained to the client   [ ]   [ ]   [ ]

71. Has the lawyer noted down the reaction of the client to the decided resulting plan of action (as a minimum, this should include the client's consent to the action going forward)?   [ ]   [ ]   [ ]

72. Were any apparent queries from the client dealt with fully, promptly and politely?   [ ]   [ ]   [ ]

73. Did the lawyer deal with any evident emotional concerns of the client?   [ ]   [ ]   [ ]

74. If it appears likely that the other side will contact the client directly, was the client advised as to what they should do in the event that the other side does contact them?   [ ]   [ ]   [ ]

III Further Action, Investigation and Research

The following criteria apply where the case extends beyond initial advice.

	Yes	No	N/a

75. Where the client wishes to appeal to an adjudicator or the Immigration Appeals Tribunal and the time limit for such applications has not already expired, is an appeal made in time?[19]　[ ]　[ ]　[ ]

76. Where the client wishes to appeal to an adjudicator or the Immigration Appeals Tribunal but the time limit for such applications has already expired, is an application made giving reasons for making an appeal out of time?　[ ]　[ ]　[ ]

77. Where the applicant has been interviewed, by immigration officials does the lawyer seek copies of interview transcripts?　[ ]　[ ]　[ ]

78. Does the lawyer seek copies of the client's, sponsor's and applicant's passports?　[ ]　[ ]　[ ]

79. Does the lawyer seek a written undertaking from the sponsor that they are prepared to support the applicant and evidence of the sponsor's financial position?　[ ]　[ ]　[ ]

80. Does the lawyer seek proof of marriage (including, where available, marriage certificates)?　[ ]　[ ]　[ ]

81. Is a statement of the client's case sent in support of the client's application?　[ ]　[ ]　[ ]

If so, does it include:

81.1 all evidence supporting the occurrence of a marriage between the client and applicant?　[ ]　[ ]　[ ]

81.2 all evidence suggesting the marriage was not entered into primarily for the purpose of gaining entry to the U.K.?　[ ]　[ ]　[ ]

81.3 evidence that the client and applicant intend to live together in the U.K.?　[ ]　[ ]　[ ]

81.4 unless a sponsor is not required, evidence that there is suitable sponsorship of the applicant and that the applicant and client will have somewhere suitable to live together (including undertakings)?　[ ]　[ ]　[ ]

81.5. Did the lawyer write to the client confirming in a comprehensible manner an outline of advice given?　[ ]　[ ]　[ ]

81.6. Was the client kept informed of any significant developments?　[ ]　[ ]　[ ]

Immigration/Nationality—Notes to the Criteria

1. Especially, Macdonald's Immigration Law and Practice (3rd Ed: Butterworths); Immigration Law Handbook (3rd Ed: Handsworth Law Centre, 1985)

2. ILPA: *Best Practice Guide to the Preparation of Asylum Applications from Arrival to First Interview* (ILPA, London 1992).

3. e.g. names, dates of birth, nationality, places of residence and jobs of parents, parents-in-law, brothers and sisters, spouse and children?

4. The client may have entered the UK as a visitor or a student, for example, before claiming political asylum.

5. e.g. did the client realise they were in the UK? was the client ill or hungry? How many hours had the client been travelling on arrival? (ILPA Guide to Best Practice)

6. The ILPA guide states that with many of these questions the aim is to take a detailed chronology with as many dates, names and addresses as possible charting the client's political involvement up to the point of escape due to persecution or fear of persecution. The aim is to show the link between actual persecution and potential persecution, the client's fears for the future and the translation of those fears into an escape (See, ILPA Guide, p.16).

7. Including quasi-political organisations such as trades unions, student unions or women's groups.

8. e.g. plane tickets, membership cards, newspaper articles, photographs, letters from friends and family containing relevant information together with the envelopes in which they arrived.

   The lawyer should discuss with client any further documents the client is able to obtain, such as letters confirming membership of political parties or a letter from any medical personnel the client may have seen in his/her country of origin following ill-treatment or torture. (see, ILPA Guide, p.20).

9. The ILPA guide states (p.24): "It is rarely easy to advise a client in certain terms whether the client will obtain refugee status or not. However some indication as to whether you believe it to be a strong or weak case should be given. You are acting as your client's adviser as well as representative. If you are completely uncertain as to whether the claim will be successful then at least communicate this to your client. Joining groups such as the Refugee Legal Group will enable you to benefit from information exchange with experienced practitioners, which in turn may make it easier to give your client an indication as to the chances of success. Advice on the chances of success should be reiterated in a subsequent letter to your client in which you inform him/her of the action it is agreed you should take on his/her behalf."

10. (Although under slightly different Home Office practices for Somali clients it is possible to lodge the claim for family reunion at the same time as the asylum claim with the hope that they will be determined simultaneously.) However if family arrive they are best advised to claim asylum as well as to request to remain as dependants on arrival; and then to contact you for full advice on any potential claims they may have. See, ILPA Guide, p.24.

11. Covering, e.g. the right to remain, family reunion, passport and that they will not be able to return to country of origin.

12. Covering, e.g., possible grant of exceptional leave to remain, effect on any other claims to remain and being excluded from Europe.

13. This is effectively an identity document enabling asylum seekers to claim income support.

14. Usually the lawyer will be seeking to demonstrate that the marriage was not entered into primarily for the purpose of gaining entry into the UK.

15. For instance, it is sometimes alleged by immigration officers that local customs make it unusual for the husband to come to live with the wife. The lawyer should be able to understand how accurate the immigration officer's views of such social/religious norms are.

16. The applicant will have a better chance of gaining leave if the couple have been *unable* to marry. (see, Macdonald, op.cit. p.256.)

17. If the applicant is appealing from within the UK, the time limit is 14 days from the date of the first instance refusal. If appealing from abroad the applicant has 3 months from the date when the notice was sent. (Immigration Appeals (Procedure) Rules 1984 [S.I. 1984/2041]).

18. Where the adjudicator dismisses an application, the applicant has 42 days from the date of the adjudicators decision in which to appeal, unless the applicant remains within the U.K. where the time limit is only 14 days. (Immigration Appeals (Procedure) Rules 1984 [S.I. 1984/2041]).

19. For an appeal to be made in time the application has to have been *received* by the Home Office (Immigration and Nationality Department) within the relevant time limits, it is not adequate that it was posted within the time limits.

Chapter Nine:
Consumer and General Contract

The transaction criteria set out in this chapter are based around a review of files, as well as a survey of literature on contract problems and general legal practice. For problems arising in connection with consumer debt and consumer credit agreements, please refer to the Debt transactions.

These criteria apply only to cases where the lawyer acts for a dissatisfied consumer. They do not apply in cases where the client is a small businessman, or a consumer being sued for withholding payment.

The transaction is divided into 3 sections:

I.   Getting Information from the Client
II. Advising On That Information
III. Further Investigation, Research and Action

I   Getting Information from the Client

General Information

		Yes	No	N/a
1.	Did the lawyer record the client's:			
1.1	full name?	[ ]	[ ]	[ ]
1.2	address and telephone number?	[ ]	[ ]	[ ]
1.3	date of birth?	[ ]	[ ]	[ ]

Contractual Information

		Yes	No	N/a
2.	Does the lawyer know the names and addresses of the parties to the contract?	[ ]	[ ]	[ ]
3.	Does the lawyer have an understanding of the following points:			
3.1	Whether and when a binding contract was concluded; including in particular:		**N/A**	[ ]
3.1.1	the nature of the offer and acceptance;	[ ]	[ ]	[ ]
3.1.2	the nature of the consideration;	[ ]	[ ]	[ ]
3.1.3	any possible problems of privity;[1]	[ ]	[ ]	[ ]
3.2	The capacity in which both parties entered into the contract;[2]	[ ]	[ ]	[ ]
3.3	What the contract was for (i.e goods and/or services) and a description of these goods/services;	[ ]	[ ]	[ ]
3.4	Where the cash price was between £100 and £30,000, how the goods[3] were purchased (cash, credit card, hire purchase or other loan);	[ ]	[ ]	[ ]

			Yes	No	N/a
4.		If the goods[3] were purchased on any form of loan, does the lawyer know:[4]		**N/A** [ ]	[ ]
	4.1	the amount of any payments outstanding?	[ ]	[ ]	[ ]
	4.2	does the lawyer have an understanding of whether the credit agreement was properly executed? i.e.: is there an understanding of:			
		4.2.1 when the contract was entered into;	[ ]	[ ]	[ ]
		4.2.2 whether it was signed by debtor and creditor/agent;	[ ]	[ ]	[ ]
		4.2.3 whether it contains the name and address of debtor and creditor;	[ ]	[ ]	[ ]
		4.2.4 description and cash price of goods;	[ ]	[ ]	[ ]
		4.2.5 timing of repayments;	[ ]	[ ]	[ ]
		4.2.6 amounts of repayments;	[ ]	[ ]	[ ]
		4.2.7 Annual Percentage Rate;	[ ]	[ ]	[ ]
		4.2.8 where the debtor signed the agreement;[5]	[ ]	[ ]	[ ]
		4.2.9 what was said by both parties before the signing of the agreement;	[ ]	[ ]	[ ]
		4.2.10 whether (and when) the debtor received a notice setting out the rights of cancellation;	[ ]	[ ]	[ ]
		4.2.11 whether the debtor received a copy of the agreement within 7 days of signing the contract;	[ ]	[ ]	[ ]
5.		The terms of the contract, i.e.:			
	5.1	the price;	[ ]	[ ]	[ ]
	5.2	the date of delivery/performance;	[ ]	[ ]	[ ]
	5.3	evidence of the terms of the contract including a copy of the contract (if available);	[ ]	[ ]	[ ]
	5.4	whether the client relied on any written description of the goods/ services;	[ ]	[ ]	[ ]
	5.5	whether any representation was made by the seller in respect of the contract goods/services before contract, and if so, what were the representations and when were they made;	[ ]	[ ]	[ ]
	5.6	whether the client sought the goods and services for a particular purpose and whether the client made that particular purpose known to the seller before contract, and if so, how;	[ ]	[ ]	[ ]
	5.7	details of advertising/promotional material in respect of the goods/ services;	[ ]	[ ]	[ ]
	5.8	whether any defects were specifically drawn to the client's attention before the contract;	[ ]	[ ]	[ ]

		Yes	No	N/a

| 5.9 | whether the client examined the goods before the contract and, if so, the nature of any defects that were revealed; | [ ] | [ ] | [ ] |

| 5.10 | whether there were any exclusion clauses. | [ ] | [ ] | [ ] |

6. When and how the client discovered the relevant defect/problem(s): [ ] [ ] [ ]

7. Details of client's loss (e.g. repair costs, personal injury, damage to property, inconvenience/disappointment); [ ] [ ] [ ]

8. Whether there is a manufacturer's guarantee, and if so what this purports to cover;[6] [ ] [ ] [ ]

9. Whether the supplier is a member of a trade association; [ ] [ ] [ ]

10. Where damage to the client's property has been sustained as a result of a mixed contract[7]/contract for services, whether the client's household insurance policy covers any of the damage; [ ] [ ] [ ]

11. Details of correspondence/communications between the parties and, in particular, details of any payments offered or accepted in relation to the goods or services in question; [ ] [ ] [ ]

12. Whether any third party has acquired rights in the contract goods (e.g. by gift, sale, pawning of the goods)? [ ] [ ] [ ]

II Advising on that Information

13. Has the lawyer explained to the client the basis of the client's claim, including:

| 13.1 | the remedies available? | [ ] | [ ] | [ ] |

| 13.2 | what will have to be shown to enable a claim to be brought?[8] | [ ] | [ ] | [ ] |

| 13.3 | the means by which such a claim can be pursued (e.g. negotiation/ litigation)? | [ ] | [ ] | [ ] |

| 13.4 | an indication of any areas of doubt in proving such a claim, when and how they might be overcome?[9] | [ ] | [ ] | [ ] |

14. Has the lawyer explained what types of claim might be recoverable as damages? [ ] [ ] [ ]

15. Has the lawyer explained the effect of any act of acceptance by the client in relation to the contract goods sold, upon the client's rights? [ ] [ ] [ ]

16. Where misrepresentation has been established, has the lawyer explained the different types of misrepresentation, and the respective remedies? [ ] [ ] [ ]

17. Has the lawyer explained the effect of any exclusion clause upon the client's remedies including the possible relevance of the Unfair Contract Terms Act 1977? [ ] [ ] [ ]

18. Where a separate creditor (e.g. the client's credit card company) has financed the purchase of goods between £100 and £30,000, and the supplier is in breach of contract, has the lawyer explained the nature of the client's remedies against the creditor? [ ] [ ] [ ]

			Yes	No	N/a

19. Where there is no privity of contract[10] between the client and the other party, has the lawyer considered a claim in tort? [ ] [ ] [ ]

20. Has the lawyer explained the way in which the client's remedies may be best enforced? [ ] [ ] [ ]

21. If the client is advised to make a claim in the small claims court or by conciliation/arbitration procedures, has the lawyer explained: N/A [ ]

     21.1   the non-availability of Legal Aid, and the restrictions under green form in respect of the claim; [ ] [ ] [ ]

     21.2   any restrictions on appeal from the district judge or arbitrator. [ ] [ ] [ ]

Costs and Funding of the Case

22. Is there an indication of advice given to the client regarding the costs and funding of the case? In particular;

     22.1   the availability of green form advice and civil legal aid: [ ] [ ] [ ]

     22.2   the limits and extent of Green Form Funding; [ ] [ ] [ ]

     22.3   the effect of the solicitor's and statutory charge on any damages received; [ ] [ ] [ ]

     22.4   the costs to the client should the case be lost; [ ] [ ] [ ]

     22.5   the duty to report changes of circumstance and address; [ ] [ ] [ ]

     22.6   if a legal aid certificate is granted the nature and consequences of discharge and revocation; [ ] [ ] [ ]

     22.7   whether or not the client will have to make a contribution to the case; [ ] [ ] [ ]

Progress of the Case

     23.1   Did the lawyer advise the client how long the claim might take to be concluded? [ ] [ ] [ ]

     23.2   Is there an indication of the steps the lawyer has agreed to take and have these been communicated to the client? [ ] [ ] [ ]

     23.3   Is there an indication of the steps the lawyer has asked the client to do? [ ] [ ] [ ]

     23.4   Is the client told when and in what form the next contact will take place? [ ] [ ] [ ]

     23.5   Has the lawyer advised the client as to more than one possible course of action?[11] [ ] [ ] [ ]

     23.6   Did the lawyer indicate the likely outcome of the case? [ ] [ ] [ ]

     23.7   Is there an indication that the client made an active choice on the lawyer's suggested mode of action? [ ] [ ] [ ]

			Yes	No	N/a
23.8		Has the lawyer noted down the reaction of the client to the decided plan of action (as a minimum, this should include the client's consent to the action going forward)?	[ ]	[ ]	[ ]
23.9		If the lawyer is not going to represent the client at any hearings, is there an indication that alternative sources of representation or assistance were explained to the client?	[ ]	[ ]	[ ]
23.10		Were any apparent queries from the client dealt with fully, promptly and politely?	[ ]	[ ]	[ ]
23.11		Did the lawyer deal with any evident emotional concerns of the client?	[ ]	[ ]	[ ]
23.12		Did the lawyer explain any contact with the other side. In particular, when the other side will be contacted and why?	[ ]	[ ]	[ ]
23.13		Did the lawyer advise the client as to what they should do in the event that the other side contacts them?	[ ]	[ ]	[ ]

III Further Investigation, Research, and Action

24.	Did the lawyer write to the client confirming in a comprehensible manner an outline of the advice given, including in particular, any areas of difficulty/ uncertainty?	[ ]	[ ]	[ ]
25.	Did the lawyer assist the client in preparing submissions in connection with conciliation/arbitration procedures, or a claim using the small claims provision of the county court?	[ ]	[ ]	[ ]
26.	Was the client kept informed of significant developments?	[ ]	[ ]	[ ]
27.	Where a term of the consumer contract has been breached, does the lawyer seek evidence of that breach?	[ ]	[ ]	[ ]
28.	Did the lawyer write to the other side setting out the nature of the client's case?	[ ]	[ ]	[ ]
29.	Where the original documents were not available at the first interview have these been sought from the client?	[ ]	[ ]	[ ]

Consumer and General Contract—Notes to the Criteria

1. e.g. Only applies where the goods were not actually bought by the person who suffered loss.

2. i.e. Whether the respective parties were private sellers, agents for private seller or selling in the course of a business or whether they were dealing as a consumer or buying in the course of business.

3. and/or services.

4. Payment by instalments does not always constitute a loan and not all instalment arrangements have to be regulated. This question applies only where a consumer credit agreement has been entered into.

5. e.g. on the suppliers trade premises.

6. A manufacturer's guarantee can only be given in respect of goods; therefore this question does not apply if the contract is for services.

7. i.e. A contract for goods and services (e.g. installing central heating).

8. e.g. Covering the contractual, statutory (e.g. product safety) law relevant to the claim and the burden of proof.

9. This might include the need to instruct experts.

10. Where the goods were not actually bought by the client.

11. i.e. on the different options for resolving the matter.

Chapter Ten:
Outcome Measures

The Board is interested in exploring the relationship between the outcome of cases, their cost, compliance levels with the transaction criteria, and other franchise requirements. Although there will inevitably be differences on individual cases, it may be possible to define a statistical relationship between outcomes, cost and levels of compliance which will allow effective comparison between firms to be made.

Outcome measures are therefore part of the independent research and development currently under way. Information on their use is being collected, initially on a voluntary basis, during audits to provide research data. They do not form part of the franchise decision making process at the moment. Research on average costs criteria is also ongoing. Pending the results of the research, average costs criteria will not be introduced as a requirement for new applicants before 1 August 1996, and for existing franchisees before 1 August 1997. Outcome measures will not by themselves be introduced as a requirement for existing franchisees until 1 August 1999. New applicants would have to meet any requirement introduced but this will not be before 1 August 1996.

We include outcome measures here in their first draft form for practitioners' information only. Any comments should be sent to the Policy and Secretariat Department, Legal Aid Head Office.

The chapter contains draft outcome measures in the three areas of Personal Injury, Matrimonial/ Family and Crime.

Personal Injury

Time Taken

The time taken to reach each stage of the case may be one indication of how well the lawyer is handling the case. There will be legitimate differences in the length of time taken between different types of case.

		Yes	No	N/a
1.	Is the case:			
1.1	a road traffic accident	[ ]	[ ]	[ ]
1.2	an accident at work case	[ ]	[ ]	[ ]
1.3	an accident at school	[ ]	[ ]	[ ]
1.4	a trip, fall or slip case	[ ]	[ ]	[ ]
1.5	industrial disease/deafness	[ ]	[ ]	[ ]
1.6	a medical negligence case	[ ]	[ ]	[ ]
1.7	general (please specify)	[ ]	[ ]	[ ]
2.	Was the case:			
2.1	pre- issue?	[ ]	[ ]	[ ]
2.2	a county court case?	[ ]	[ ]	[ ]
2.3	transferred to the county court?	[ ]	[ ]	[ ]
2.4	a High Court case?	[ ]	[ ]	[ ]
2.5	transferred to the High Court?	[ ]	[ ]	[ ]

3.   Also the nature of the client's injuries should be recorded on a scale of 1 to 4:   ____

1 = relatively minor
2 = fairly serious
3 = serious
4 = very serious/catastrophic

4.   How complex was the case on a scale of 1— 4:   ____

1 = simple
2 = less simple
3 = complex
4 = highly complex

5.   Was there ever a settled prognosis?   Yes [ ] No [ ]

6.   Was it a fatal accident?   Yes [ ] No [ ]

7.   The auditor should then record the dates as and when the following steps occurred:

			Day	Month	Year
7.1	initial instructions	Date	___	___	___
7.2	date legal aid certificate granted	Date	___	___	___
7.3	in medical negligence cases, when were medical records received?	Date	___	___	___
7.4	the first medical report obtained	Date	___	___	___
7.5	issuing of proceedings	Date	___	___	___
7.6	close of pleadings[1]	Date	___	___	___
7.7	setting down for trial	Date	___	___	___
7.8	settlement	Date	___	___	___
7.9	trial	Date	___	___	___
7.10	when prognosis became settled[2]	Date	___	___	___

8. On receipt of a payment into court was there a need to seek further evidence, advice from Counsel, etc.?[3]   Yes [ ]   No [ ]

9. On receipt of a payment into court, how long from the receipt of notice of payment in was:

9.1 Client advised on the payment in: In days _____

9.2 A decision taken to reject/accept: In days _____

9.3 Action taken on a decision to accept: In days _____

Matrimonial/Family

Divorce Proceedings

		Yes	No
1.	Is the client petitioner	[ ]	[ ]
	or respondent?:	[ ]	[ ]

2. How long have the parties been married (years & months)?   Years _____ months_____

3. Were there any exceptional behaviourial circumstances that the court took into account when making the financial settlement?   Yes [ ]   No [ ]

4. Please record the parties' financial position prior to their relationship breakdown:

CLIENT:

4.1	Income: (£s) (If on Welfare Benefits, please state which one(s).)	
4.2	Outgoing: (£'s)	
4.3	Capital: (£'s) e.g. Equity in Home Pension Savings	
4.4	Unsecured Debts: (£'s) e.g. Overdrafts Credit Cards	
4.5	Secured Debts: (£'s) e.g. 1st mortgage 2nd mortgage 3rd mortgage Loans	

4.6   OTHER PARTY:

4.7	Income: (£'s) If on Welfare Benefits please state which one(s).	
4.8	Outgoings: (£'s)	

4.9	Capital: (£'s) e.g. Equity in Home Pension Savings	
4.10	Unsecured Debts: (£'s) e.g. Overdrafts Credit Cards	
4.11	Secured Debts: (£'s) e.g. 1st mortgage 2nd mortgage 3rd mortgage Loans	

Following a settlement or court order please
record details of the settlement/order:

5.   Where the client has to pay periodical payments: **N/A** [ ]

    5.1   how much is ordered to be paid by the other party?   monthly £ _____

    5.2   how much is ordered to be paid to the children?   monthly £ _____

6.   Where the client receives periodical payments: **N/A** [ ]

    6.1   how much is received for the client?   monthly £ _____

    6.2   how much is received for the children?   monthly £ _____

7.   Where the client has to transfer or receives property, what is its net value (i.e.   **N/A** [ ]
after deducting mortgages and other charges)?   amount £'s _____

8.   Where the client has to pay or receives a lump sum payment: **N/A** [ ]

    8.1   what was the amount?   amount £'s _____

        Yes   No   N/a

9.   Is there a transfer involving the matrimonial home: [ ]   [ ]   [ ]

If so:

    9.1   what was the size of the share: amount £'s _____

        9.1.1   of the other side? (if none, write none)   _____

        9.1.2   of the client? (if none, write none)   _____

    9.2   did the client obtain the right to occupy the home?   [ ]   [ ]   [ ]

9.3 which of the following circumstances triggered the sale of the home or the realisation of the charge attached to the property?

      9.3.1 youngest child reaches 17 years or ceases full-time education.   [ ]   [ ]   [ ]

      9.3.2 if the wife dies, remarries or commences permanent co-habitation with another man.   [ ]   [ ]   [ ]

      9.3.3 other (please specify)

_____

_____

10. How much (in £'s) of the client's settlement was recoverable under the statutory charge?   amount £'s _____

Time Taken

The time taken to reach each stage of the case may be one indication of how well the lawyer is handling the case. There will be legitimate differences in the length of time taken between different types of case.

*Where lawyer acting for **petitioner**:*

			Day	Month	Year
11.	The auditor should record the dates as and when the following occurred:				
	11.1 date of client's first visit to lawyer	Date	___	___	___
	11.2 filing of petition	Date	___	___	___
	11.3 acknowledgement of service served	Date	___	___	___
	11.4 application for directions and submission of affidavit	Date	___	___	___
	11.5 decree nisi pronounced	Date	___	___	___
	11.6 decree absolute	Date	___	___	___
	11.7 date file closed	Date	___	___	___

12. *Where lawyer acting for **respondent**:*

		Day	Month	Year
12.1 Date of client's first visit to lawyer	Date	___	___	___
12.2 receipt of petition	Date	___	___	___
12.3 acknowledgement of service made	Date	___	___	___
12.4 date file closed	Date	___	___	___

13. Where children were affected by the family breakdown how long after the filing of the divorce petition were residence/contact issues between the parties resolved?   _____

14. If the other side made a Calderbank letter or open offer:

     14.1 how many working days did it take the lawyer to inform the client thereof?   Date   ___ ___ ___

     14.2 how many working days did the lawyer take to advise the client as to whether or not to accept the offer?   Date   ___ ___ ___

14.3   how many working days did it take before the lawyer responded to the other side indicating whether the offer was declined or accepted or further information was required?

Date   ____ _____ ____

15.1   Did the court return any documents due to procedural irregularities or requests for further information or requests for further copies for service?[4]

[ ]   [ ]   [ ]

15.2   If so, how many times?

_____

	Yes	No	N/a
16. If there was any delay did the lawyer explain to the client why?	[ ]	[ ]	[ ]

17.   Which documents did the court return, if any?

_____

18.   If there were any factors beyond the control of the lawyer which caused delay, what were they?

_____

Crime

Time Taken

The time taken to reach each stage of the case may be one indication of how well the lawyer is handling the case. There will be legitimate differences in the length of time taken between different types of case.

1. How long (in days) after giving first instructions was full criminal legal aid sought or received?   Number: [ ]

2. How long (in days) after giving full instructions after the date of charge was it before advance disclosure (or a summary of evidence) was sought or received?[5]   Number: [ ]

3. If there was a conference with counsel, how long before trial (in days):
    3.1   was the brief delivered?[6]   Number: [ ]
    3.2   did the conference take place?[7]   Number: [ ]

Advice at the Police Station

		Yes	No	N/a
10.1	Was advice at the police station given:			
	a) in person?	[ ]	[ ]	[ ]
	b) over the telephone?	[ ]	[ ]	[ ]
10.2	At the police station, was advice given to the client in the capacity of:[8]			
	a) Duty Solicitor?	[ ]	[ ]	[ ]
	b) own Solicitor?	[ ]	[ ]	[ ]
10.3	What is the status of the person attending the police station:[9]			
	a) solicitor?	[ ]	[ ]	[ ]
	b) trainee solicitor?	[ ]	[ ]	[ ]
	c) Fellow of the Institute of Legal Executives	[ ]	[ ]	[ ]
	d) Associate of the Institute of Legal Executives or trainee legal executive	[ ]	[ ]	[ ]
	e) Duty Solicitor authorised representative?	[ ]	[ ]	[ ]
	f) other?	[ ]	[ ]	[ ]

10.4   What is the experience of that person in this type of work in number of years?   Number: [ ]

		Yes	No	N/a
10.5	If there was an identification procedure which could have been attended by the lawyer. Did they attend?	[ ]	[ ]	[ ]

10.6   How many adjournments were there in the case?   Number: [ ]

The Board is currently considering the possibility of including some outcome measures and measures of case seriousness. The following section reflects current thinking on variables relevant in considering such data.[10]

Seriousness

The following table provides a banding for seriousness of offence types.[11]

BAND A   Murder, Serious Violence and other Grave Crimes: e.g. Aggravated Burglary, Arson, Rape, Manslaughter, S18 Wounding with Intent, Arson with Intent, Possessing Arms and Explosives, Importing Dangerous Drugs

BAND B	Blackmail, Robbery and Kidnapping
BAND C	Supplying Drugs
BAND D	Sexual Offences (other than Rape)
BAND E	S.20 wounding (Grievous Bodily Harm)
BAND F	Death by Dangerous Driving, Dangerous Driving, Causing Death by Careless Driving whilst under the influence of drink or drugs.
BAND G	Public Disorder (Affray and Violent Disorder, Criminal Damage and Perverting the Course of Justice)
BAND H	Household Burglary
BAND I	Other Burglaries and Thefts Frauds and Handling Stolen Goods
BAND J	Minor Violence (S.47 Assaults Occasioning Actual Bodily Harm, Common Assault), Threats to Kill
BAND K	Other Offences (all with very low rates of custody)

The following grid is used to indicate which offences the client was initially charged with and the outcome of those charges. The number of charges falling under each grade and the outcome of each of those charges will be recorded.

BAND	Initially Charged With	Charge Dropped	Not Guilty Plea- Aquitted	Not Guilty Plea- Convicted	Guilty Plea	Other (Please Specify)
A						
B						
C						
D						
E						
F						
G						
H						
I						
J						
K						
Other (Please Specify)						

3. If the client pleaded guilty[12], at what stage was this decision taken for each charge: **N/A** [ ]

		Yes	No	N/a
3.1	at the outset	[ ]	[ ]	[ ]
3.2	after police interview	[ ]	[ ]	[ ]
3.3	after giving advice outside the police station	[ ]	[ ]	[ ]
3.4	after advance disclosure	[ ]	[ ]	[ ]
3.5	after conference with counsel	[ ]	[ ]	[ ]
3.6	after committal (up until trial)	[ ]	[ ]	[ ]
3.7	during the trial	[ ]	[ ]	[ ]

4. How many previous convictions of a
similar type does the client have?[13]   Number: [ ]

Violence

5.1 Do(es) the charge(s) involve an offence against the person (i.e. violence)?   [ ] [ ] [ ]

5.2 If so, did the violence:

5.2.1 arise from a personal dispute?   [ ] [ ] [ ]

5.2.2 arise from other motives: e.g. theft, sexual gratification, resisting arrest, or an unprovoked attack?   [ ] [ ] [ ]

5.3 what degree of injury did the violence lead to:

5.3.1 Violence Threatened, no Harm Caused   [ ] [ ] [ ]

5.3.2 Bruises/Grazes/Cuts not requiring Stitches   [ ] [ ] [ ]

5.3.3 Wounds requiring Stitches   [ ] [ ] [ ]

5.3.4 Broken Bones/Fractured Limbs/Skull/Severe Internal Injuries   [ ] [ ] [ ]

5.4 did violence lead to continuing impairment of the victim?   [ ] [ ] [ ]

6. Do(es) the charge(s) involve a sexual offence?   [ ] [ ] [ ]

Financial Loss

7. Where there was some financial loss as a result of the offence, was the amount involved: **N/A** [ ]

7.1 Less than £499   [ ] [ ] [ ]

7.2 £500-£999   [ ] [ ] [ ]

7.3	£1,000-£9,999	[ ]	[ ]	[ ]
7.4	£10,000 plus	[ ]	[ ]	[ ]

Vulnerability of Victim(s):

8.	In crimes of violence:		N/A	[ ]
8.1	was the victim a child of 16 or under?	[ ]	[ ]	[ ]
8.2	an adult of 65 plus?	[ ]	[ ]	[ ]
8.3	female?	[ ]	[ ]	[ ]

Trial and/or Sentencing

9.	If the client was tried, was the case tried in:		N/A	[ ]
9.1	Magistrates' Court?	[ ]	[ ]	[ ]
9.2	Crown Court?	[ ]	[ ]	[ ]
10.	If the client was sentenced was this:		N/A	[ ]
10.1	at the Magistrates Court?	[ ]	[ ]	[ ]
10.2	at the Crown Court?	[ ]	[ ]	[ ]
10.3	at the Crown Court after being committed for sentencing by the Magistrates?	[ ]	[ ]	[ ]
11.	Was the client's remand status:		N/A	[ ]
11.1	appeared for Sentence on Remand in Custody?	[ ]	[ ]	[ ]
11.2	appeared for Sentence on Bail?	[ ]	[ ]	[ ]
12.	Was the client in breach of a court order?	[ ]	[ ]	[ ]
13.	Was previous custodial history for similar type of offence:		N/A	[ ]
13.1	no prior custodial sentence for similar offence?	[ ]	[ ]	[ ]
13.2	one or more prior custodial sentence for similar offence?	[ ]	[ ]	[ ]
14.	Where the client has previously breached a Community Service Order, did the client have:		N/A	[ ]
14.1	No Previous CSO	[ ]	[ ]	[ ]
14.2	Previous CSO without breaching?	[ ]	[ ]	[ ]
14.3	Previous CSO breached?	[ ]	[ ]	[ ]
15.	If convicted, what sentence was received:[14]		N/A	[ ]
15.1	absolute discharge?	[ ]	[ ]	[ ]

		Yes	No	N/a
15.2	conditional discharge?	[ ]	[ ]	[ ]
15.3	a fine?	[ ]	[ ]	[ ]
15.4	other non- custodial orders?	[ ]	[ ]	[ ]
15.5	suspended custodial sentences?	[ ]	[ ]	[ ]
15.6	custodial sentence (length in months)?	[ ]	[ ]	[ ]

16. Was identification in dispute? [ ] [ ] [ ]

17. Were any expert witnesses used? [ ] [ ] [ ]

18. Was there any forensic evidence? [ ] [ ] [ ]

19. On a scale of 1 to 4, how complex was the case? Number: [ ]

1 = straightforward,
2 = less straightforward
3 = complex
4 = highly complex

20. How many defence witnesses were there? [ ]

21. How many prosecution witnesses were there? [ ]

22. If there was a trial, how long did it take (in days)? [ ]

Outcome Measures—Notes to the Criteria

Personal Injury

1. Close of pleadings occurs 14 days after the last pleading of the proceedings.

2. If prognosis was always settled this date should be the date of initial instructions.

3. Time taken to respond to a payment it may well differ if there is a need to seek further evidence, advice from Counsel, etc.

Matrimonial/Family

4. The court may have returned documents because of defects or requesting further information.

Crime

5. Advance disclosure only applies to either way offences.

6. See, paras 21 and 32, pp. 166 and 108: *The Royal Commission on Criminal Justice*, (HMSO 1993).

7. Auditors will record the date of the first conference if there was more than one.

8. See "Advice At Police Stations Report" Form DSPS 1.

9. It is intended that firms be monitored on the number of occasions different levels of staff are sent down to the police station with a view to establishing their approach to such work. Such data will be analysed by case type. This information is not expected to appear on each file as long as it may be found out from, for example, a central record of employees of firms.

10. See, e.g. Hood, *Race and Sentencing* (Clarendon Press, Oxford 1992). In Hood's study 18 judges were compared on their sentencing decisions. Having controlled for the seriousness of the offence, certain judges were shown to have markedly different sentencing patterns for black, white and Asian offenders.

11. See, Hood, R: op. cit., p.70.

12. If the client pleads guilty to more than one charge at different times in the procedure.

13. The importance of previous convictions appears for the present time to have been dramatically reduced by the Criminal Justice Act 1991. However, the vigour of a prosecution might still depend upon previous convictions and this might have an effect on the seriousness of the case.

14. A sentence may consist of a combination of the following.

Transaction Criteria Auditor Guidelines

The Transaction Criteria audit will be carried out by the Board's Quality Auditors. The general guidance provided to auditors for the purposes of the pre-contract audit is set out below. The Board will be defining the level of compliance for the franchise categories of legal aid work probably in August 1994. The levels of compliance required will be set out in the Franchising Specification and will form an integral part of the overall assessment of the quality of the organisation and its work.

Overview

1. Although the method of developing the transaction criteria means that they are an indicator of the steps which should be carried out in particular cases, they are not intended to be an exhaustive check-list of issues which must be addressed, neither are they intended to indicate the only way in which work on a case should be structured. It follows that it is not necessary for files to contain check-lists based on the transaction criteria—auditors will be expected to find the information wherever it may appear on the files and this should be possible providing files are kept in reasonable order.

2. The transaction criteria have not been set in such a way that a single omission would by itself indicate a major difficulty in relation to the adviser or the organisation's work. The audit will therefore be looking for either a large number of non-systematic omissions on files or a number of systematic omissions covering answers to particular transaction criteria or particular groups of transaction criteria. A systematic omission occurs where the same piece of essential information is omitted from a majority of case files audited. Non-systematic omissions are random omissions across some or all files.

Objective Evidence

3. In order for the Board's auditors to verify compliance with the transaction criteria, there must be objective evidence on the file which demonstrates how the firm complies with the criteria. The objective evidence may take any one of a number of forms and need not be a document generated by the caseworker who dealt with the client. It can just as easily be an item which exists in a document or letter from the other side or elsewhere. Provided the information is in the file, it is available to the lawyer. It is not necessary for the caseworker to note that a particular criterion is 'not applicable' as the Board's auditors will make this allowance where appropriate.

4. In each set of transaction criteria there are two types of question. The first type asks "does the file show . . .?" The second asks "does the file show some understanding of . . .?" The difference between these is the level of information that is required. For example, it is not always necessary to obtain as much detail on certain points at the early stages of a case. A general view of something from the client may be asked for to give the lawyer "an understanding" of what is necessary later. Similarly the second type of question may be used in relation to an issue which may not be easily described in specific terms such as the atmosphere of a relationship and it is, therefore, sufficient for the auditor to be satisfied that there is objective evidence that the lawyer has addressed the issue in more general terms.

5. The following examples may help to interpret the requirement for objective evidence of compliance at the transaction criteria audit:

   a. The Personal Injury transaction criteria ask if the lawyer has noted down the reaction of the client to the decided plan of action (as a minimum this should include the client's consent to the action going forward). A signature on the legal aid application is not objective evidence of consent, because it does not demonstrate that the lawyer has specifically addressed this issue. The application may after all have been dealt with only through the post. In this situation organisations can demonstrate compliance by simply noting on the file the clients reaction to the proposed plan of action or noting in a letter the points made by the lawyer at interview and the clients agreement to these.

   b. The Crime transaction criteria ask if the lawyer has made a note of whether or not he or she intervened during the police interrogation of the client. The organisation can demonstrate compliance by simply noting on the file that intervention occurred or that no intervention was necessary. If the file is completely silent on this point then this would be recorded as a non compliance.

6. The Board's auditors follow the general principle that the objective evidence required to satisfy a particular criterion may be found at any point in the file. This will not, however, be the case if compliance must occur at a particular stage. So, for example, under the heading of first interview at the police station the Crime transaction criteria ask if the suspect and police were informed or aware of the representative's status. This information may be found much later on the file in the context perhaps of the trial, but a non-compliance would still be recorded because it is clear from the criterion that the information should have been given at a particular time. Auditors will keep in mind whether or not the criteria assume that compliance must occur at a particular stage.

7. Of course, in some situations auditors will need to exercise their judgement to determine what constitutes compliance. Some of the criteria inevitably require this, and auditors are always guided by commonsense and reasonableness.

8. In some circumstances, probably infrequently, the Board's auditors may come across handwriting or documents which are simply illegible. Where this is the case the auditor will attempt to determine from the context in which the handwritten document appears if compliance has been demonstrated on the file. The principle must be that it should always be possible for another case worker to pick up a file and take it over. If the auditor cannot make out the content nor assess its relevance from the context within which the handwritten note appears the Board's auditor will raise the issue at the closing meeting of the audit if it appears to be important to do so. If all reasonable attempts to understand the content and context should fail then it would be appropriate for the auditor to disregard the handwritten note as a source of objective evidence.

9. It may be that there will sometimes be files which have been the subject of a change of solicitor, and the previous solicitor's file is contained within the new solicitor's file. Pragmatism dictates that all factual information, for example, the name and address of the client detailed in the previous solicitor's file should be credited to the new solicitor. Other matters, however, might not be treated in this way. For example, if the previous solicitor has dealt with the statutory charge, there must as a minimum be an indication on the new solicitor's file that he or she has confirmed that the previous information given is correct.

"Yes"/"No"/"Not Applicable"

10. Auditors should indicate for each element whether the criterion has been met or not, or indicate "not applicable". For the avoidance of doubt, the "not applicable" option is intended

for use only where the circumstances indicated by the criteria do not arise in the particular case. It is not expected that the lawyer would note within the file that a not applicable issue has been considered and rejected, auditors will recognise when criteria do not apply in particular cases or circumstances. In some sections of the criteria a "not applicable" answer rules out a number of consequential elements which may as a result be ignored.

Serial Questions

11. Some questions contained in the criteria are contingent upon organisations dealing with a preliminary lead question, for example;

Lead question   a) does the file show whether there were any witnesses?

Contingent questions b) does the lawyer know whether the client objects to contacting the witnesses?

        c) did the lawyer attempt to contact and interview witnesses?

12. The purpose of these questions is to encourage the lawyer to consider the important lead question when dealing with the particular type of case. In conducting the transaction criteria audit it will therefore be important that the file demonstrates that the lawyer has considered these lead questions. Where the auditor can see this from the file, a compliance will be recorded for the lead question but where there is no information then a non-compliance will be recorded.

13. The auditor will then seek objective evidence that the contingent questions have been addressed. As before, evidence of compliance with these might be anywhere on the file. If the auditor can see from the file that the lawyer did consider the contingent issues then a compliance will be recorded but if no evidence can be found on the file the auditor cannot assume compliance.

14. For the example at paragraph 11 this means that if the lawyer knows that the answer to the lead question was that there were no witnesses or even that there could not have been any witnesses, the lawyer must still make a note of this on the file. The auditor will not be able to assume that because the file is silent on the issue the answer to the lead question is that there were no witnesses. A non-compliance will therefore be recorded, not only against the lead question but also against all the contingent questions as well. However, where the circumstances of the case recorded on the file are such that it is clear that there were no witnesses or could not have been any, the auditor should be able to deduce this from the evidence on the file and record a "not applicable" for the lead question and then also record all the contingent questions as "not applicable".

Safeguards

15. The Board recognises that many organisations, particularly those that have not had the benefit of participating in a transaction criteria audit, feel concerned that the success of their application for a franchise, or its retention, could depend solely on compliance with the transaction criteria. It is therefore proposed to introduce the following procedures as safeguards.

16. The Board will use a standard sampling technique which will ensure that the fact that all files cannot be examined is taken into account. This standard statistical technique recognises that since a sample of files only is examined the audit result can only be an estimate of the actual

level of compliance. In recognising this fact the statistical technique ensures that the organisation is not unfairly penalised because the random sample chosen happens to include one or two low scoring files.

17. If the organisation fails to achieve the required compliance rate in a particular category, and this is the sole reason for refusing, suspending or ending the franchise, then a second transaction criteria audit will be undertaken as quickly as possible. In this the audit of the original sample of files will be checked jointly by the organisation and an auditor under the supervision of the Liaison Manager. Any discrepancies found will be used to adjust the audit score.

18. If the organisation is still unable to meet the compliance rate, the Board will take another audit sample focused on more recent work.

19. If the organisation remains unable to demonstrate compliance with the transaction criteria, and this is the sole reason for the refusal or loss of a franchise, the organisation will be able to elect to have its files reviewed by a panel of franchised solicitors, who may also be members of a Law Society specialist panel.

20. The panel will carry out an assessment of the same files used in the transaction criteria audit to determine whether, in their opinion, the work was of acceptable competence.

21. If non-compliance with the transaction criteria was the only reason for refusing a franchise, the panel will also be asked to advise the Franchise Appeal Body whether the transaction criteria audit result should be disregarded and the organisation granted a franchise in the appropriate category.

22. In any event, the auditors' mark books will be left with the organisation after the audit as a computerised record will be kept by the Board. This will allow organisations to check individual scores on files where they have concerns about the process should they wish to do so.